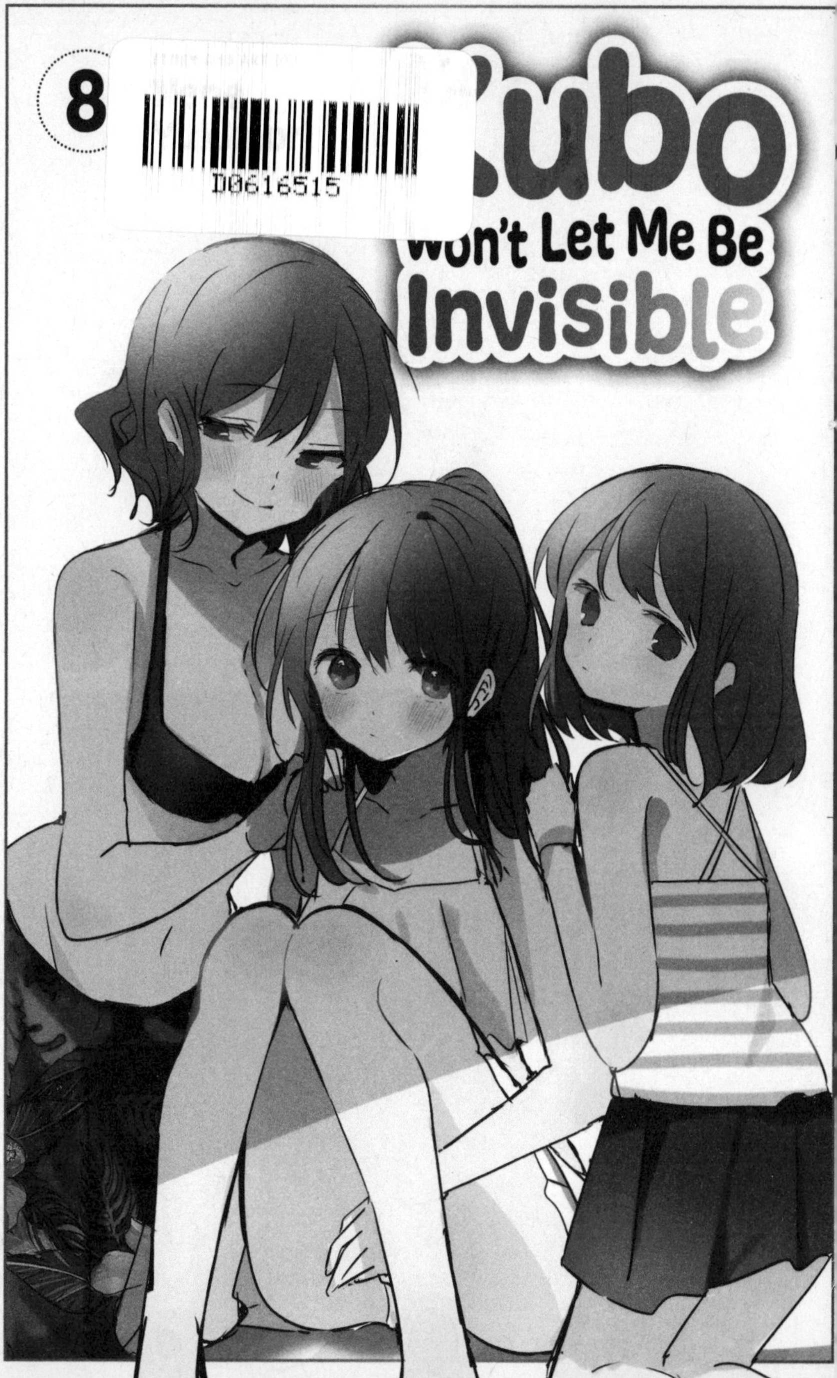
8
Kubo Won't Let Me Be Invisible

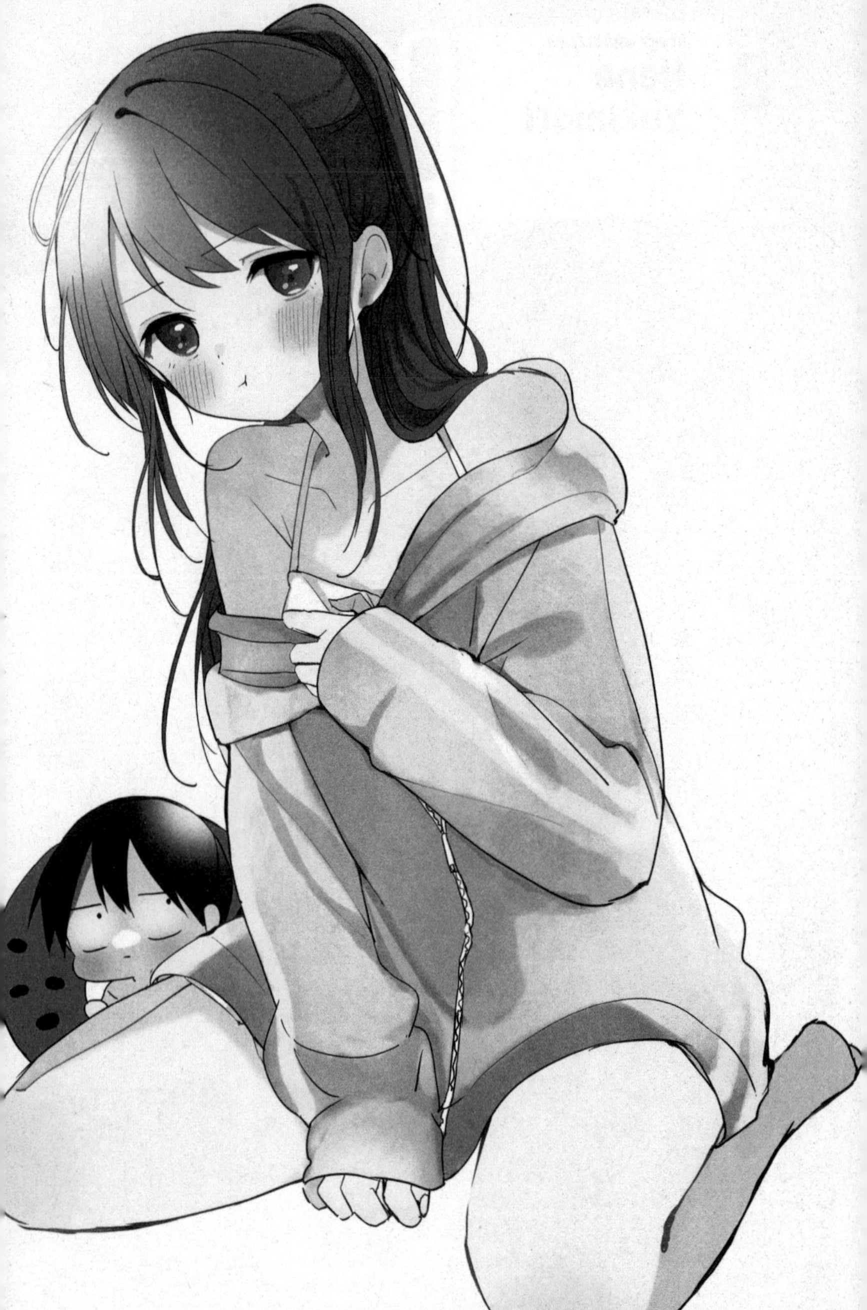

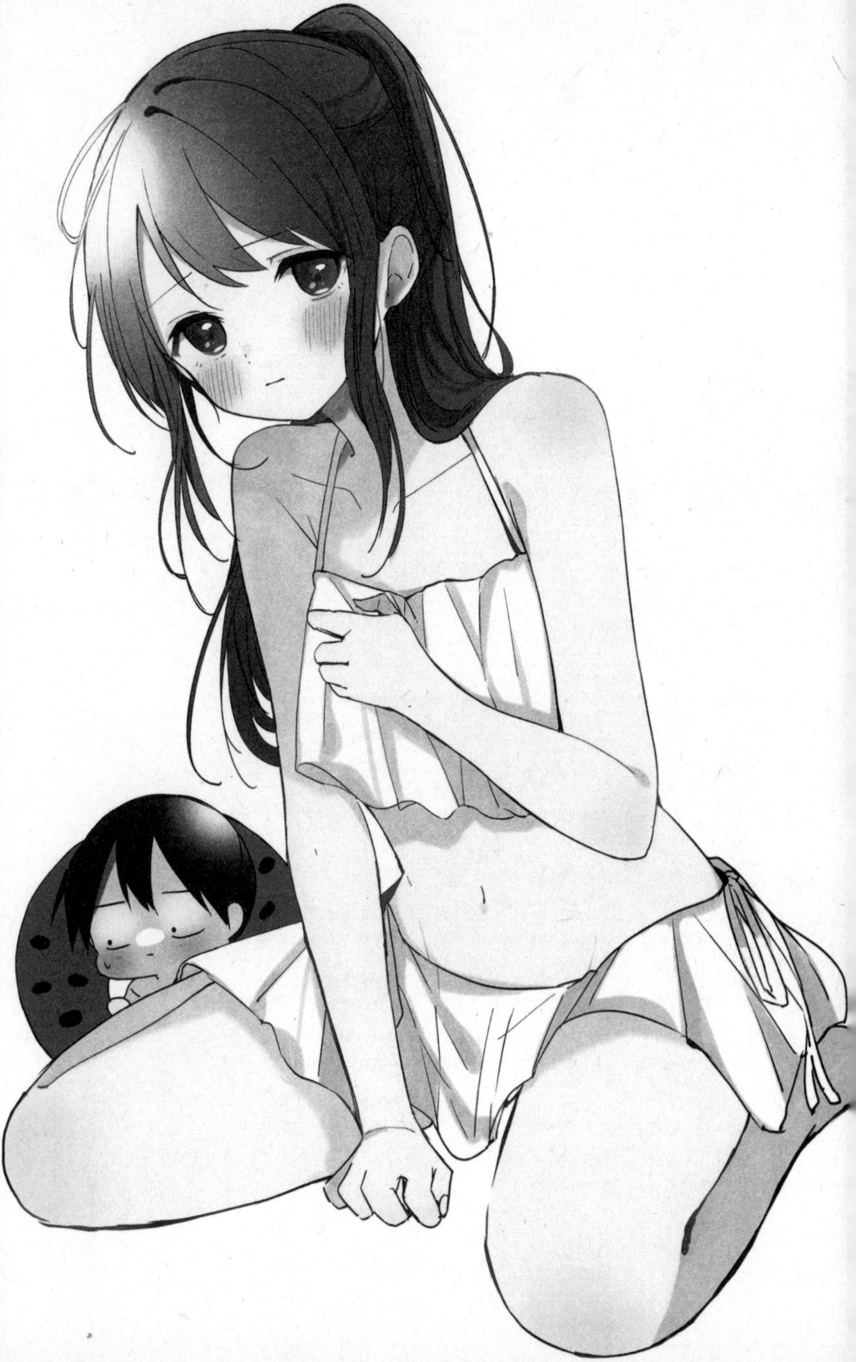

CONTENTS

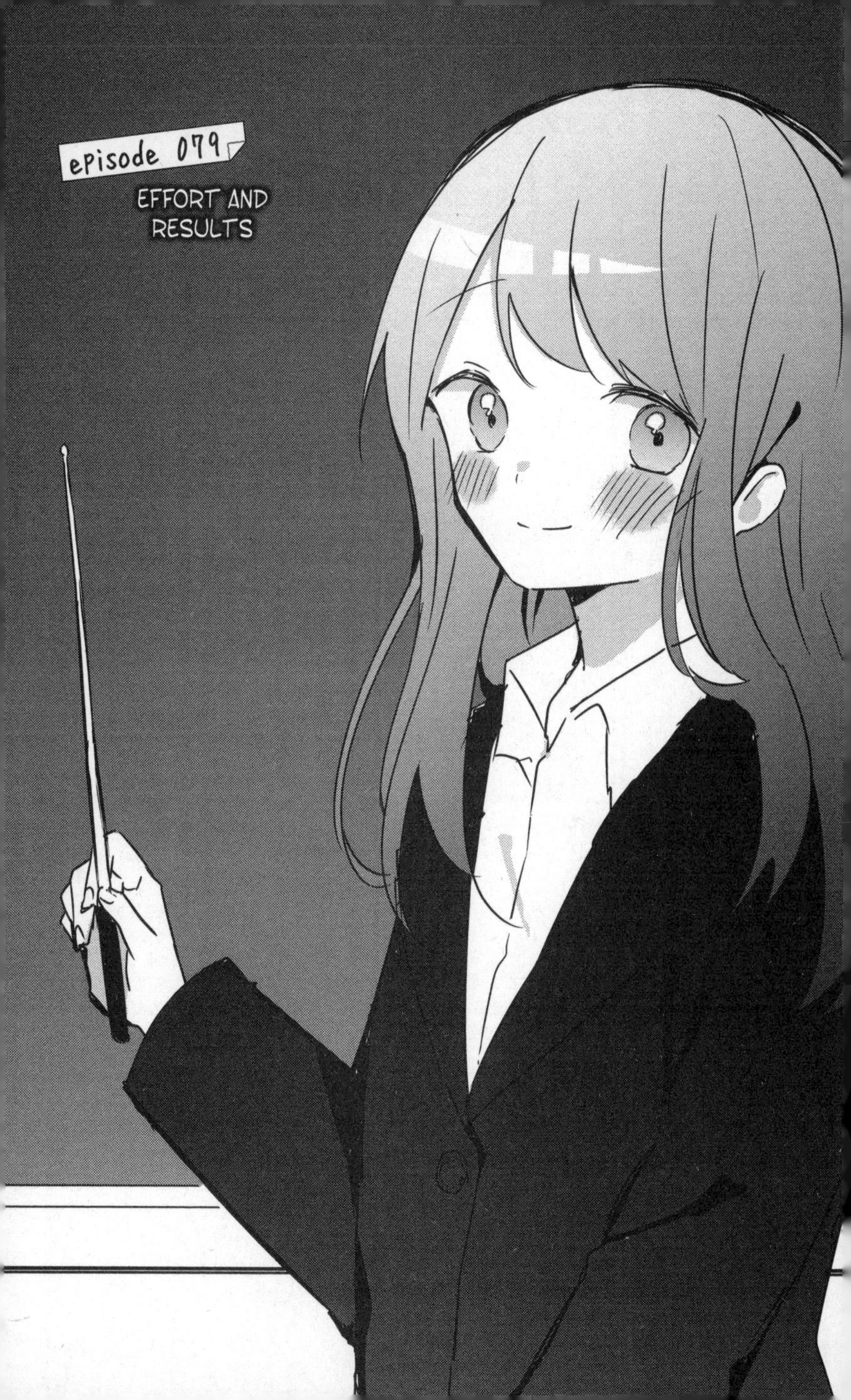
episode 079
EFFORT AND RESULTS

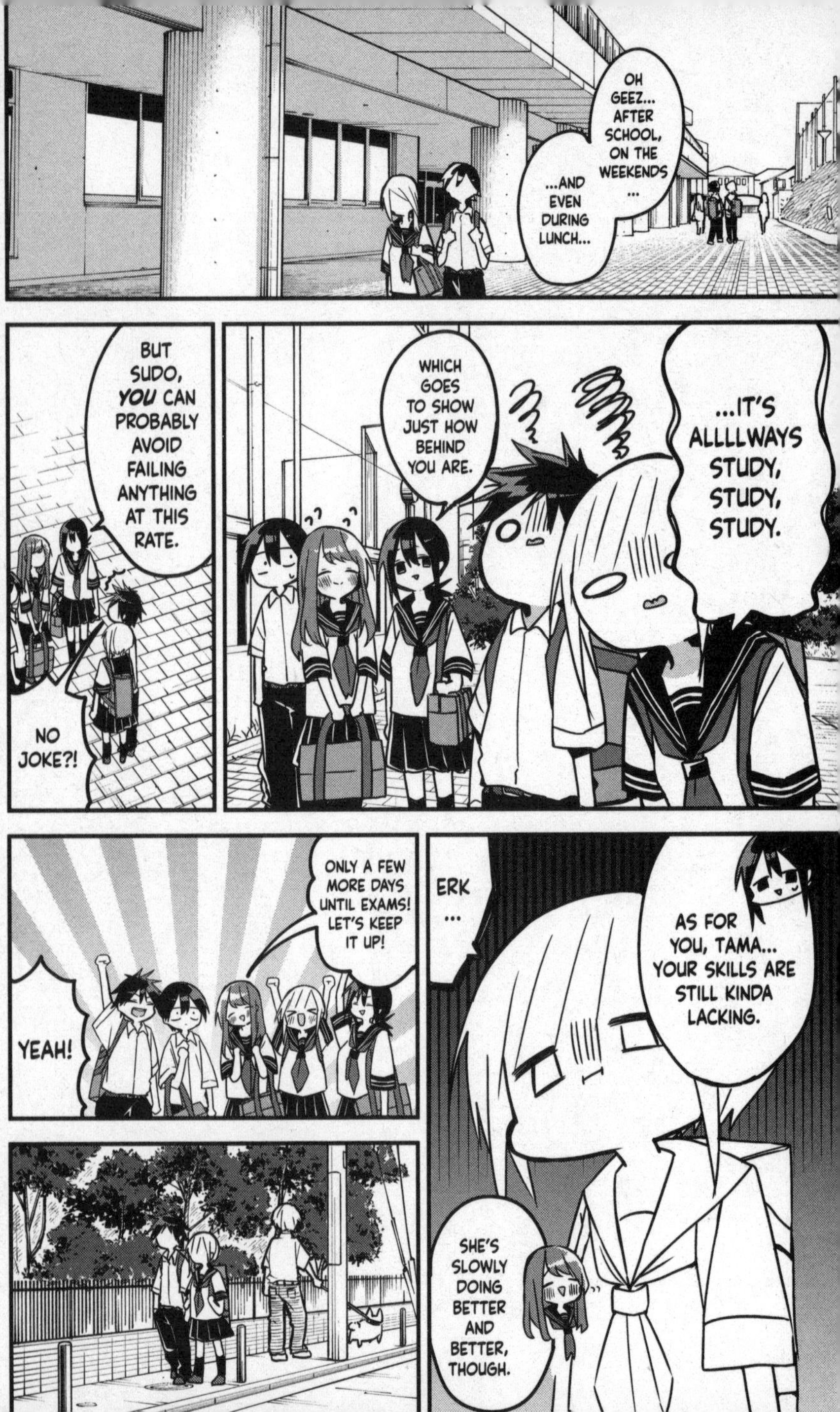
OH GEEZ... AFTER SCHOOL, ON THE WEEKENDS...
...AND EVEN DURING LUNCH...
...IT'S ALLLLWAYS STUDY, STUDY, STUDY.
WHICH GOES TO SHOW JUST HOW BEHIND YOU ARE.
BUT SUDO, *YOU* CAN PROBABLY AVOID FAILING ANYTHING AT THIS RATE.
NO JOKE?!
AS FOR YOU, TAMA... YOUR SKILLS ARE STILL KINDA LACKING.
ERK...
SHE'S SLOWLY DOING BETTER AND BETTER, THOUGH.
ONLY A FEW MORE DAYS UNTIL EXAMS! LET'S KEEP IT UP!
YEAH!

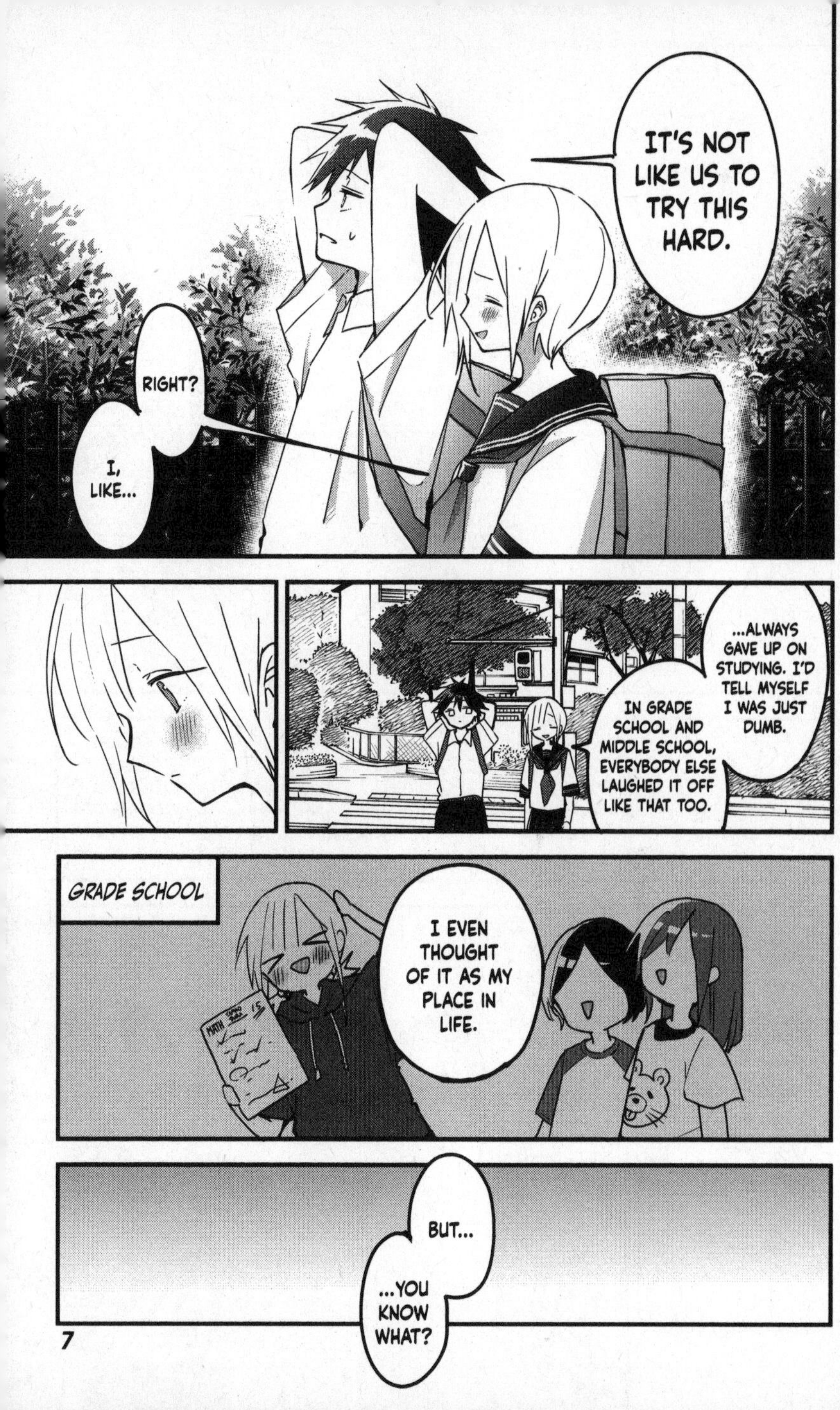
IT'S NOT LIKE US TO TRY THIS HARD.
RIGHT?
I, LIKE...
...ALWAYS GAVE UP ON STUDYING. I'D TELL MYSELF I WAS JUST DUMB.
IN GRADE SCHOOL AND MIDDLE SCHOOL, EVERYBODY ELSE LAUGHED IT OFF LIKE THAT TOO.
GRADE SCHOOL
I EVEN THOUGHT OF IT AS MY PLACE IN LIFE.
BUT...
...YOU KNOW WHAT?

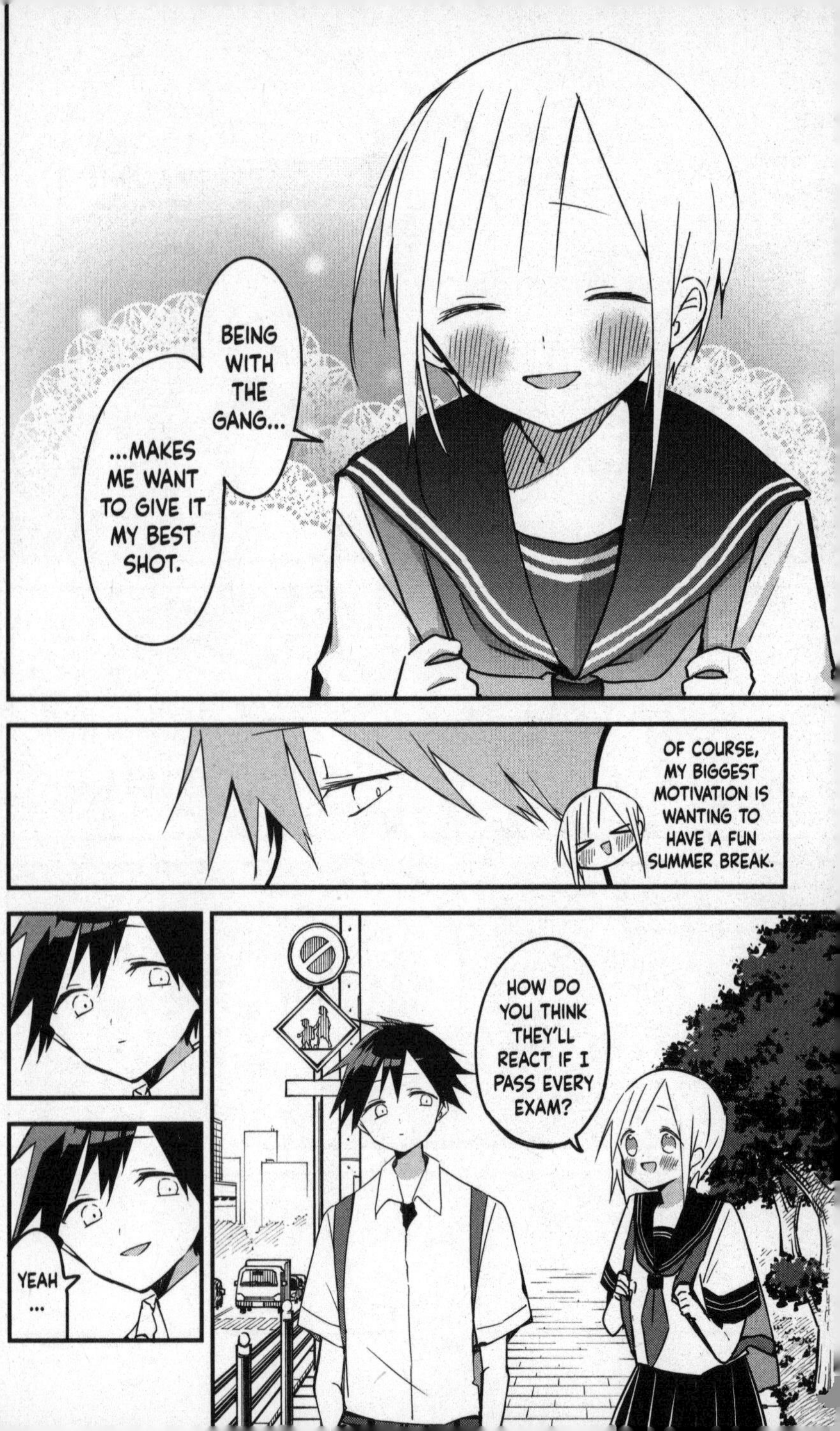
BEING WITH THE GANG...
...MAKES ME WANT TO GIVE IT MY BEST SHOT.
OF COURSE, MY BIGGEST MOTIVATION IS WANTING TO HAVE A FUN SUMMER BREAK.
HOW DO YOU THINK THEY'LL REACT IF I PASS EVERY EXAM?
YEAH...

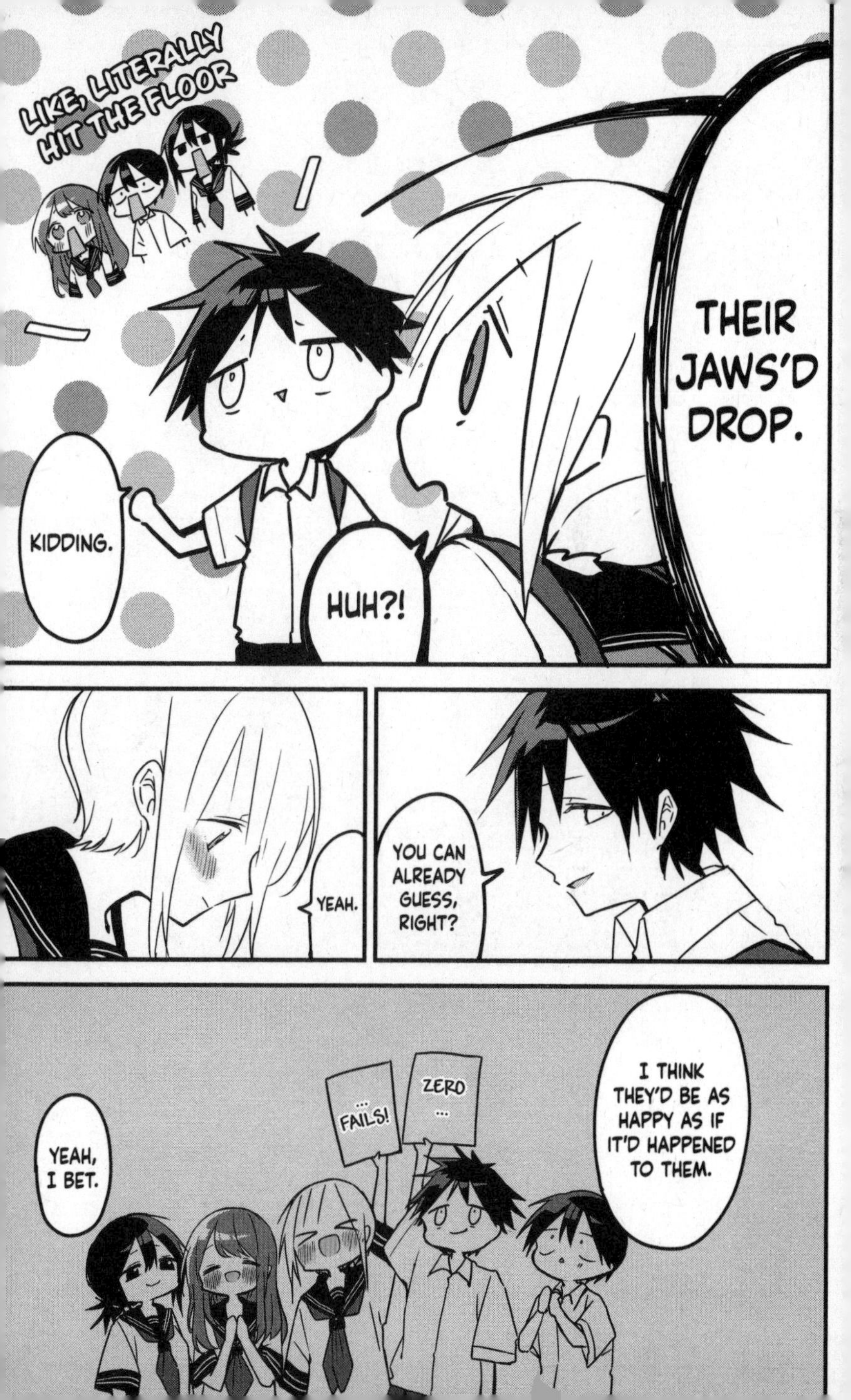
THEIR JAWS'D DROP.
LIKE, LITERALLY HIT THE FLOOR
HUH?!
KIDDING.
YOU CAN ALREADY GUESS, RIGHT?
YEAH.
I THINK THEY'D BE AS HAPPY AS IF IT'D HAPPENED TO THEM.
ZERO ...
... FAILS!
YEAH, I BET.

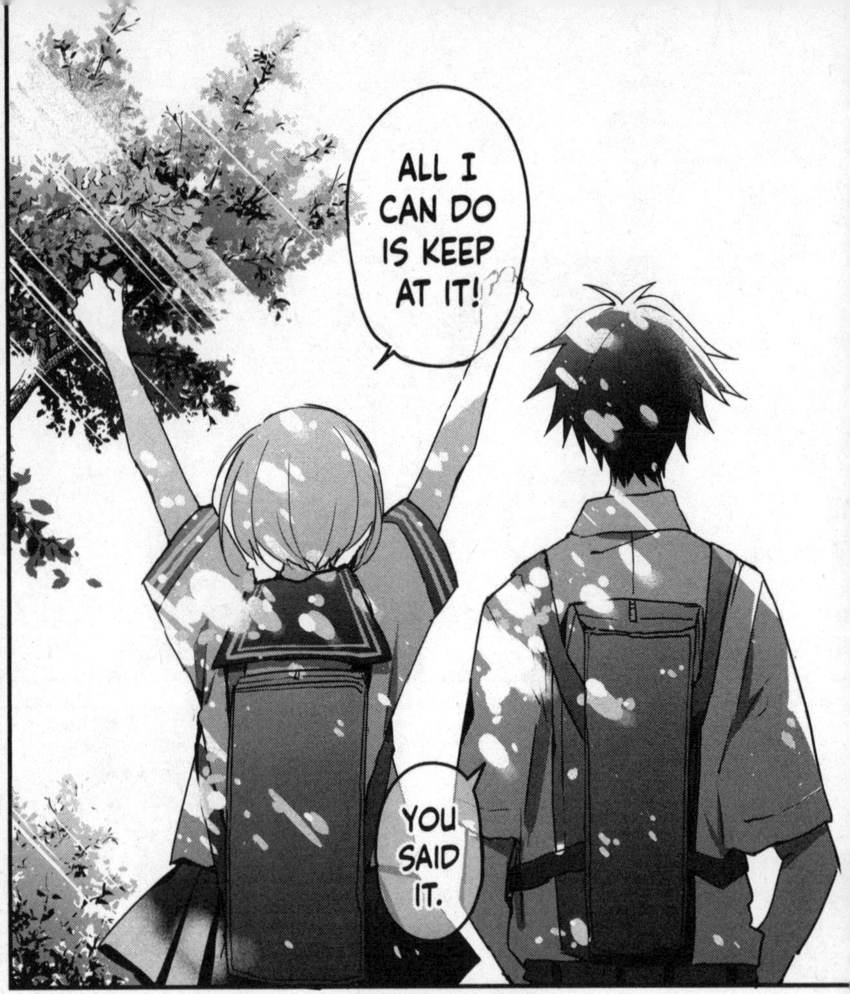
ALL I CAN DO IS KEEP AT IT!
YOU SAID IT.
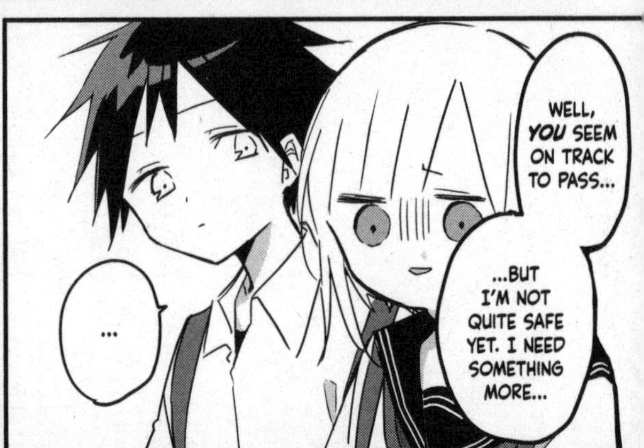
WELL, ***YOU*** SEEM ON TRACK TO PASS...
...BUT I'M NOT QUITE SAFE YET. I NEED SOMETHING MORE...
...
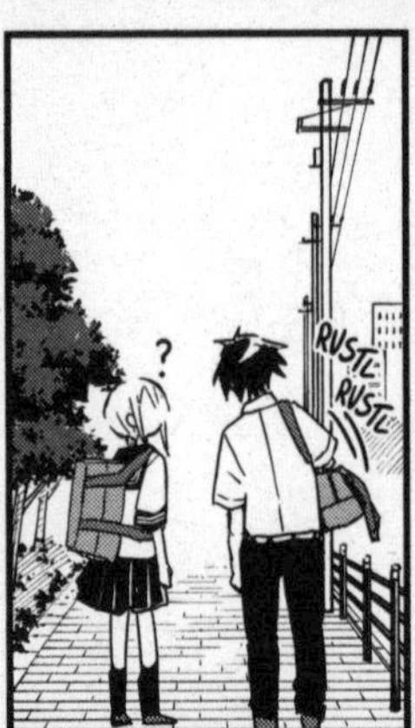
?
RUSTL
RUSTL

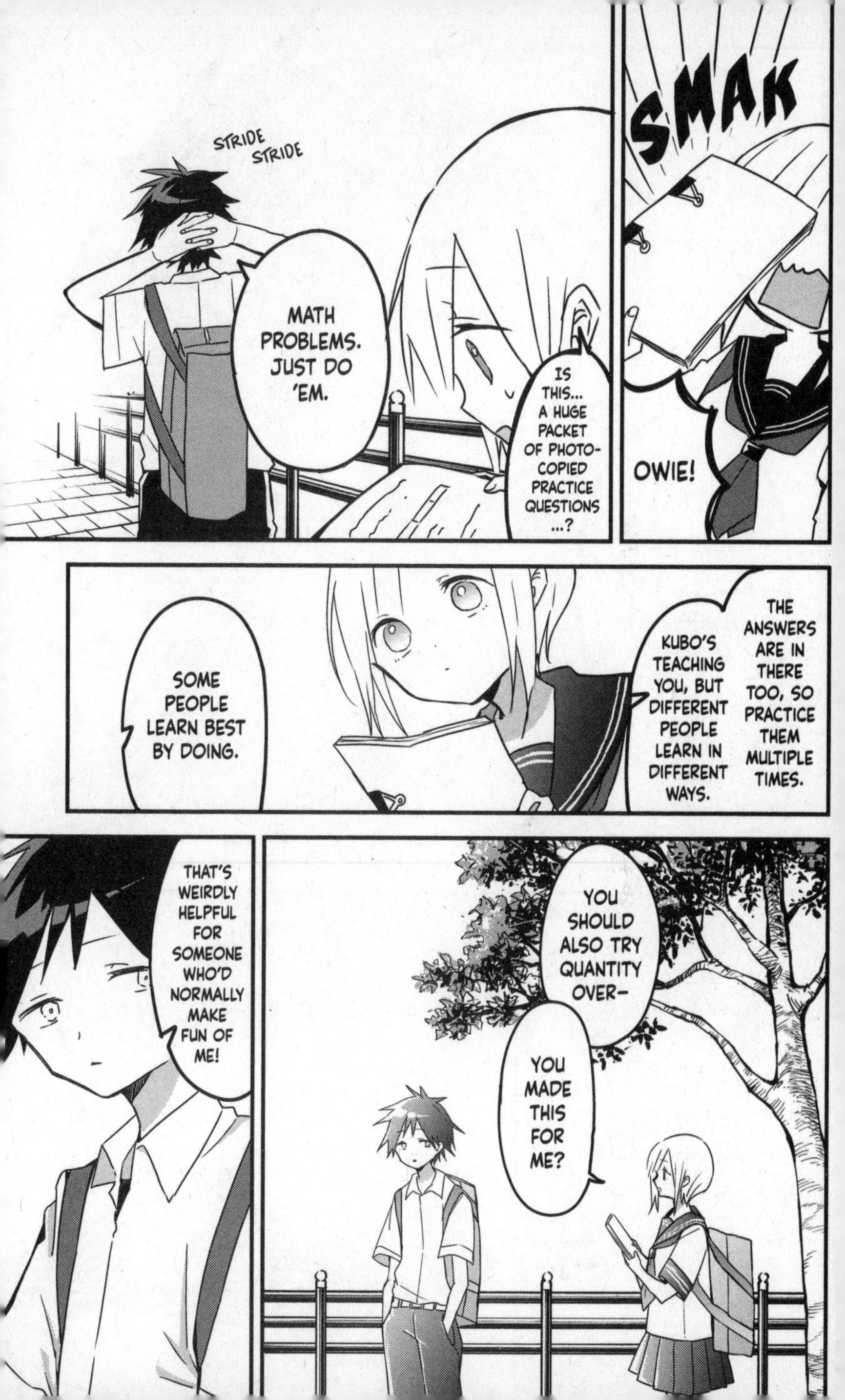
SMAK
OWIE!
IS THIS... A HUGE PACKET OF PHOTO-COPIED PRACTICE QUESTIONS ...?
MATH PROBLEMS. JUST DO 'EM.
STRIDE STRIDE
THE ANSWERS ARE IN THERE TOO, SO PRACTICE THEM MULTIPLE TIMES.
KUBO'S TEACHING YOU, BUT DIFFERENT PEOPLE LEARN IN DIFFERENT WAYS.
SOME PEOPLE LEARN BEST BY DOING.
YOU SHOULD ALSO TRY QUANTITY OVER—
YOU MADE THIS FOR ME?
THAT'S WEIRDLY HELPFUL FOR SOMEONE WHO'D NORMALLY MAKE FUN OF ME!

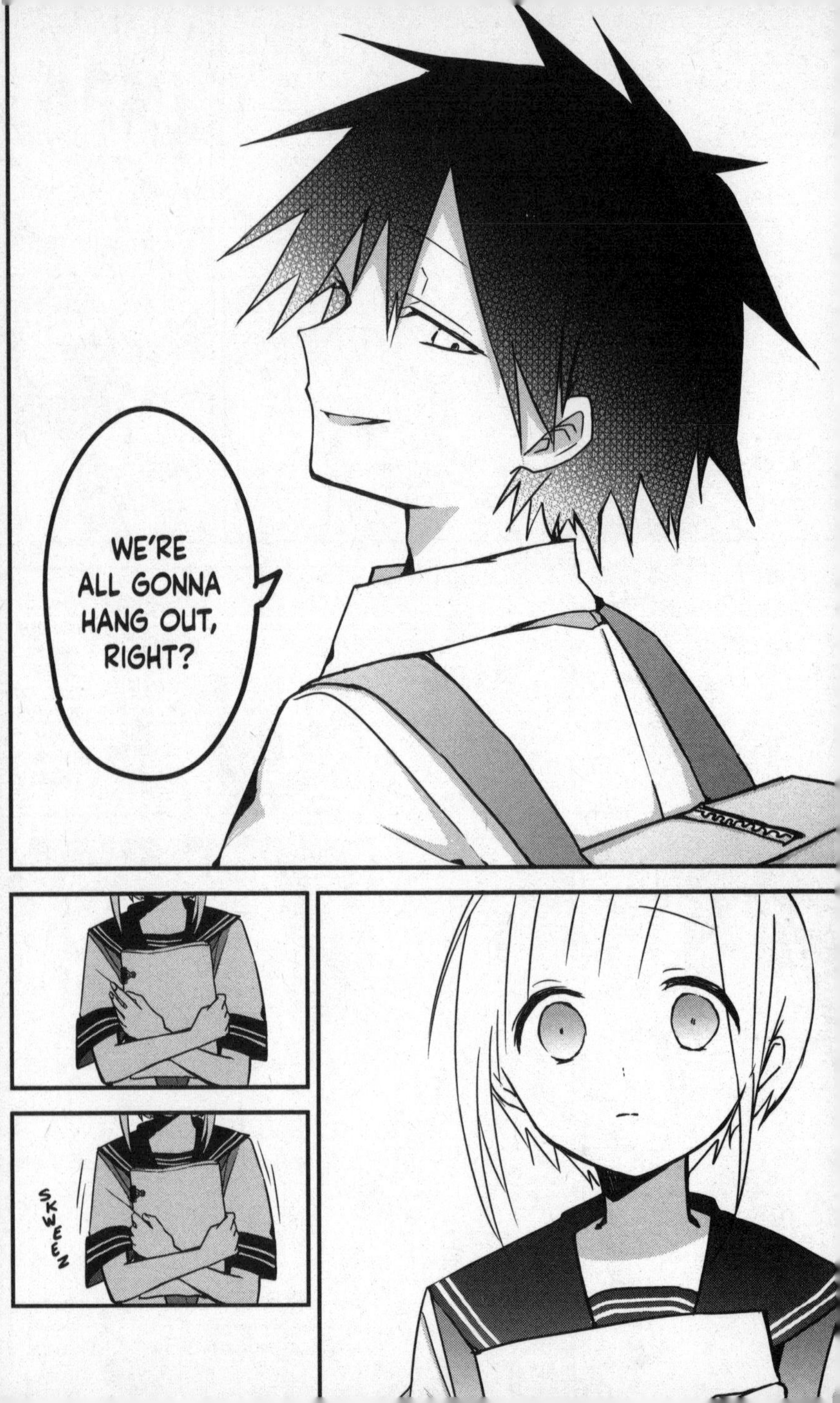
WE'RE ALL GONNA HANG OUT, RIGHT?
SKWEEZ

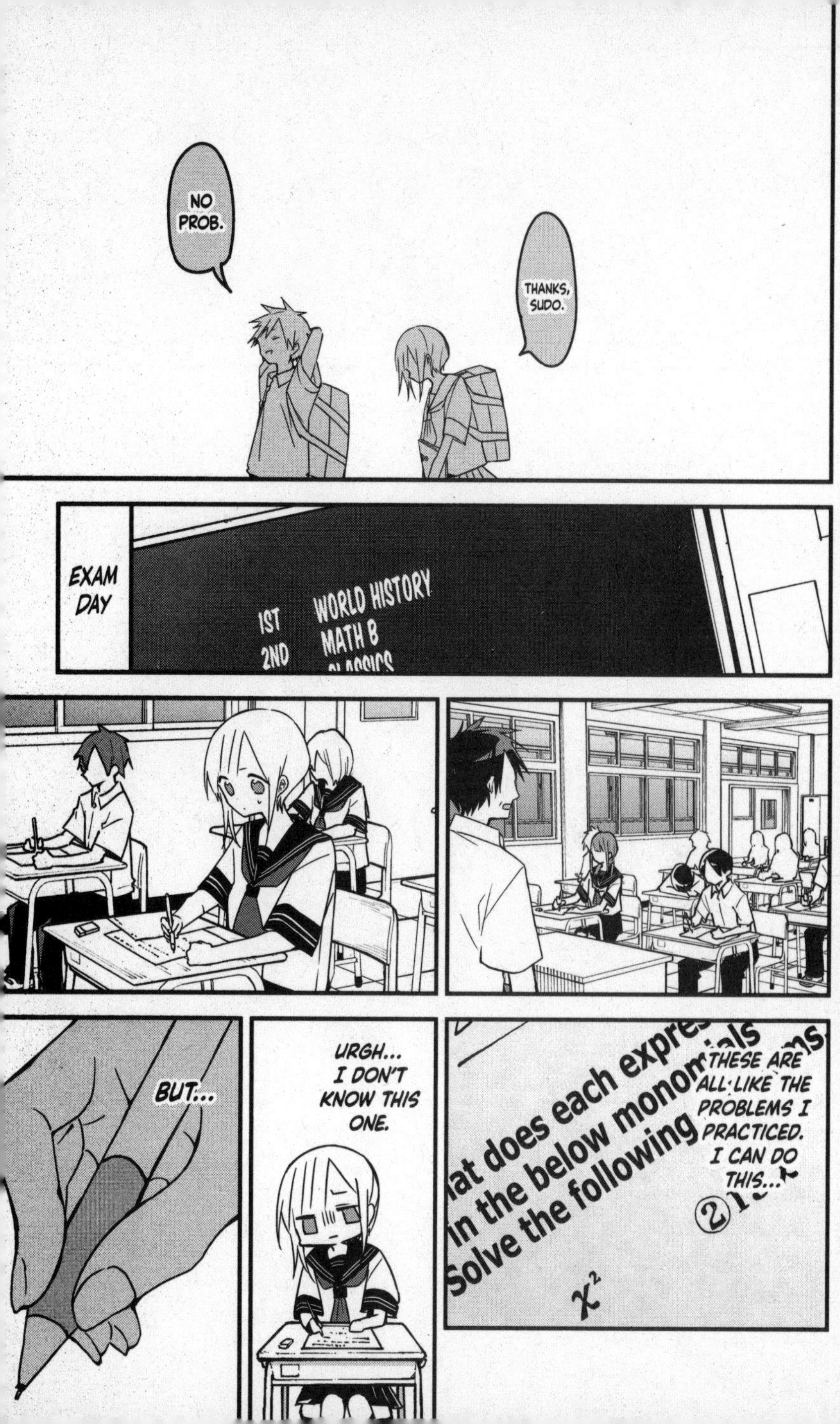
THANKS, SUDO.
NO PROB.
1ST WORLD HISTORY
2ND MATH B
EXAM DAY
Solve the following
THESE ARE ALL LIKE THE PROBLEMS I PRACTICED. I CAN DO THIS...
URGH... I DON'T KNOW THIS ONE.
BUT...

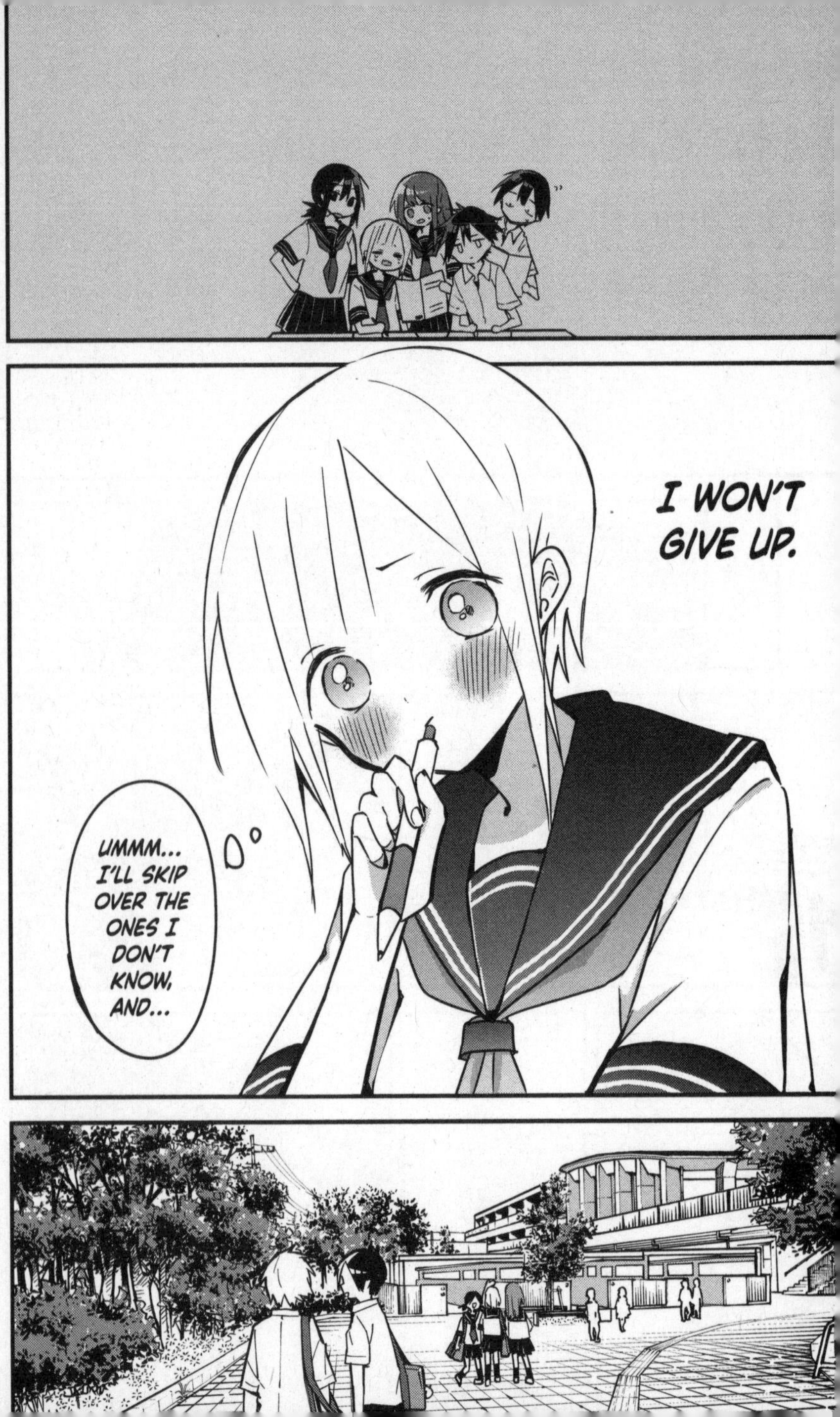
I WON'T GIVE UP.
UMMM... I'LL SKIP OVER THE ONES I DON'T KNOW, AND...

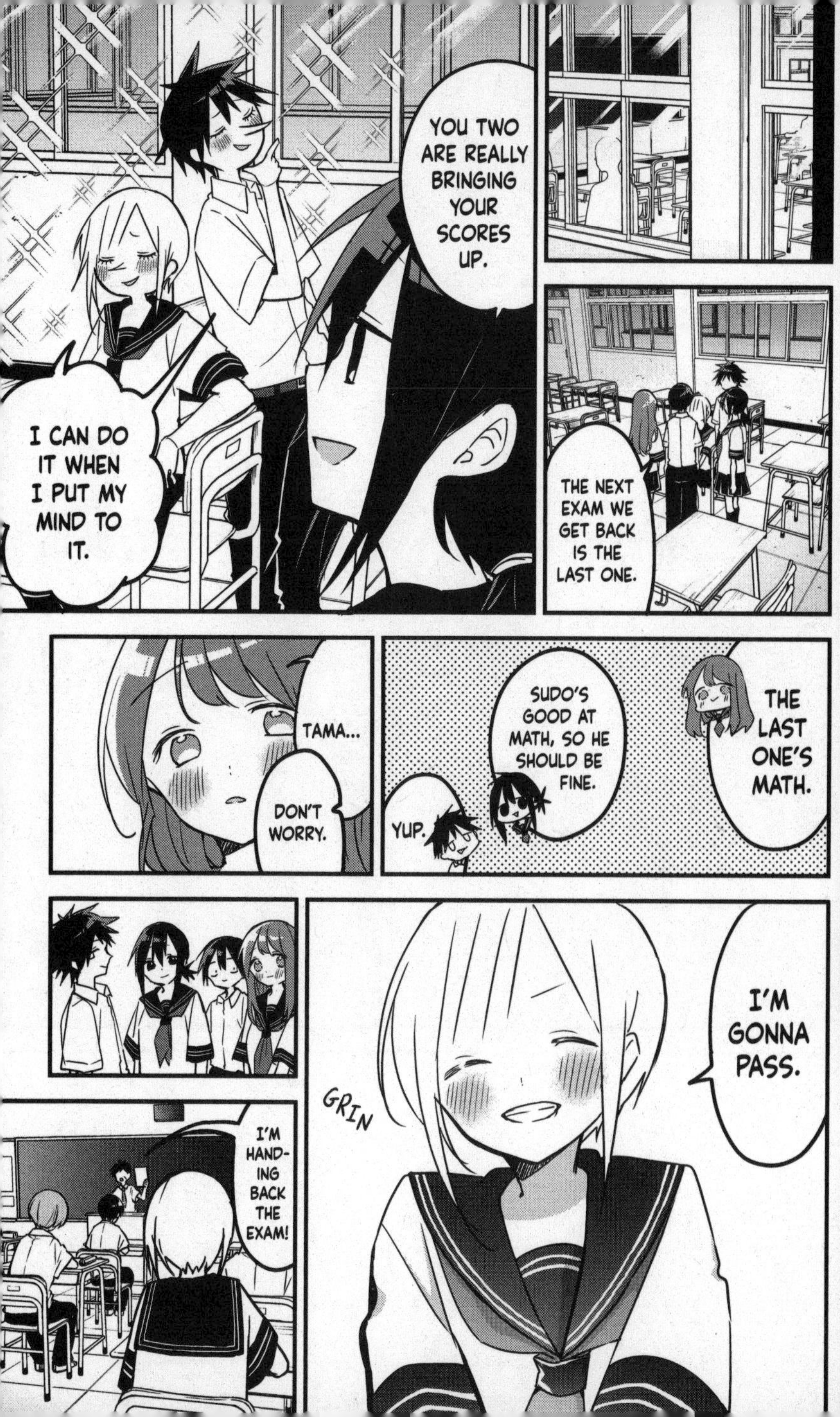
THE NEXT EXAM WE GET BACK IS THE LAST ONE.
YOU TWO ARE REALLY BRINGING YOUR SCORES UP.
I CAN DO IT WHEN I PUT MY MIND TO IT.
THE LAST ONE'S MATH.
SUDO'S GOOD AT MATH, SO HE SHOULD BE FINE.
YUP.
TAMA...
DON'T WORRY.
I'M GONNA PASS.
GRIN
I'M HAND-ING BACK THE EXAM!

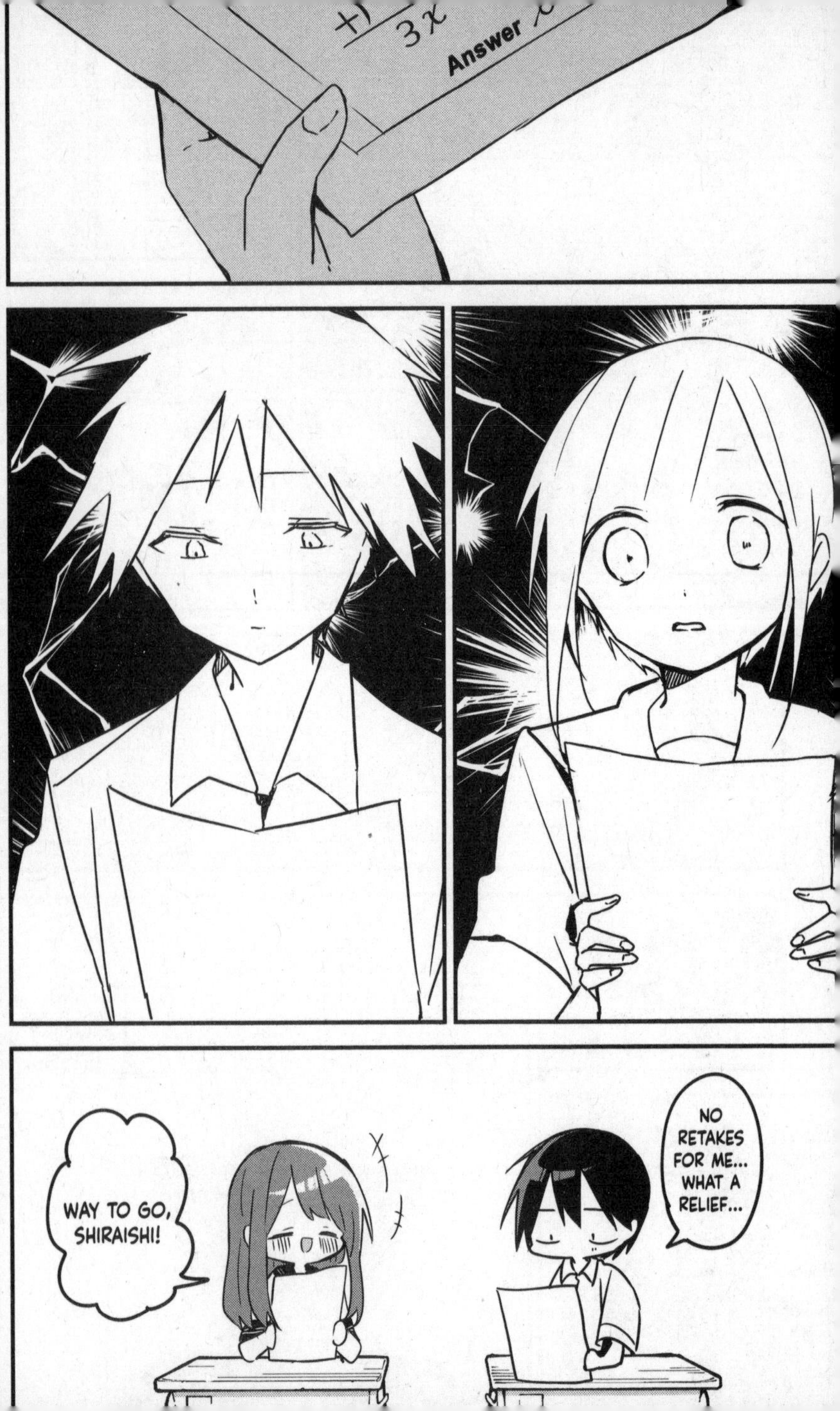
3x
Answer
NO RETAKES FOR ME... WHAT A RELIEF...
WAY TO GO, SHIRAISHI!

SUDO AND TAMA ARE OFTEN ENERGETIC EVEN IN THE ROUGH DRAFTS.

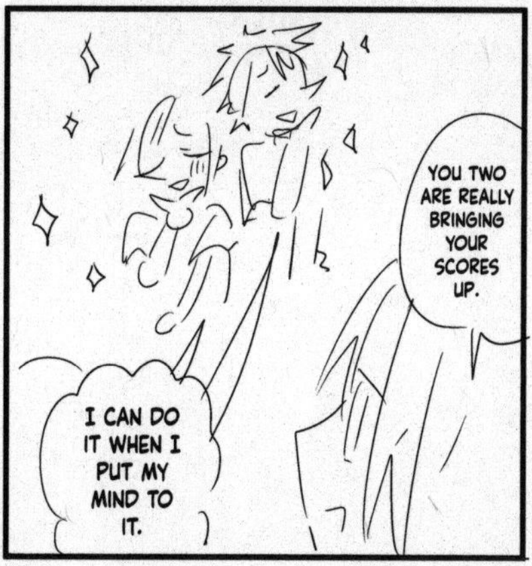
YOU TWO ARE REALLY BRINGING YOUR SCORES UP.
I CAN DO IT WHEN I PUT MY MIND TO IT.

SUDO AND TAMA'S PARENTS ARE FRIENDS. (INFO SURE TO NEVER COME UP IN THE MAIN STORY)

WE GREW UP TOGETHER.

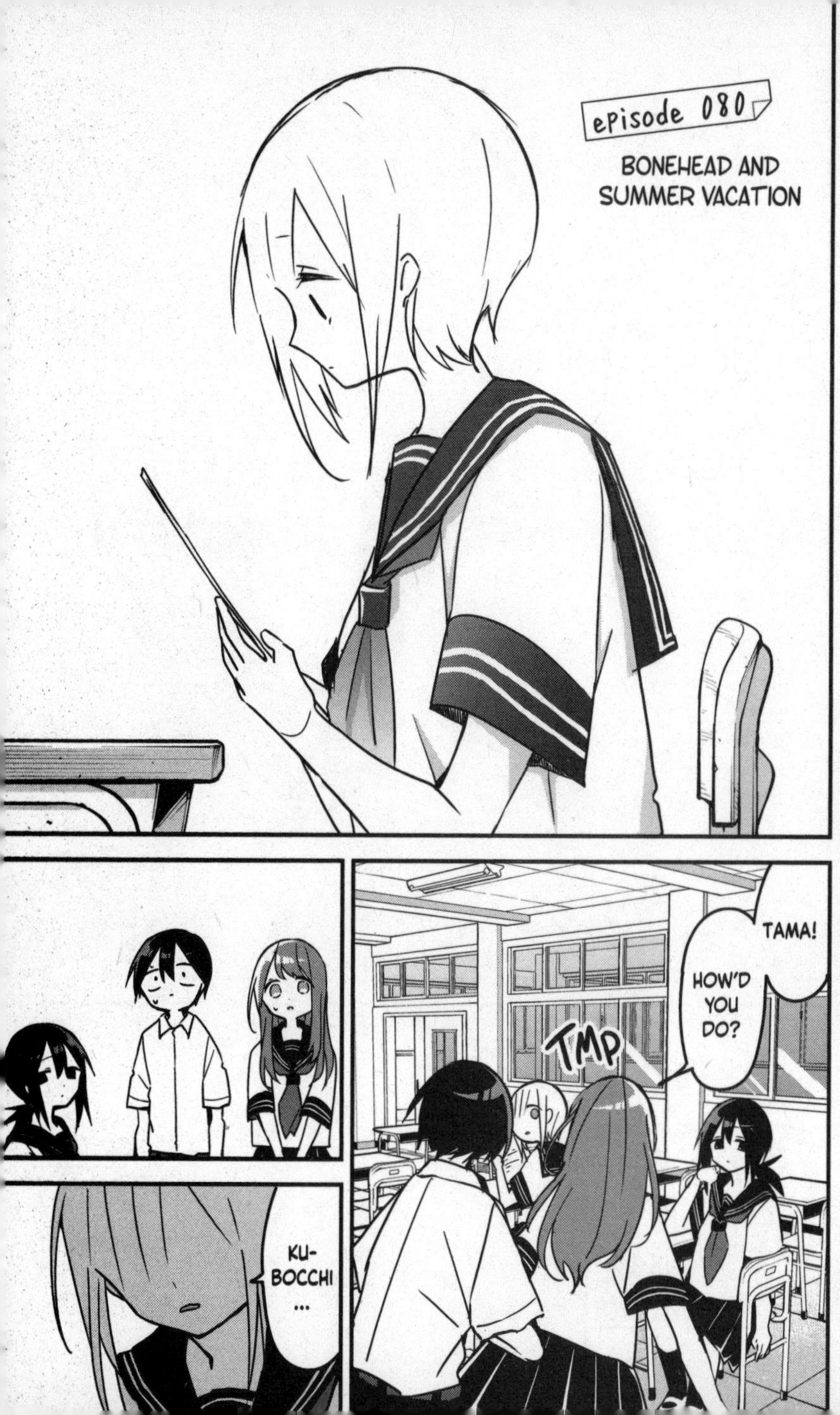
episode 080
BONEHEAD AND SUMMER VACATION
TAMA!
HOW'D YOU DO?
TMP
KU-BOCCHI...

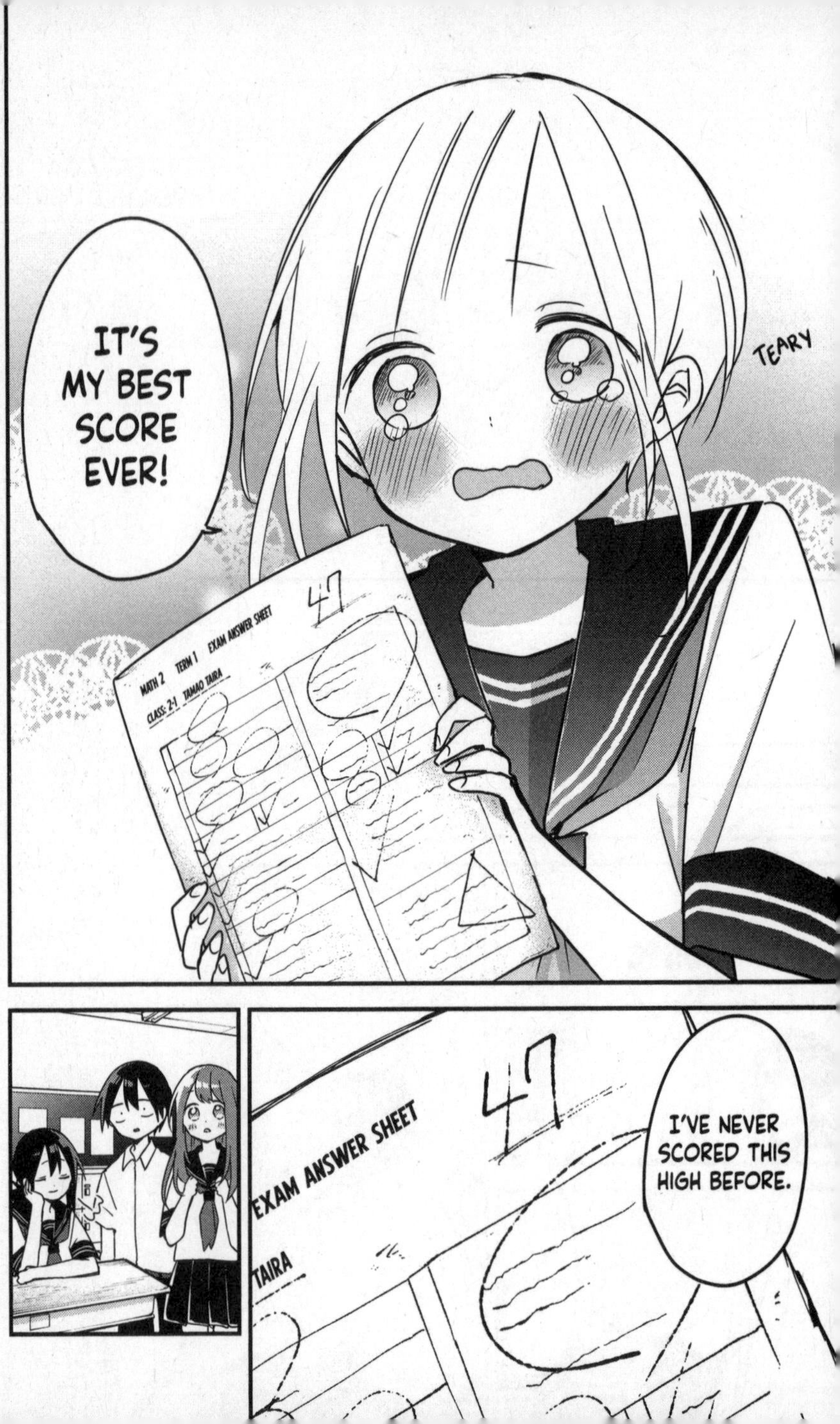
IT'S MY BEST SCORE EVER!
TEARY
47
MATH 2 TERM 1 EXAM ANSWER SHEET
CLASS: 2-1 TAMAO TAIRA
I'VE NEVER SCORED THIS HIGH BEFORE.
47
EXAM ANSWER SHEET
TAIRA

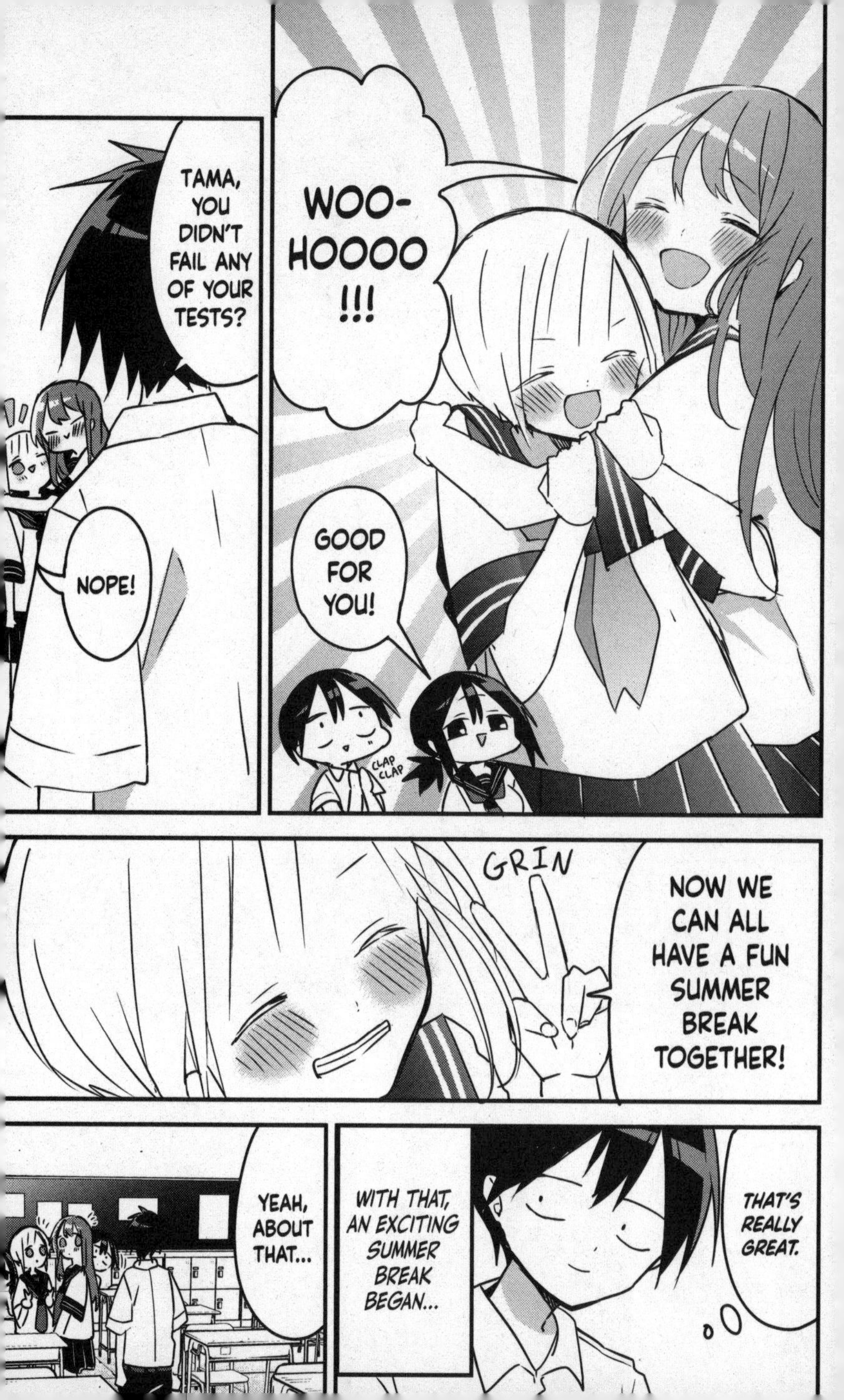
WOO-HOOOO!!!
GOOD FOR YOU!
CLAP CLAP
TAMA, YOU DIDN'T FAIL ANY OF YOUR TESTS?
NOPE!
NOW WE CAN ALL HAVE A FUN SUMMER BREAK TOGETHER!
GRIN
THAT'S REALLY GREAT.
WITH THAT, AN EXCITING SUMMER BREAK BEGAN...
YEAH, ABOUT THAT...

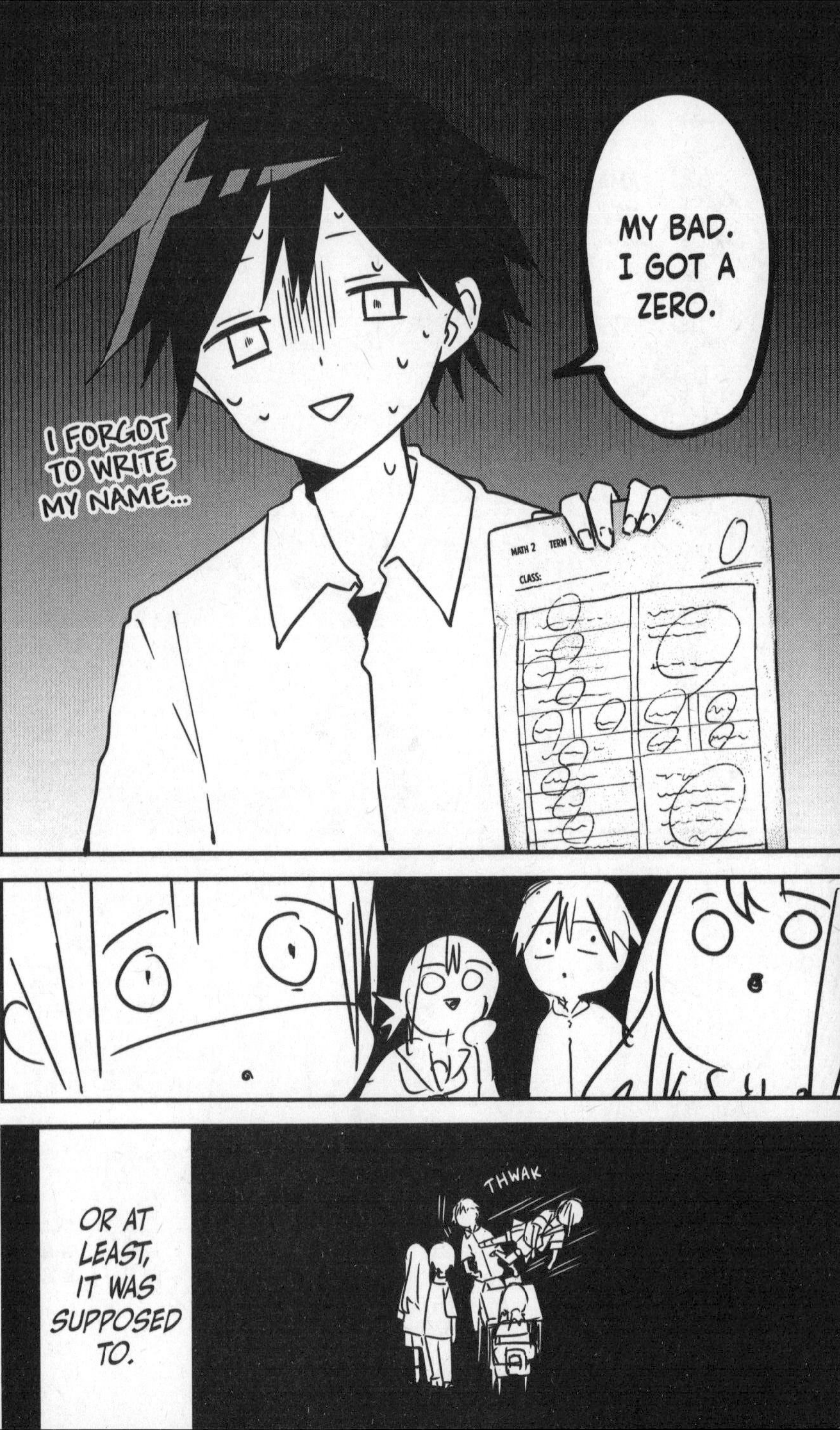
MY BAD. I GOT A ZERO.
I FORGOT TO WRITE MY NAME...
MATH 2 TERM 1
CLASS:
0
THWAK
OR AT LEAST, IT WAS SUPPOSED TO.

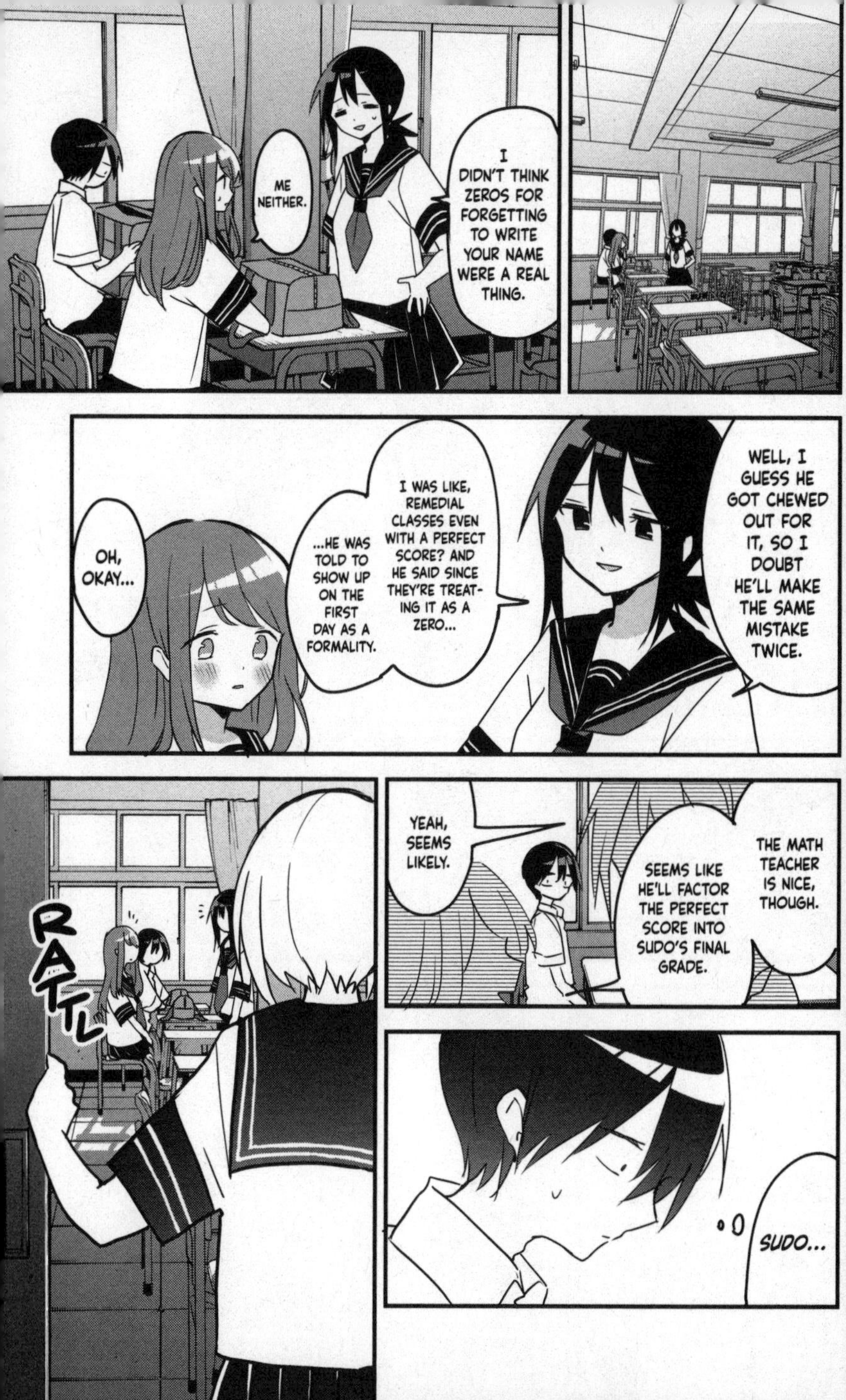
I DIDN'T THINK ZEROS FOR FORGETTING TO WRITE YOUR NAME WERE A REAL THING.
ME NEITHER.
WELL, I GUESS HE GOT CHEWED OUT FOR IT, SO I DOUBT HE'LL MAKE THE SAME MISTAKE TWICE.
I WAS LIKE, REMEDIAL CLASSES EVEN WITH A PERFECT SCORE? AND HE SAID SINCE THEY'RE TREATING IT AS A ZERO...
...HE WAS TOLD TO SHOW UP ON THE FIRST DAY AS A FORMALITY.
OH, OKAY...
THE MATH TEACHER IS NICE, THOUGH.
SEEMS LIKE HE'LL FACTOR THE PERFECT SCORE INTO SUDO'S FINAL GRADE.
YEAH, SEEMS LIKELY.
SUDO...
RATTL

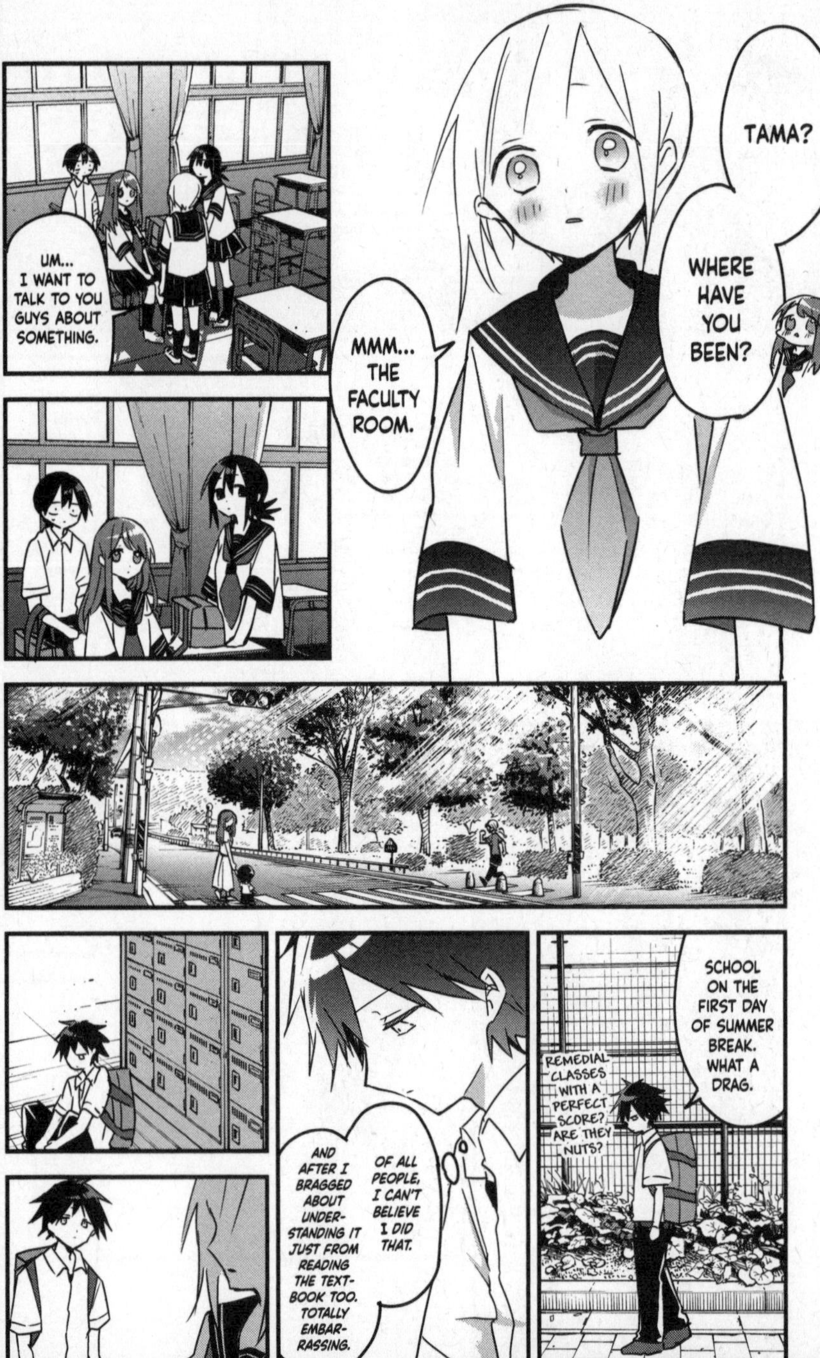
TAMA?
WHERE HAVE YOU BEEN?
MMM... THE FACULTY ROOM.
UM... I WANT TO TALK TO YOU GUYS ABOUT SOMETHING.
SCHOOL ON THE FIRST DAY OF SUMMER BREAK. WHAT A DRAG.
REMEDIAL CLASSES WITH A PERFECT SCORE? ARE THEY NUTS?
OF ALL PEOPLE, I CAN'T BELIEVE I DID THAT.
AND AFTER I BRAGGED ABOUT UNDER-STANDING IT JUST FROM READING THE TEXT-BOOK TOO. TOTALLY EMBAR-RASSING.

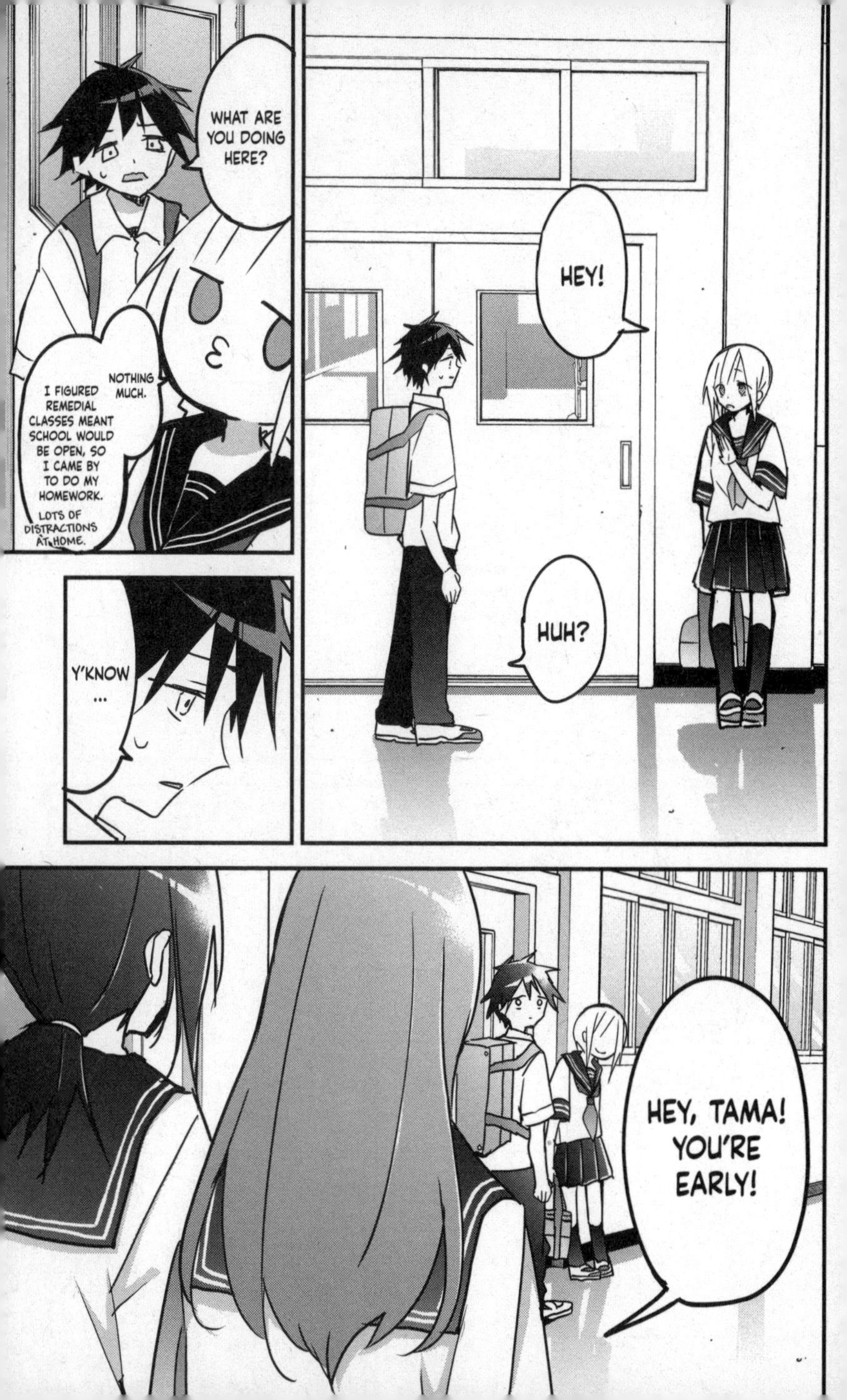
HEY!
HUH?
WHAT ARE YOU DOING HERE?
NOTHING MUCH.
I FIGURED REMEDIAL CLASSES MEANT SCHOOL WOULD BE OPEN, SO I CAME BY TO DO MY HOMEWORK.
LOTS OF DISTRACTIONS AT HOME.
Y'KNOW...
HEY, TAMA! YOU'RE EARLY!

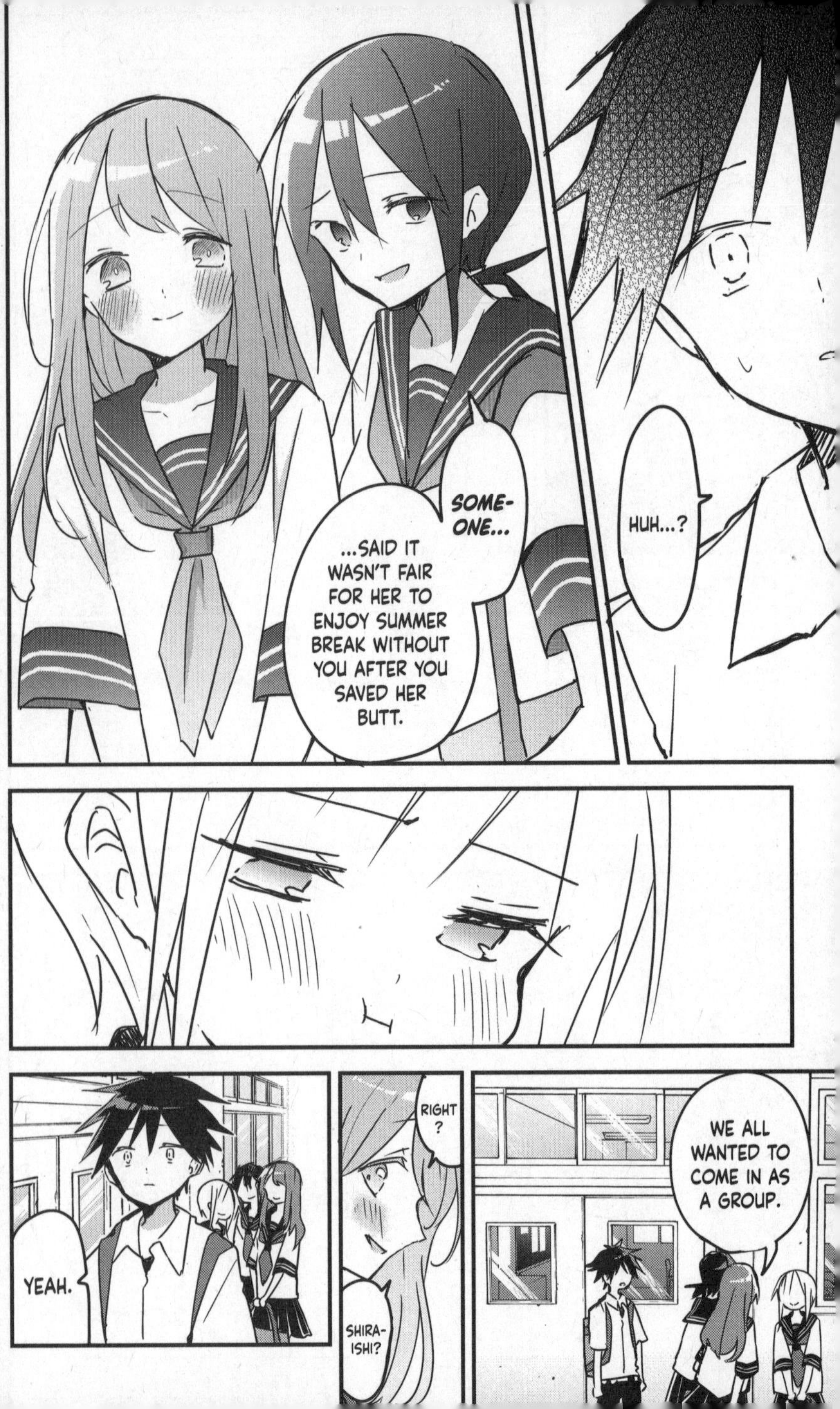
HUH...?
SOME-ONE...
...SAID IT WASN'T FAIR FOR HER TO ENJOY SUMMER BREAK WITHOUT YOU AFTER YOU SAVED HER BUTT.
WE ALL WANTED TO COME IN AS A GROUP.
RIGHT?
SHIRA-ISHI?
YEAH.

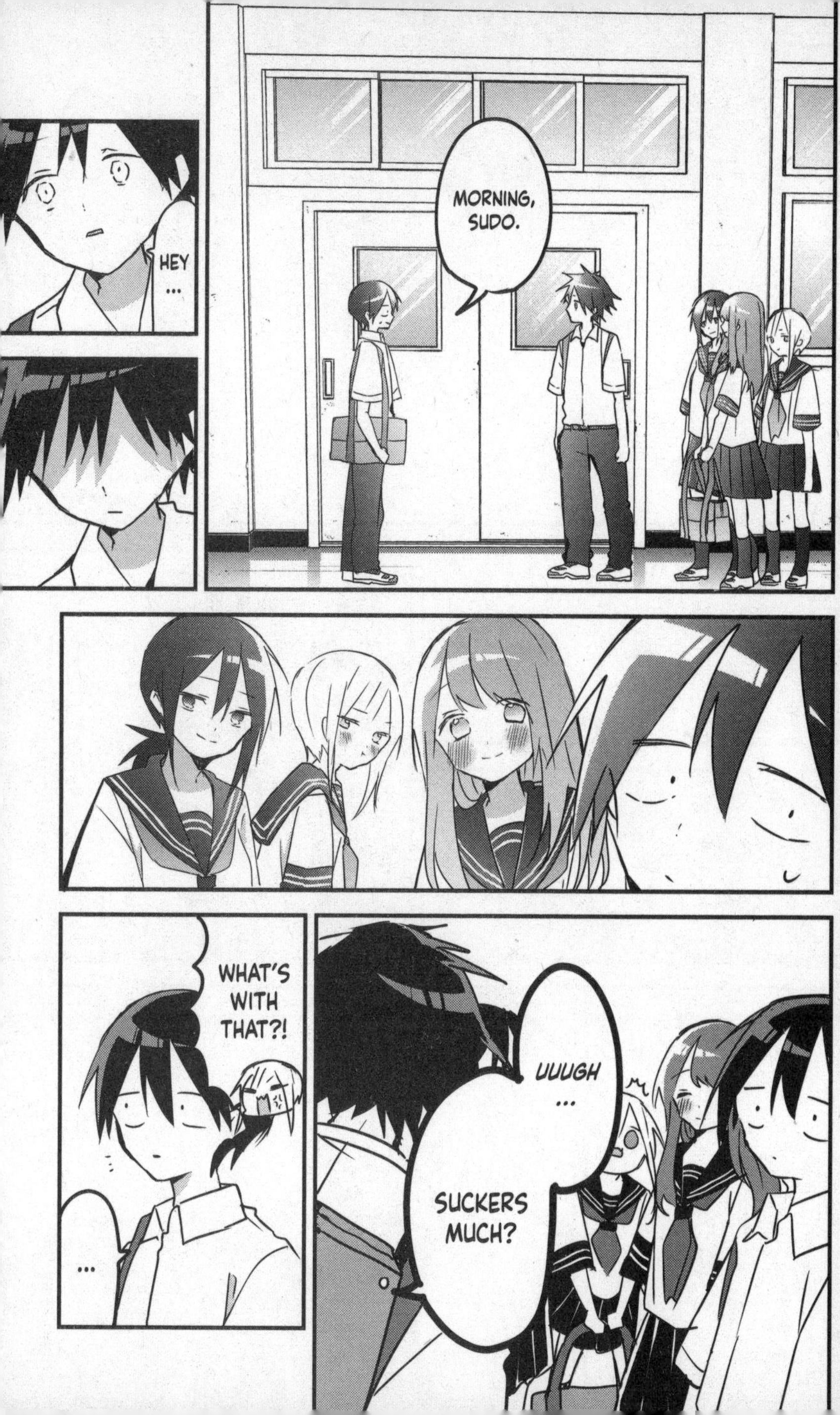
MORNING, SUDO.
HEY...
UUUGH...
SUCKERS MUCH?
WHAT'S WITH THAT?!
...

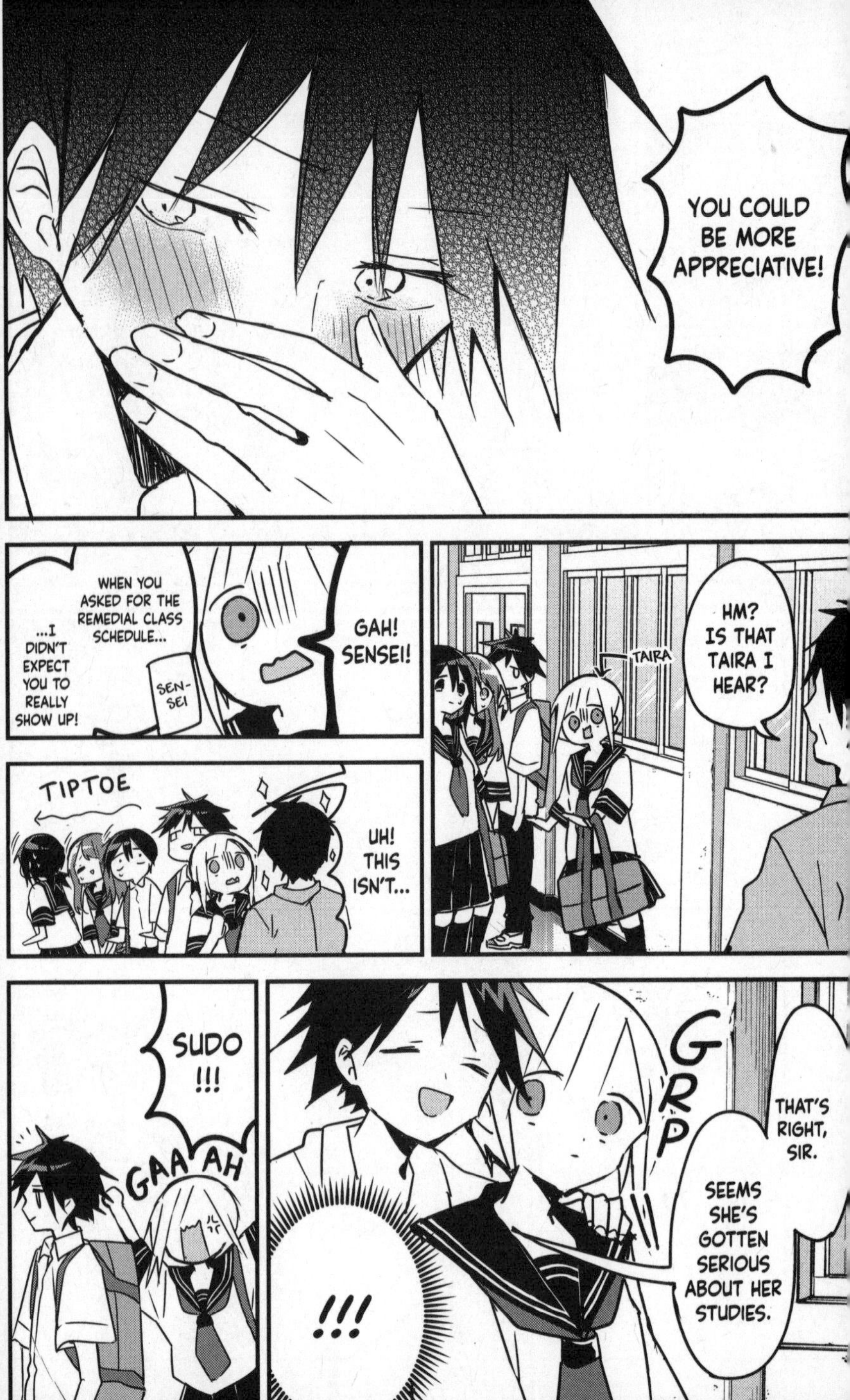
YOU COULD BE MORE APPRECIATIVE!
HM? IS THAT TAIRA I HEAR?
TAIRA
GAH! SENSEI!
WHEN YOU ASKED FOR THE REMEDIAL CLASS SCHEDULE...
...I DIDN'T EXPECT YOU TO REALLY SHOW UP!
SEN-SEI
UH! THIS ISN'T...
TIPTOE
THAT'S RIGHT, SIR.
SEEMS SHE'S GOTTEN SERIOUS ABOUT HER STUDIES.
GRP
!!!
SUDO !!!
GAAAH

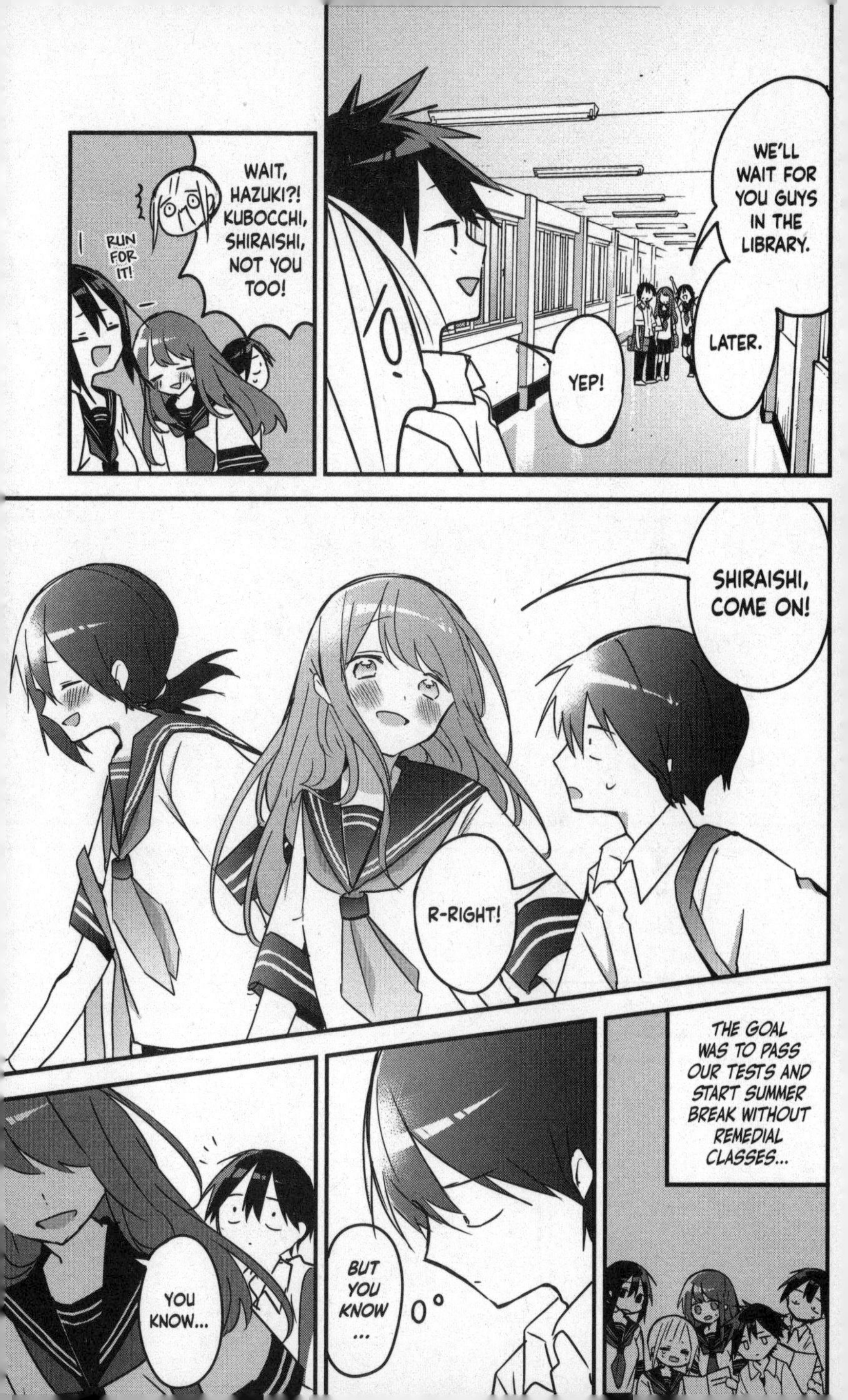
WE'LL WAIT FOR YOU GUYS IN THE LIBRARY.
LATER.
YEP!
WAIT, HAZUKI?! KUBOCCHI, SHIRAISHI, NOT YOU TOO!
RUN FOR IT!
SHIRAISHI, COME ON!
R-RIGHT!
THE GOAL WAS TO PASS OUR TESTS AND START SUMMER BREAK WITHOUT REMEDIAL CLASSES...
BUT YOU KNOW ...
YOU KNOW...

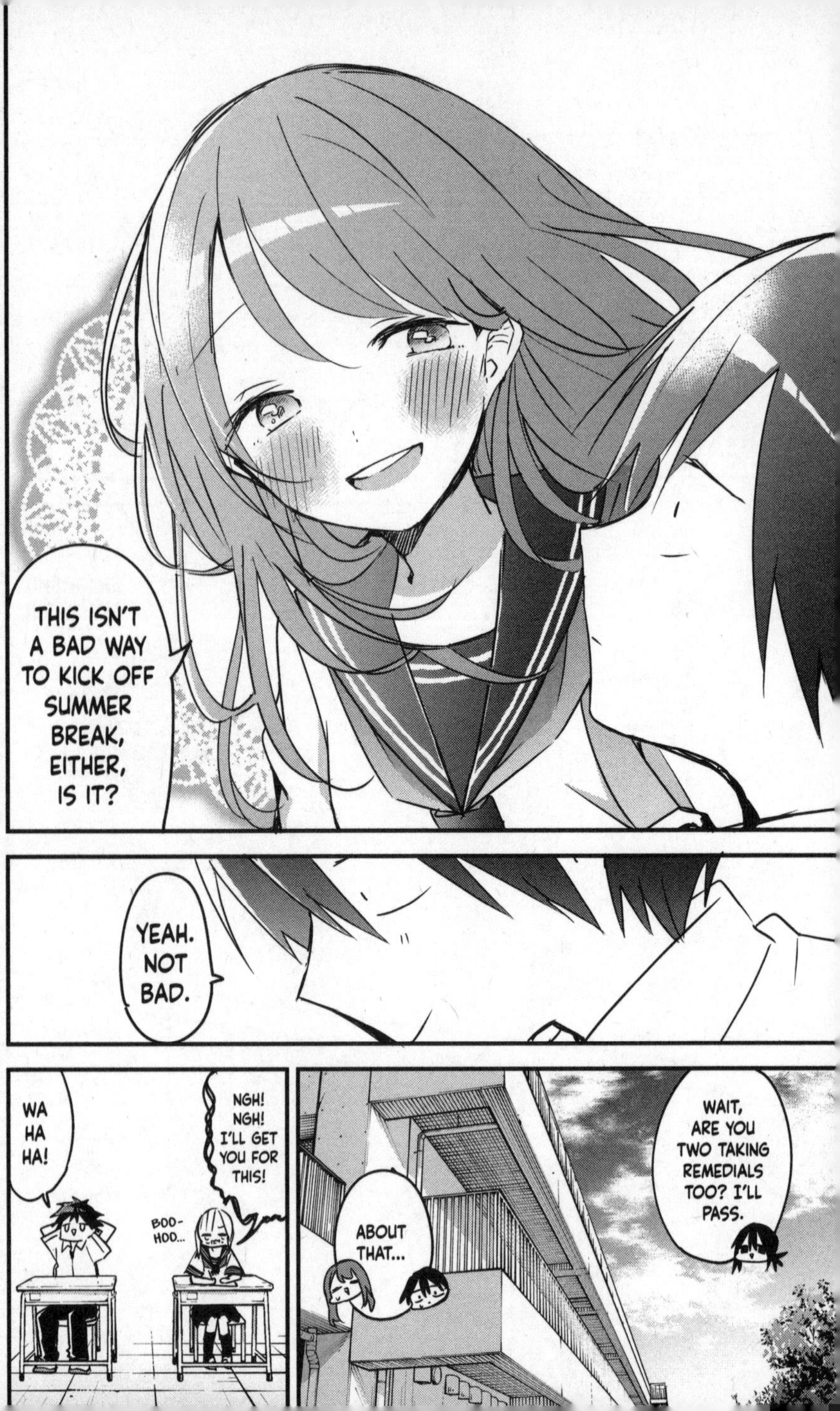
THIS ISN'T A BAD WAY TO KICK OFF SUMMER BREAK, EITHER, IS IT?
YEAH. NOT BAD.
WAIT, ARE YOU TWO TAKING REMEDIALS TOO? I'LL PASS.
ABOUT THAT...
NGH! NGH! I'LL GET YOU FOR THIS!
BOO-HOO...
WA HA HA!

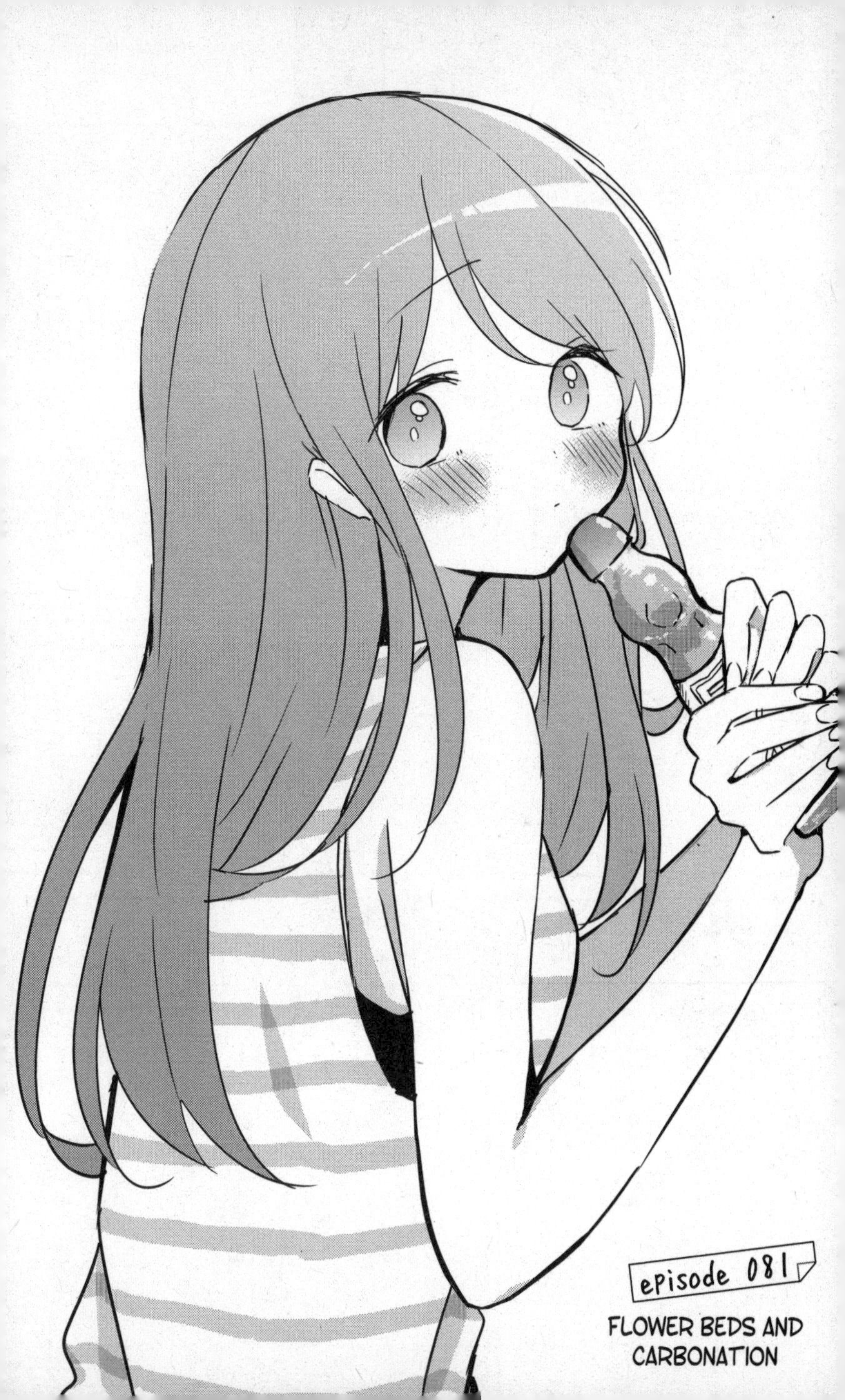

episode 081

FLOWER BEDS AND CARBONATION

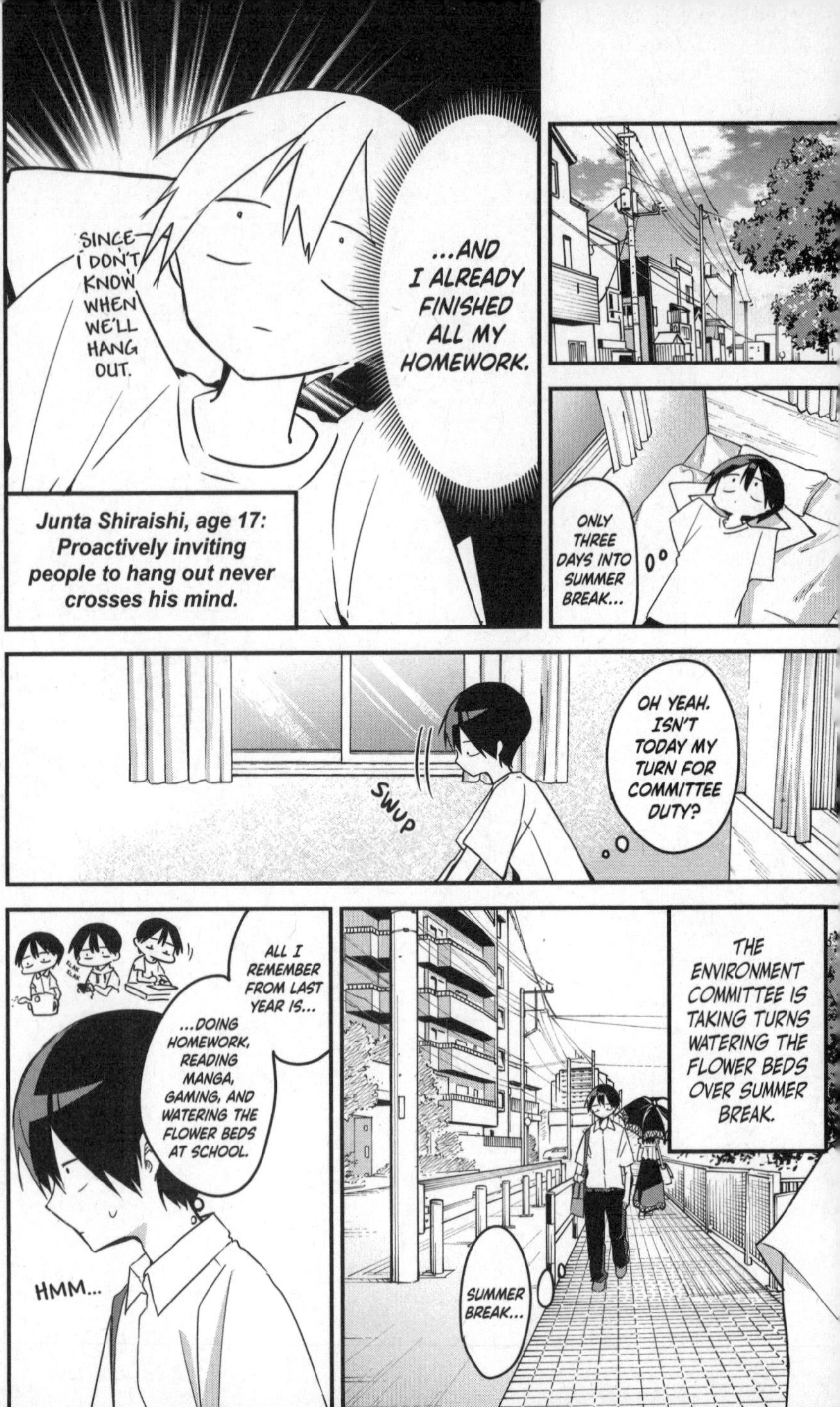
ONLY THREE DAYS INTO SUMMER BREAK...
...AND I ALREADY FINISHED ALL MY HOMEWORK.
SINCE I DON'T KNOW WHEN WE'LL HANG OUT.
Junta Shiraishi, age 17: Proactively inviting people to hang out never crosses his mind.
OH YEAH. ISN'T TODAY MY TURN FOR COMMITTEE DUTY?
SWUP
THE ENVIRONMENT COMMITTEE IS TAKING TURNS WATERING THE FLOWER BEDS OVER SUMMER BREAK.
SUMMER BREAK...
ALL I REMEMBER FROM LAST YEAR IS...
...DOING HOMEWORK, READING MANGA, GAMING, AND WATERING THE FLOWER BEDS AT SCHOOL.
HMM...

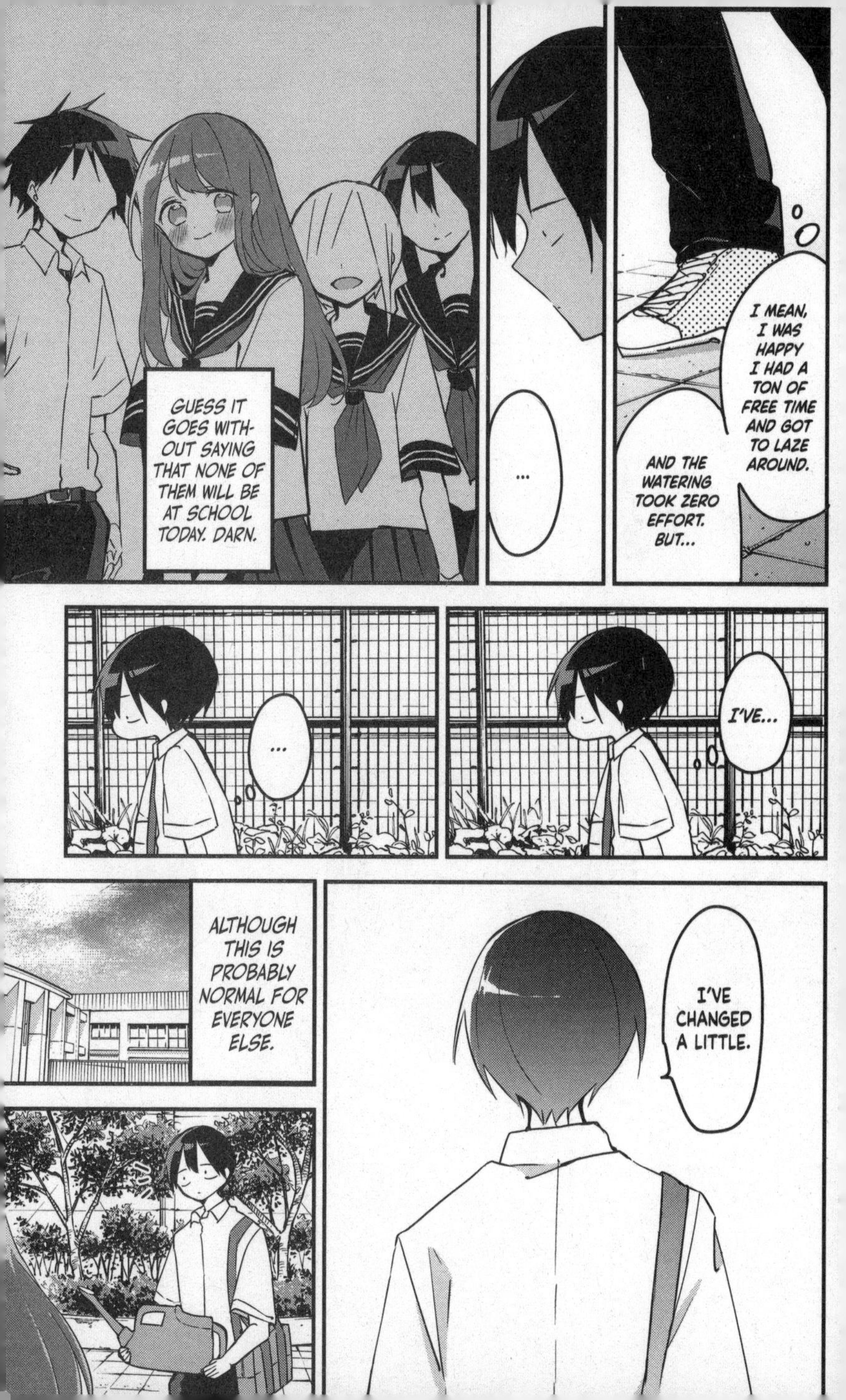
I MEAN, I WAS HAPPY I HAD A TON OF FREE TIME AND GOT TO LAZE AROUND.
AND THE WATERING TOOK ZERO EFFORT. BUT...
...
GUESS IT GOES WITH-OUT SAYING THAT NONE OF THEM WILL BE AT SCHOOL TODAY. DARN.
I'VE...
...
I'VE CHANGED A LITTLE.
ALTHOUGH THIS IS PROBABLY NORMAL FOR EVERYONE ELSE.

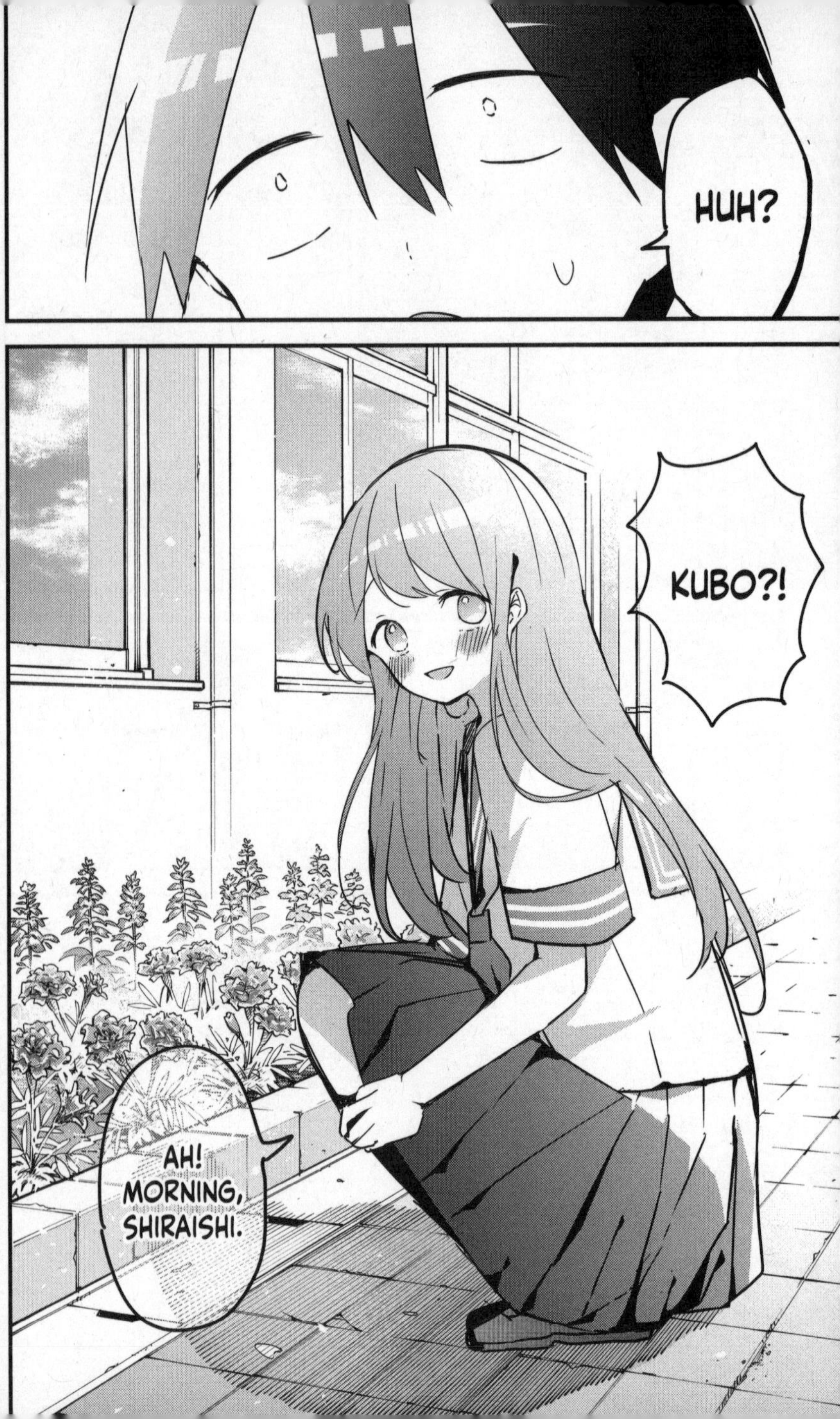
HUH?
KUBO?!
AH! MORNING, SHIRAISHI.

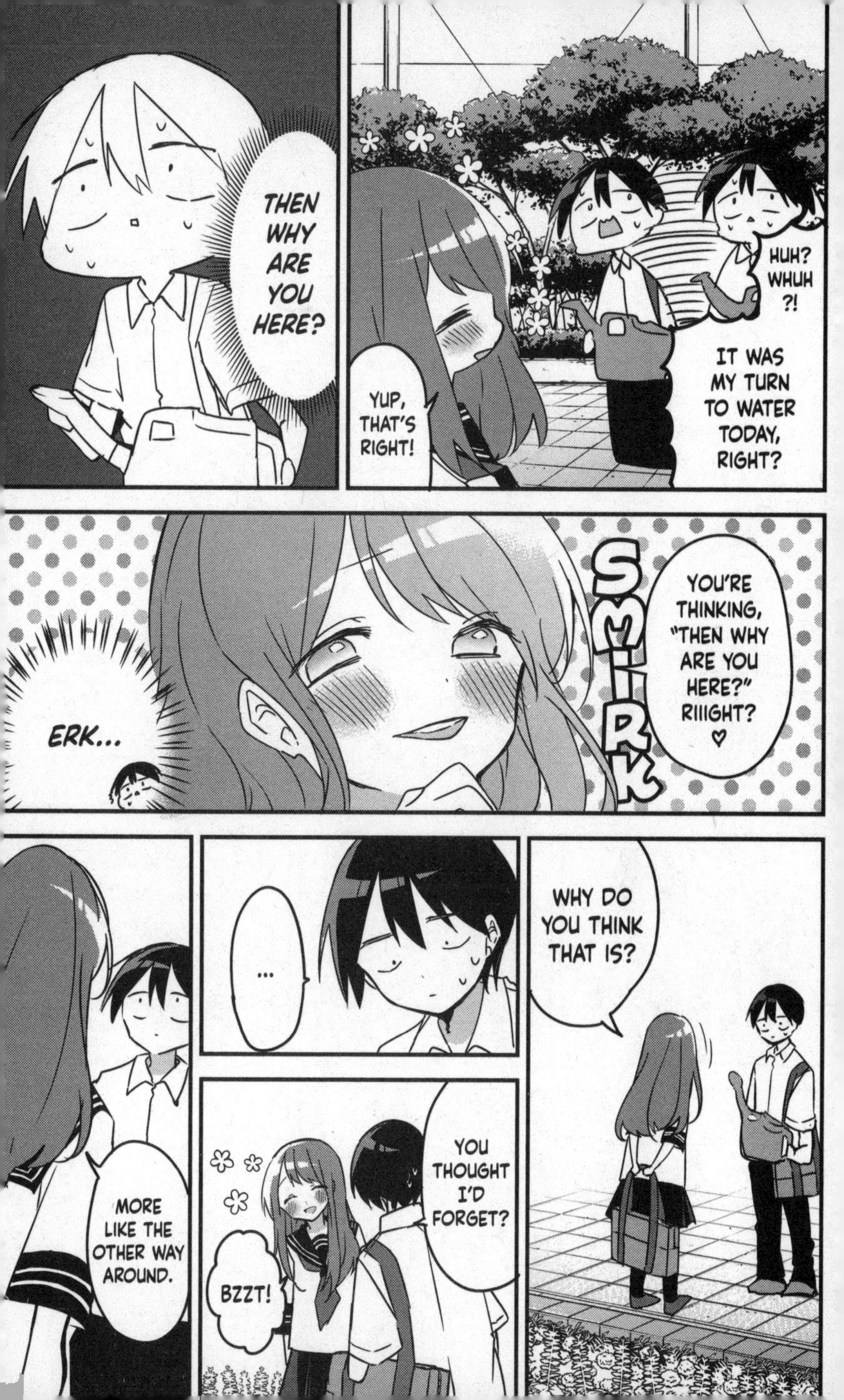
HUH? WHUH?!
IT WAS MY TURN TO WATER TODAY, RIGHT?
YUP, THAT'S RIGHT!
THEN WHY ARE YOU HERE?
SMIRK
YOU'RE THINKING, "THEN WHY ARE YOU HERE?" RIIIGHT? ♡
ERK...
WHY DO YOU THINK THAT IS?
...
YOU THOUGHT I'D FORGET?
BZZT!
MORE LIKE THE OTHER WAY AROUND.

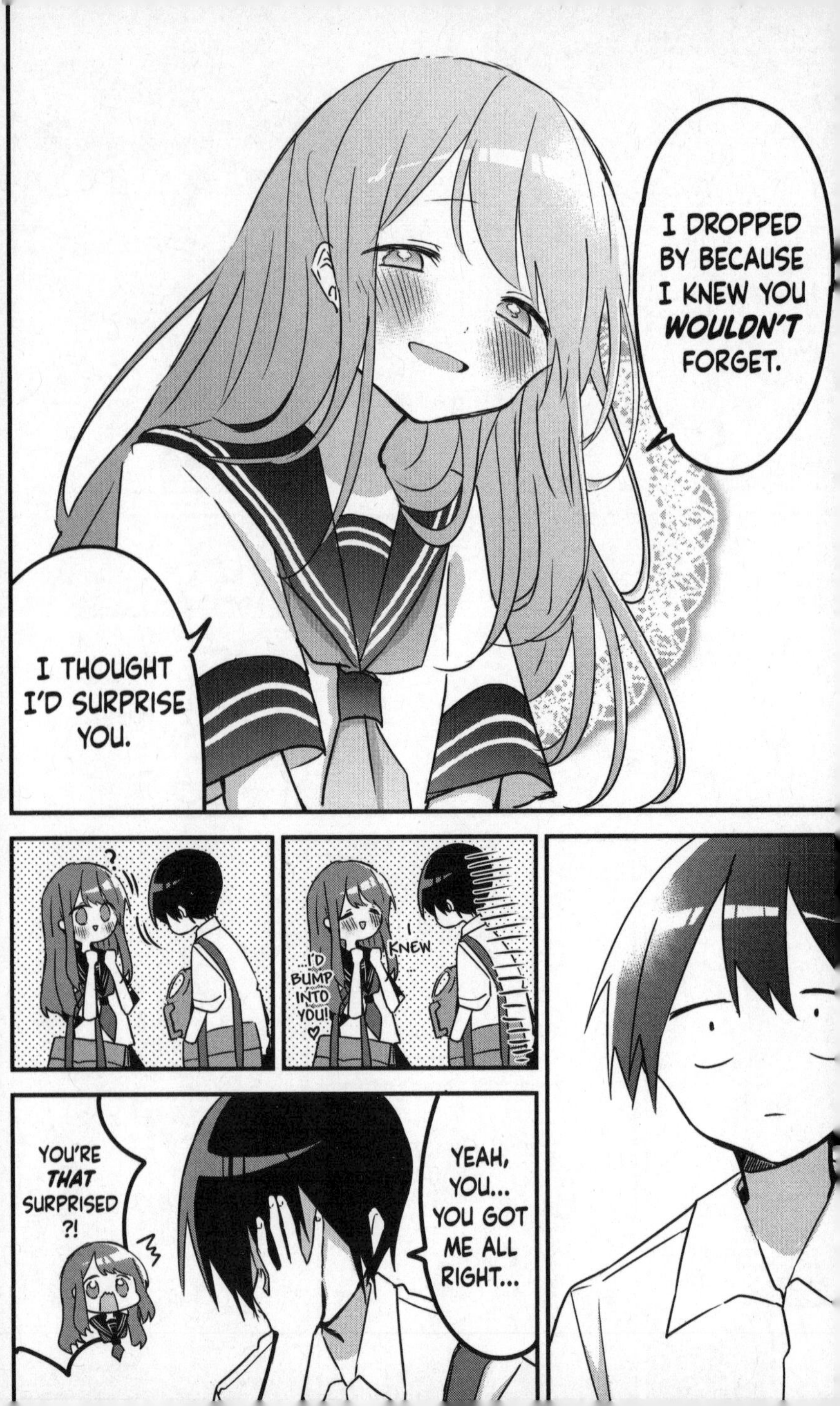
I DROPPED BY BECAUSE I KNEW YOU ***WOULDN'T*** FORGET.
I THOUGHT I'D SURPRISE YOU.
I KNEW...
...I'D BUMP INTO YOU! ♥
?
YEAH, YOU... YOU GOT ME ALL RIGHT...
YOU'RE ***THAT*** SURPRISED?!

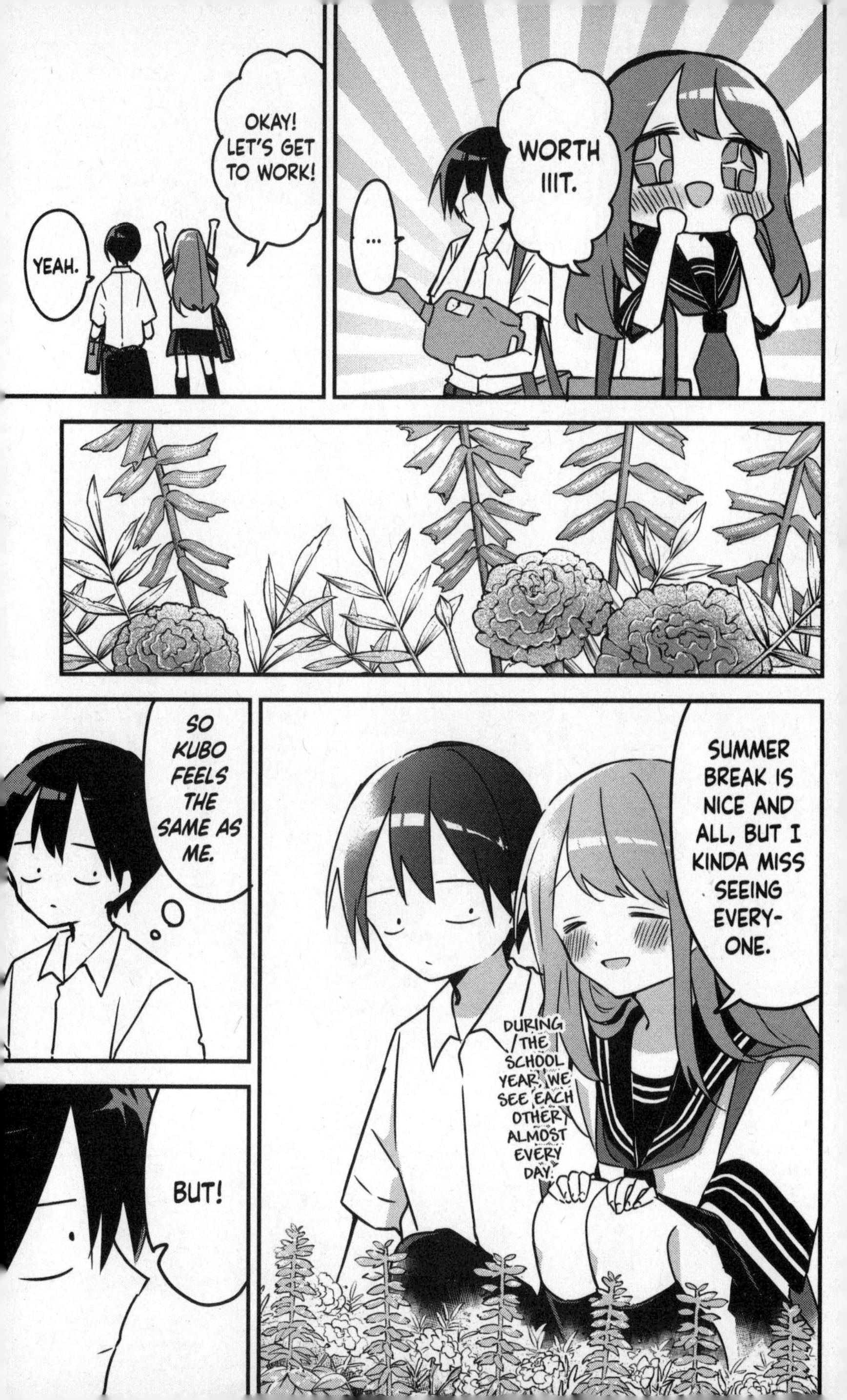
WORTH IIIT.
...
OKAY! LET'S GET TO WORK!
YEAH.
SUMMER BREAK IS NICE AND ALL, BUT I KINDA MISS SEEING EVERY-ONE.
DURING THE SCHOOL YEAR, WE SEE EACH OTHER ALMOST EVERY DAY.
SO KUBO FEELS THE SAME AS ME.
BUT!

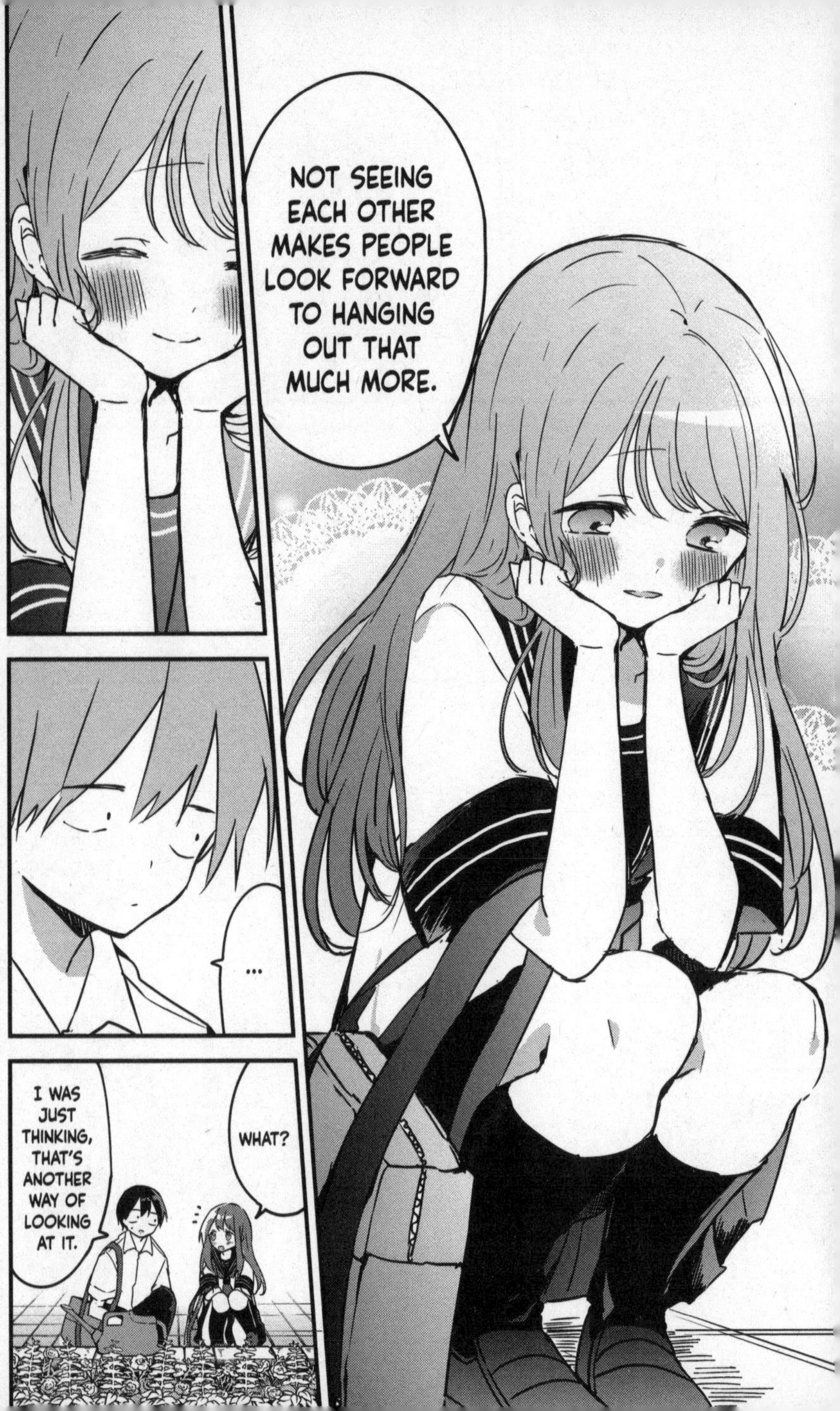
NOT SEEING EACH OTHER MAKES PEOPLE LOOK FORWARD TO HANGING OUT THAT MUCH MORE.
...
WHAT?
I WAS JUST THINKING, THAT'S ANOTHER WAY OF LOOKING AT IT.

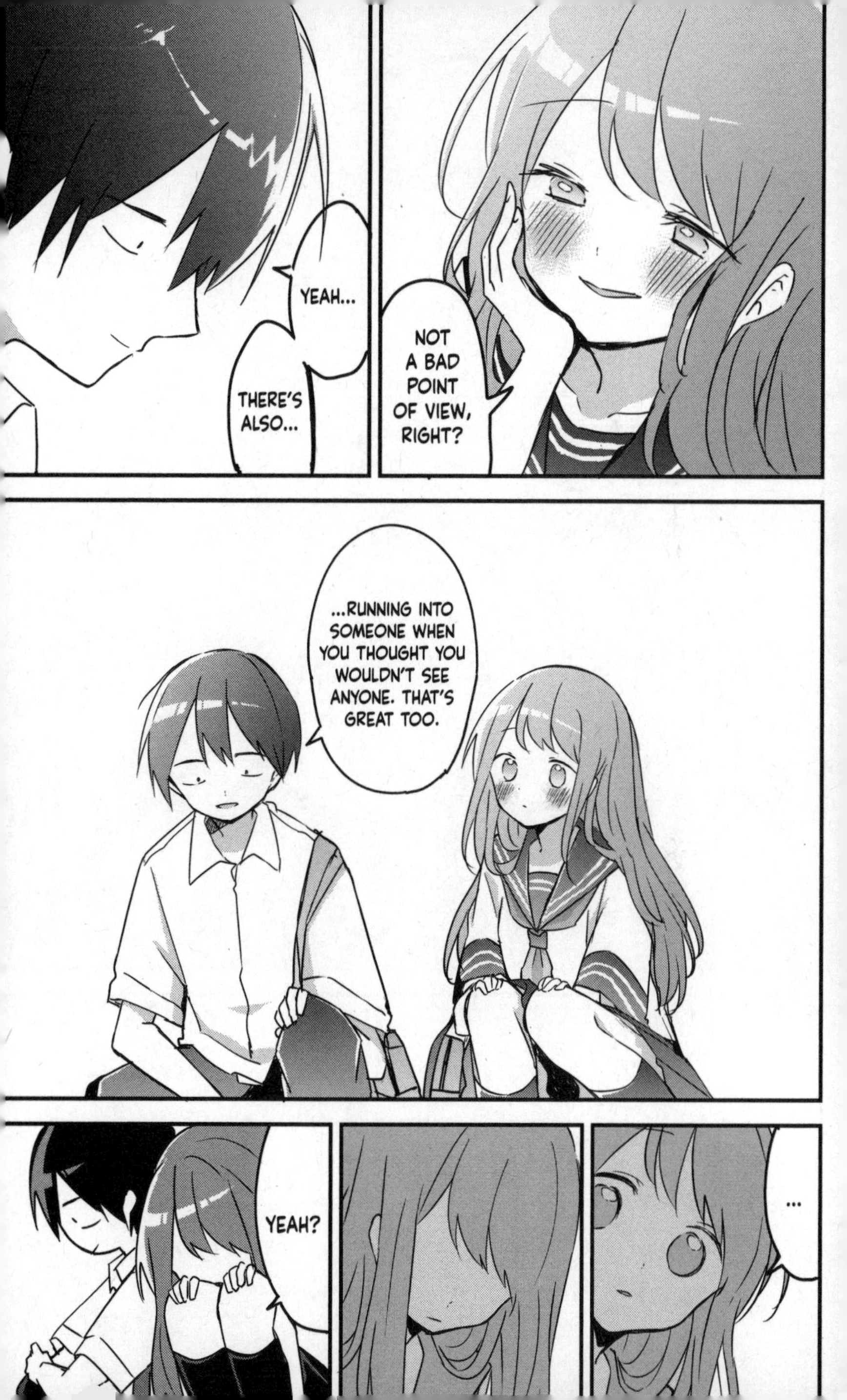
NOT A BAD POINT OF VIEW, RIGHT?
YEAH...
THERE'S ALSO...
...RUNNING INTO SOMEONE WHEN YOU THOUGHT YOU WOULDN'T SEE ANYONE. THAT'S GREAT TOO.
...
YEAH?

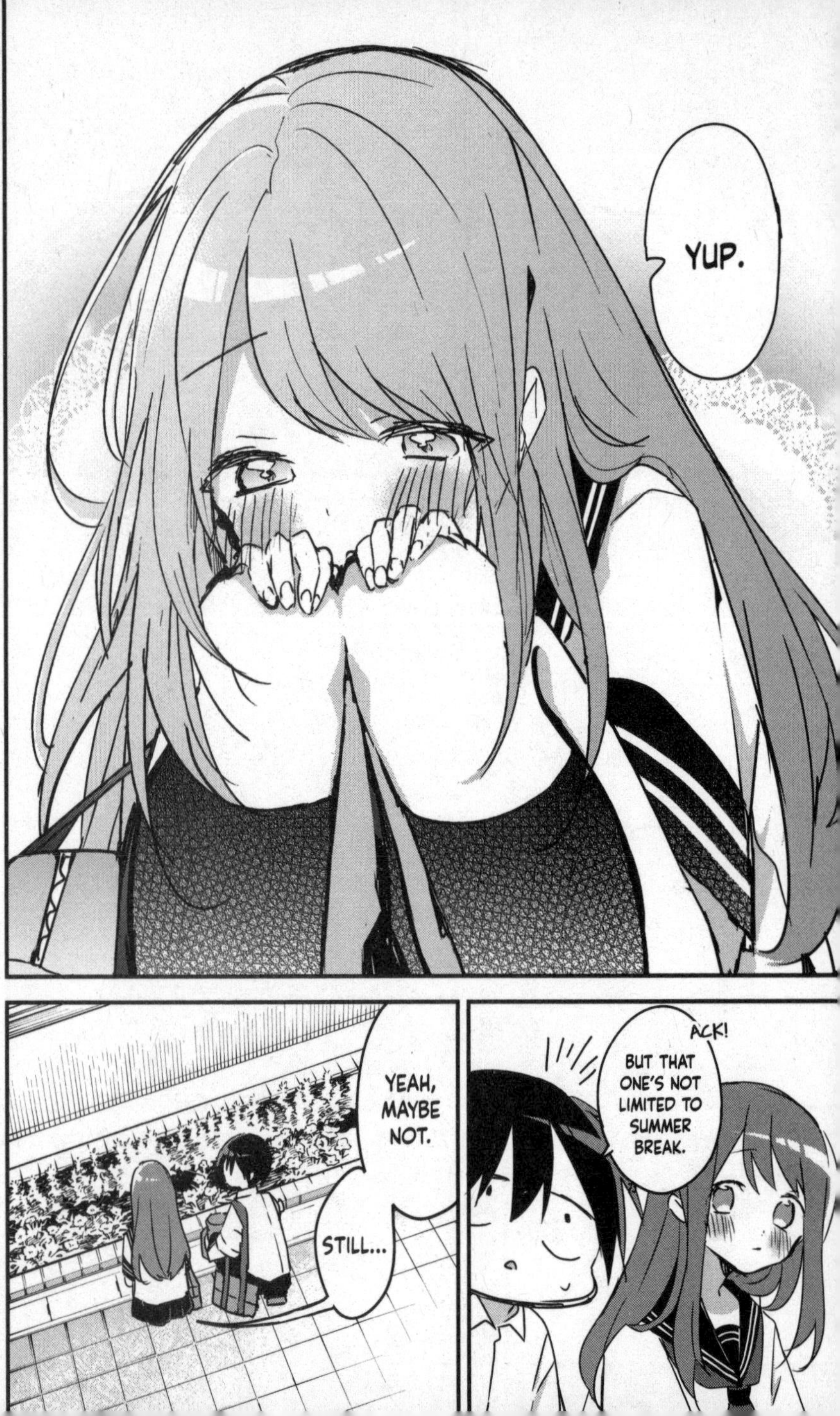
YUP.
ACK!
BUT THAT ONE'S NOT LIMITED TO SUMMER BREAK.
YEAH, MAYBE NOT.
STILL...

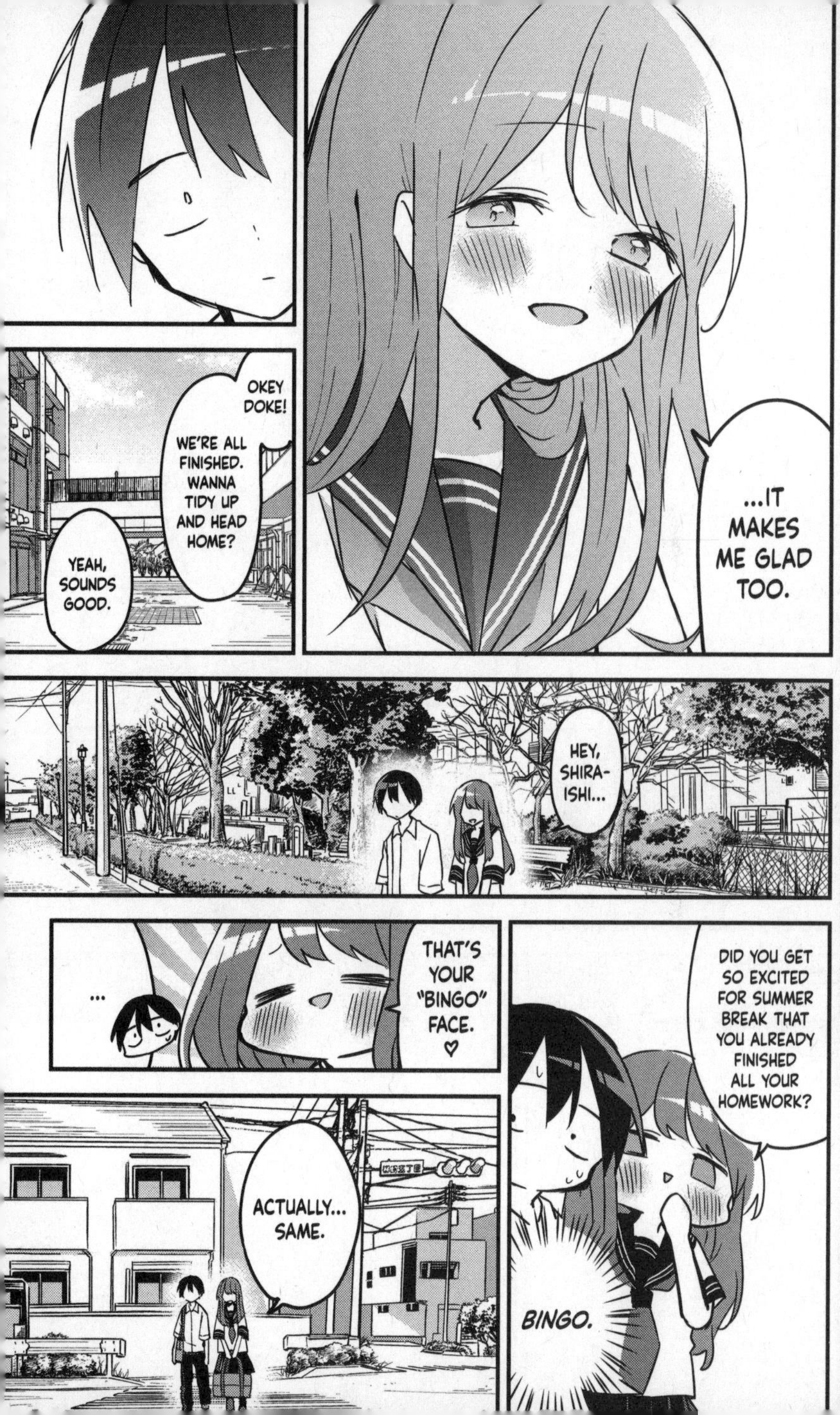
...IT MAKES ME GLAD TOO.
OKEY DOKE!
WE'RE ALL FINISHED. WANNA TIDY UP AND HEAD HOME?
YEAH, SOUNDS GOOD.
HEY, SHIRA-ISHI...
DID YOU GET SO EXCITED FOR SUMMER BREAK THAT YOU ALREADY FINISHED ALL YOUR HOMEWORK?
BINGO.
THAT'S YOUR "BINGO" FACE. ♡
...
ACTUALLY... SAME.

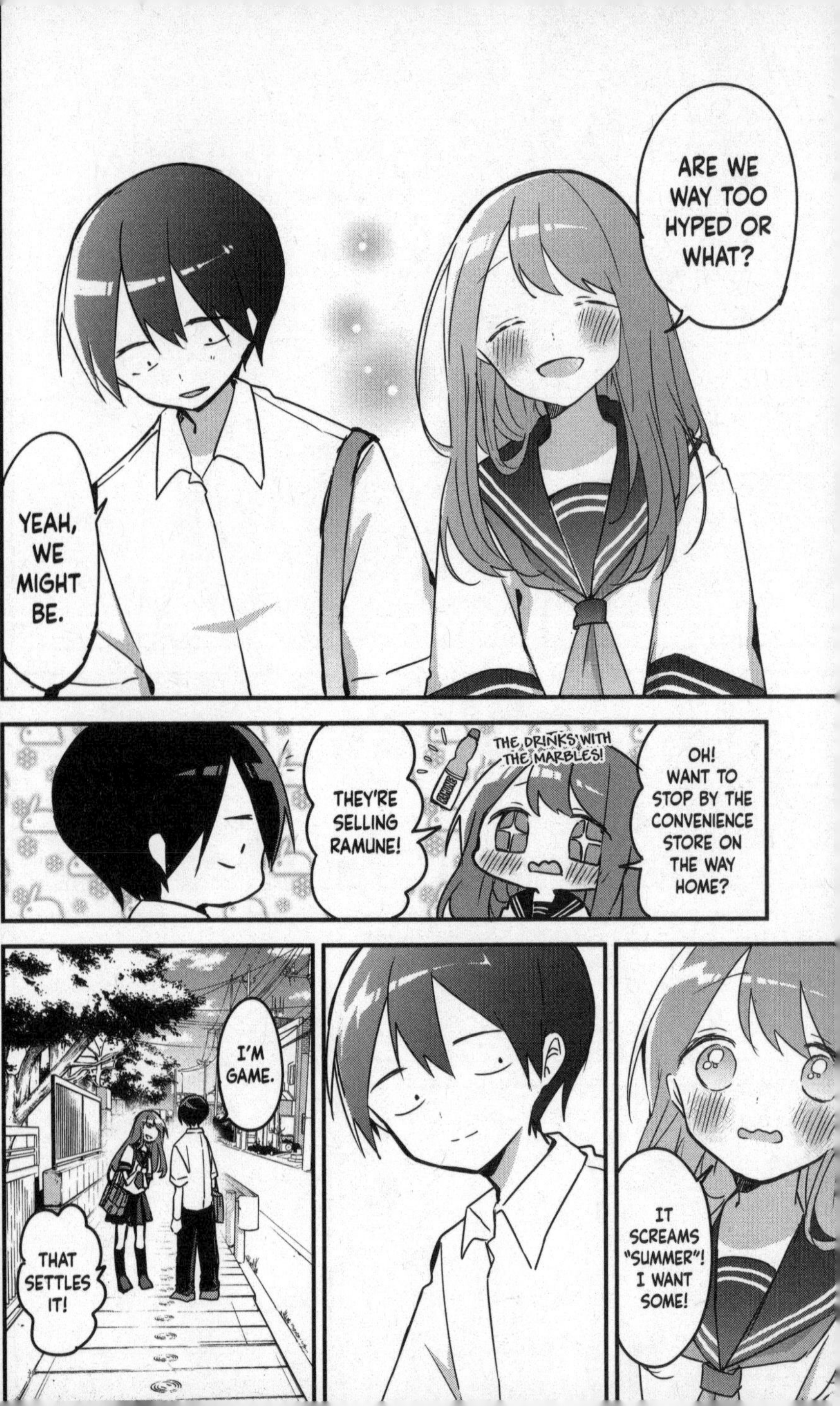
ARE WE WAY TOO HYPED OR WHAT?
YEAH, WE MIGHT BE.
OH! WANT TO STOP BY THE CONVENIENCE STORE ON THE WAY HOME?
THE DRINKS WITH THE MARBLES!
THEY'RE SELLING RAMUNE!
IT SCREAMS "SUMMER"! I WANT SOME!
I'M GAME.
THAT SETTLES IT!

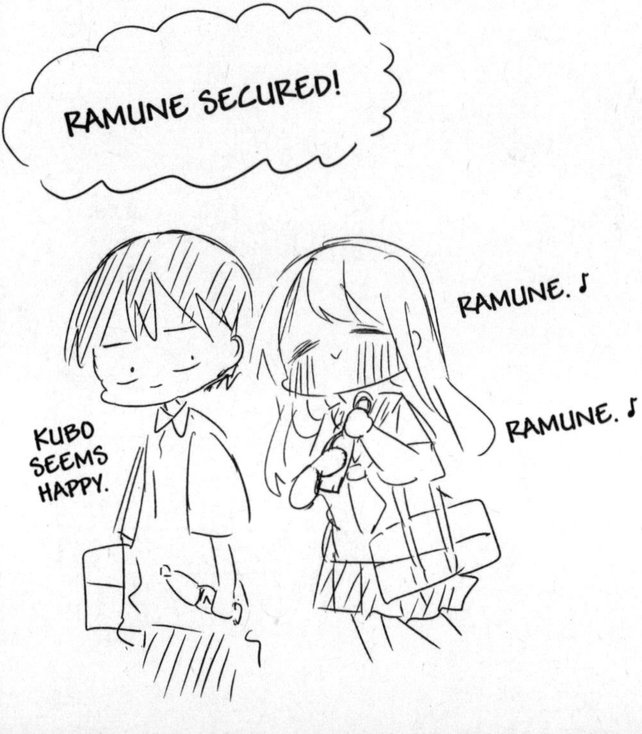
RAMUNE SECURED!
RAMUNE. ♪
RAMUNE. ♪
KUBO SEEMS HAPPY.

AFTERWARD, THEY DRANK THEIR
RAMUNE AT THE PARK BEFORE
CONTINUING HOME.

IT
SURE
IS.

IT'S
BUBBLY.
♡

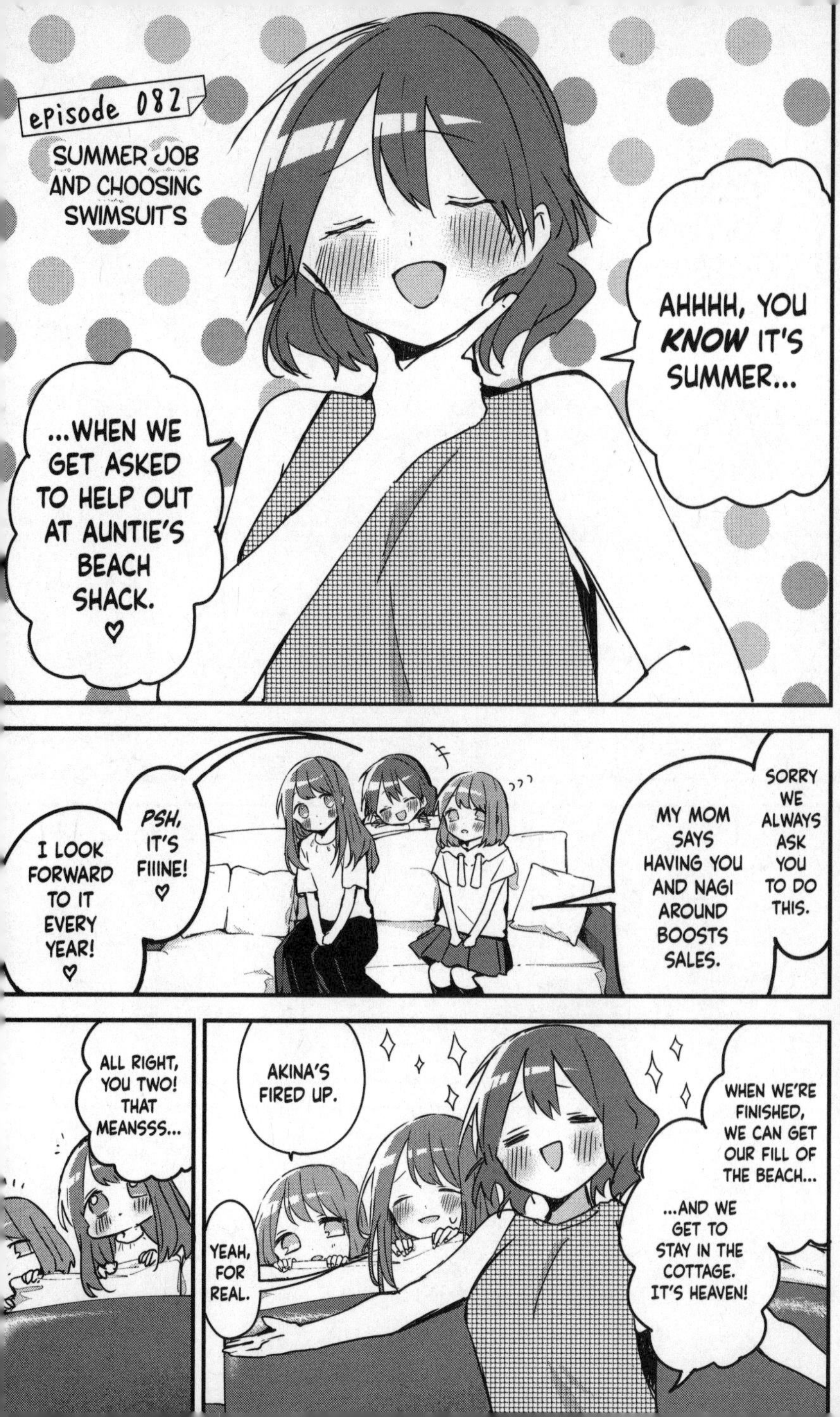
episode 082
SUMMER JOB AND CHOOSING SWIMSUITS
AHHHH, YOU *KNOW* IT'S SUMMER...
...WHEN WE GET ASKED TO HELP OUT AT AUNTIE'S BEACH SHACK. ♡
SORRY WE ALWAYS ASK YOU TO DO THIS.
MY MOM SAYS HAVING YOU AND NAGI AROUND BOOSTS SALES.
PSH, IT'S FIIINE! ♡
I LOOK FORWARD TO IT EVERY YEAR! ♡
WHEN WE'RE FINISHED, WE CAN GET OUR FILL OF THE BEACH...
...AND WE GET TO STAY IN THE COTTAGE. IT'S HEAVEN!
AKINA'S FIRED UP.
YEAH, FOR REAL.
ALL RIGHT, YOU TWO! THAT MEANSSS...

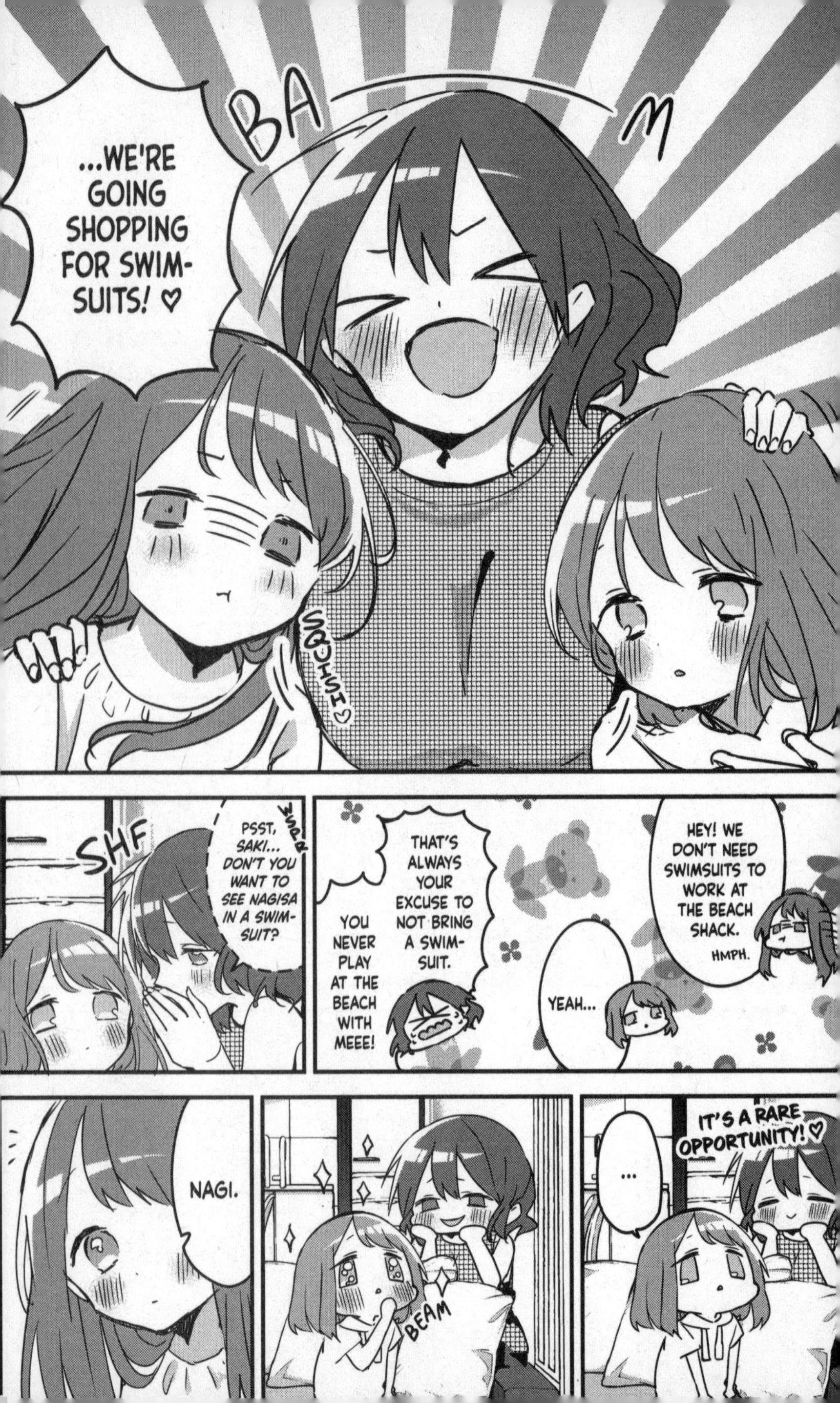
...WE'RE GOING SHOPPING FOR SWIM-SUITS! ♡
BAM
SQUISH ♡
HEY! WE DON'T NEED SWIMSUITS TO WORK AT THE BEACH SHACK.
HMPH.
YEAH...
THAT'S ALWAYS YOUR EXCUSE TO NOT BRING A SWIM-SUIT.
YOU NEVER PLAY AT THE BEACH WITH MEEE!
WSPR
PSST, SAKI... DON'T YOU WANT TO SEE NAGISA IN A SWIM-SUIT?
SHF
IT'S A RARE OPPORTUNITY! ♡
...
BEAM
NAGI.

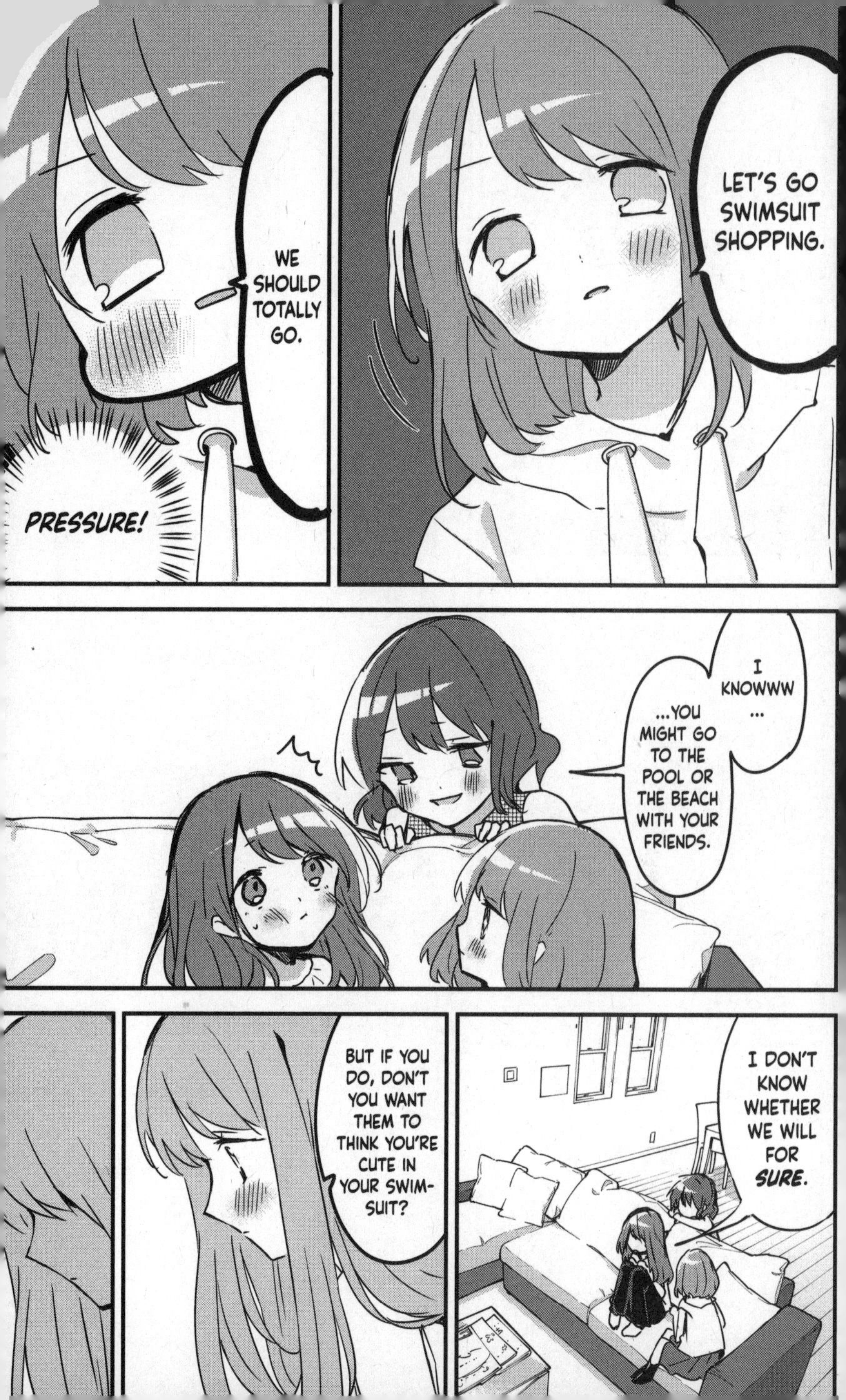
LET'S GO SWIMSUIT SHOPPING.
WE SHOULD TOTALLY GO.
PRESSURE!
I KNOWWW...
...YOU MIGHT GO TO THE POOL OR THE BEACH WITH YOUR FRIENDS.
I DON'T KNOW WHETHER WE WILL FOR **SURE**.
BUT IF YOU DO, DON'T YOU WANT THEM TO THINK YOU'RE CUTE IN YOUR SWIM-SUIT?

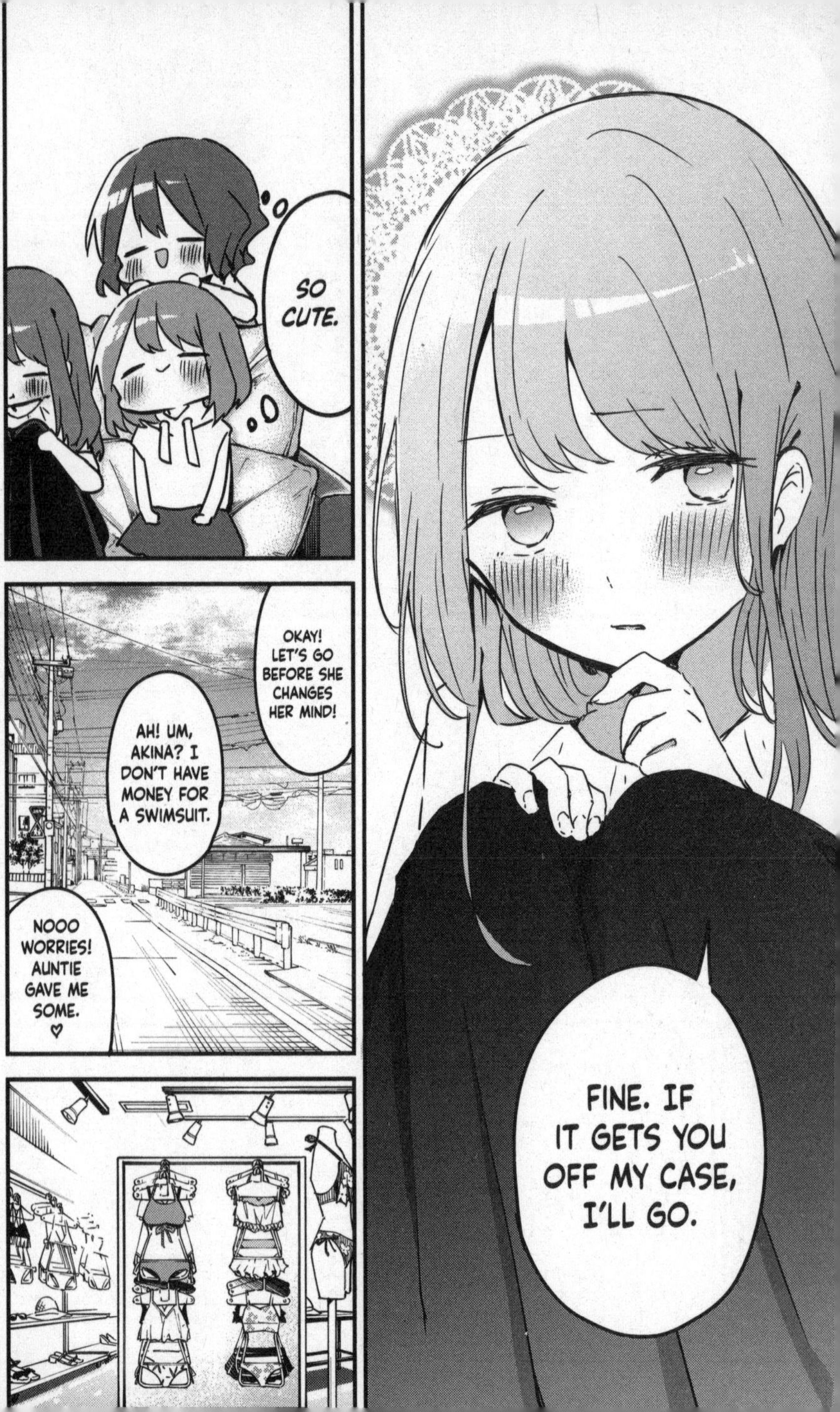
FINE. IF IT GETS YOU OFF MY CASE, I'LL GO.
SO CUTE.
OKAY! LET'S GO BEFORE SHE CHANGES HER MIND!
AH! UM, AKINA? I DON'T HAVE MONEY FOR A SWIMSUIT.
NOOO WORRIES! AUNTIE GAVE ME SOME. ♡

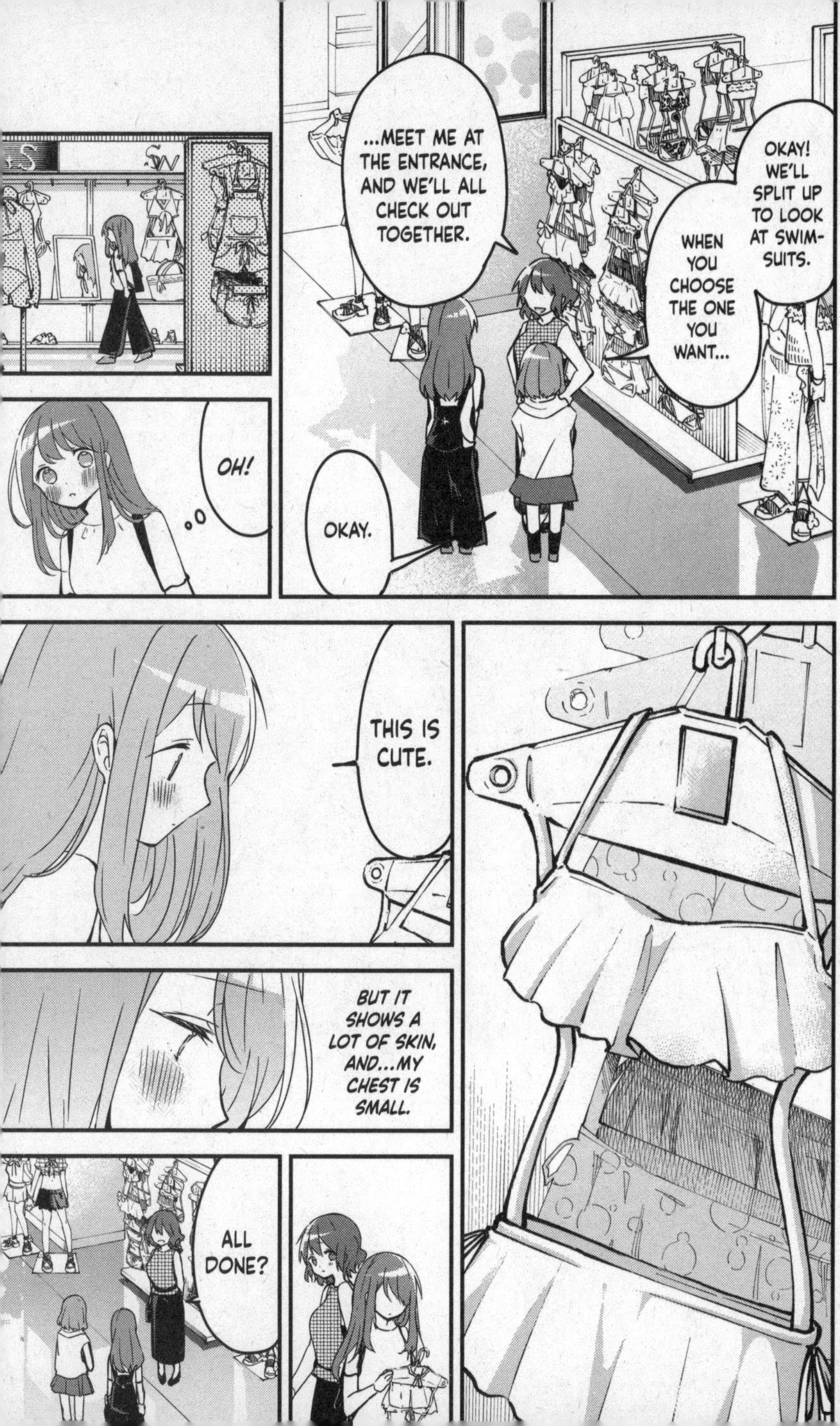
OKAY! WE'LL SPLIT UP TO LOOK AT SWIM-SUITS.
WHEN YOU CHOOSE THE ONE YOU WANT...
...MEET ME AT THE ENTRANCE, AND WE'LL ALL CHECK OUT TOGETHER.
OKAY.
OH!
THIS IS CUTE.
BUT IT SHOWS A LOT OF SKIN, AND...MY CHEST IS SMALL.
ALL DONE?

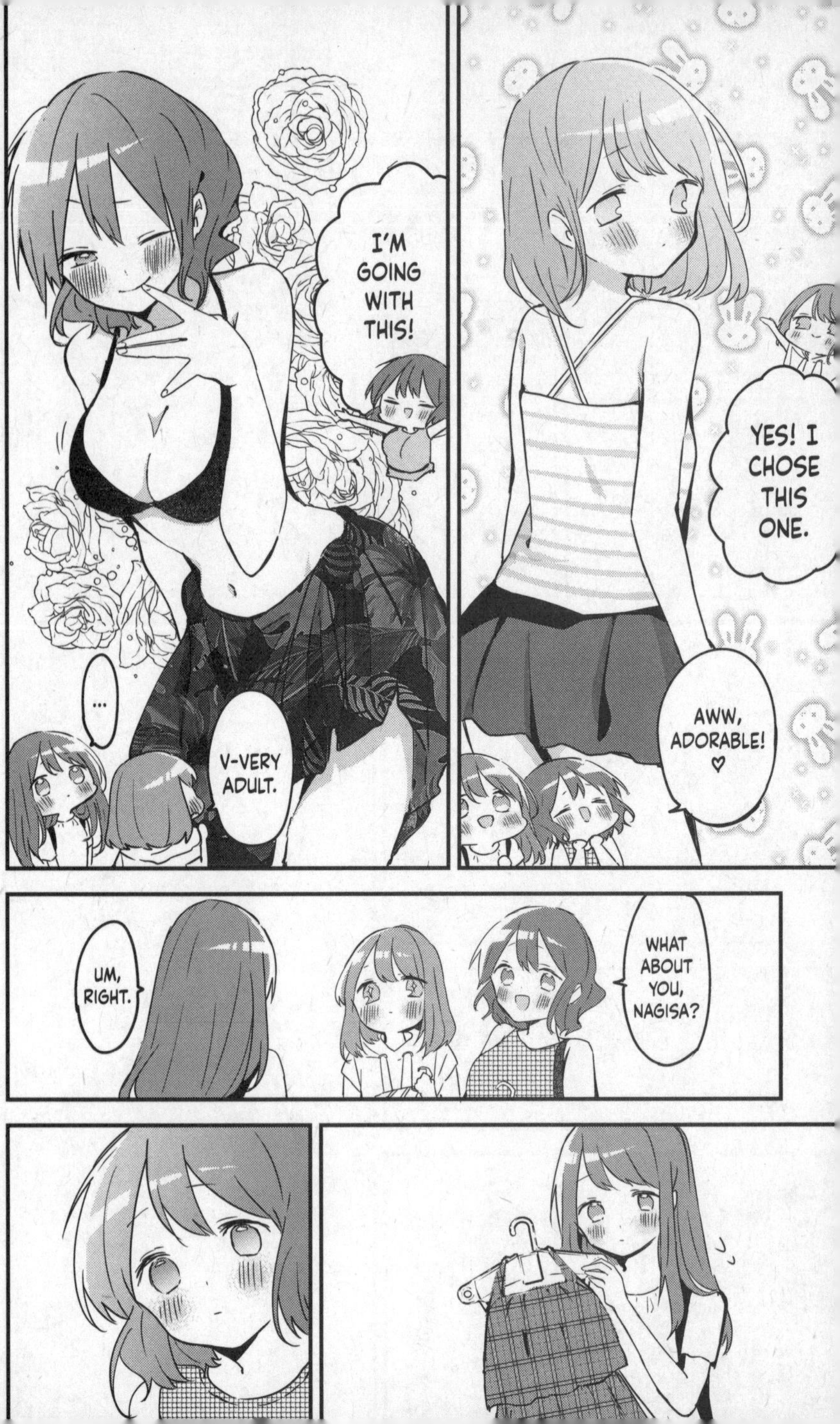
YES! I CHOSE THIS ONE.
AWW, ADORABLE! ♡
I'M GOING WITH THIS!
V-VERY ADULT.
...
WHAT ABOUT YOU, NAGISA?
UM, RIGHT.

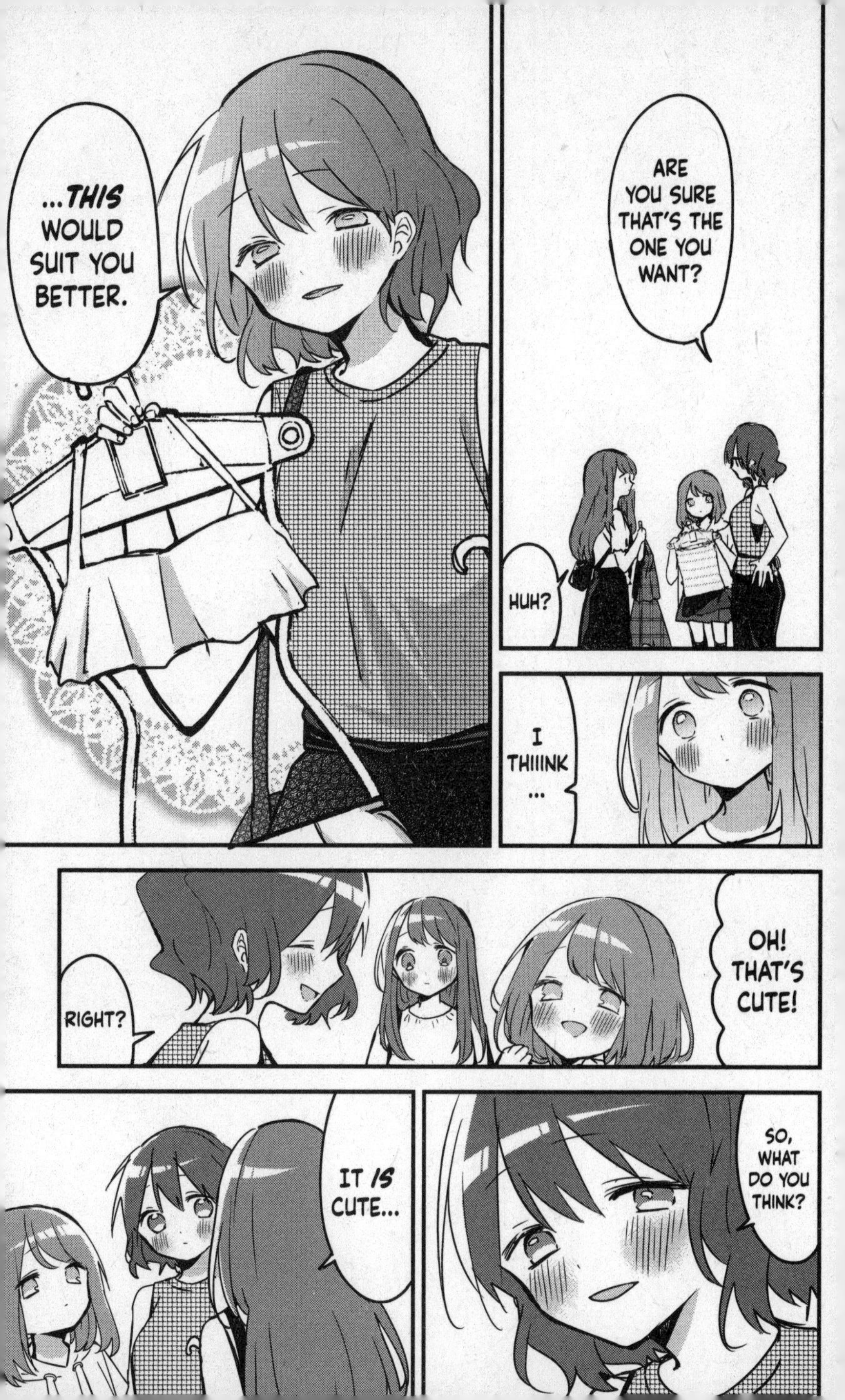
ARE YOU SURE THAT'S THE ONE YOU WANT?
HUH?
I THIIINK ...
...*THIS* WOULD SUIT YOU BETTER.
OH! THAT'S CUTE!
RIGHT?
SO, WHAT DO YOU THINK?
IT *IS* CUTE...

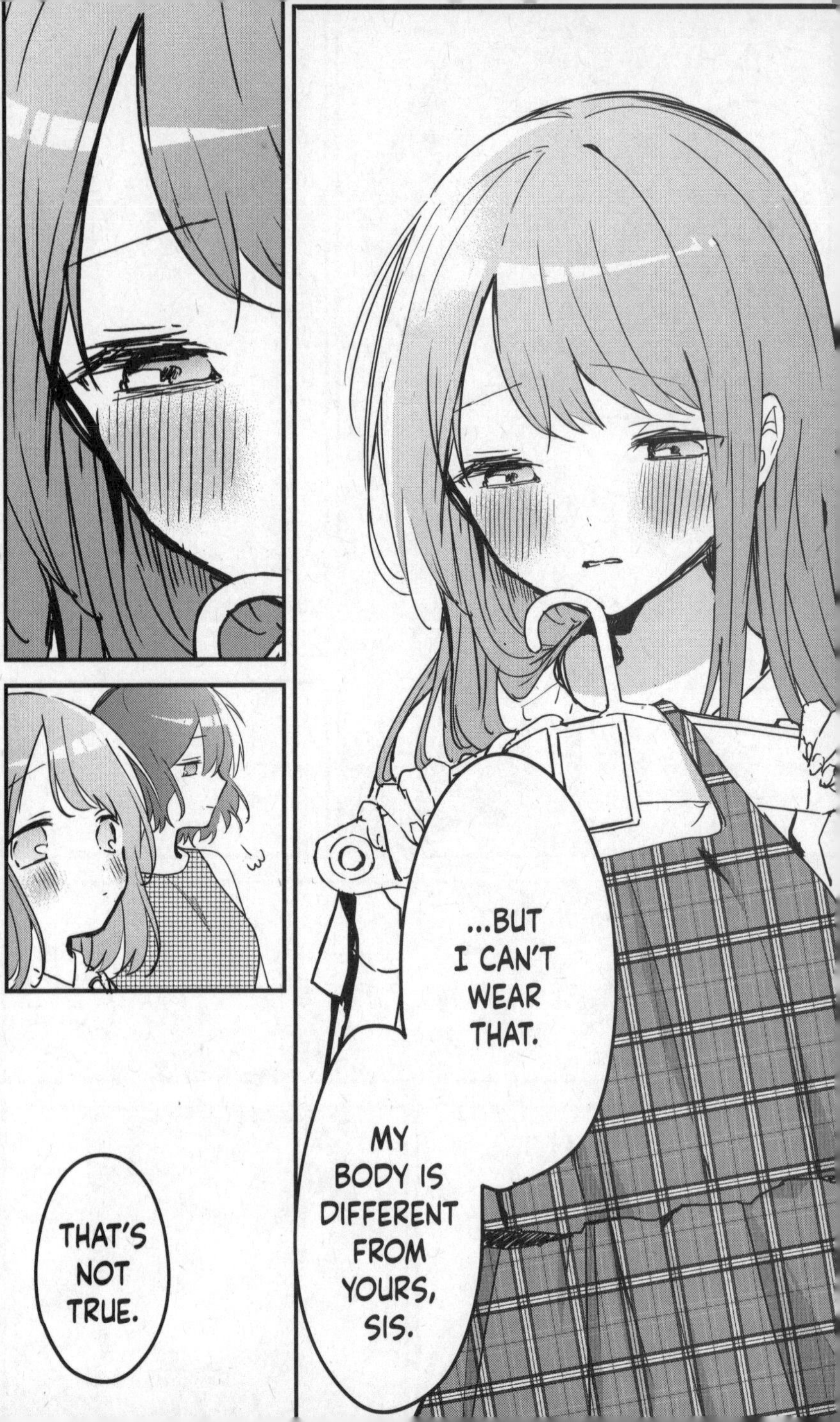
...BUT I CAN'T WEAR THAT.
MY BODY IS DIFFERENT FROM YOURS, SIS.
THAT'S NOT TRUE.

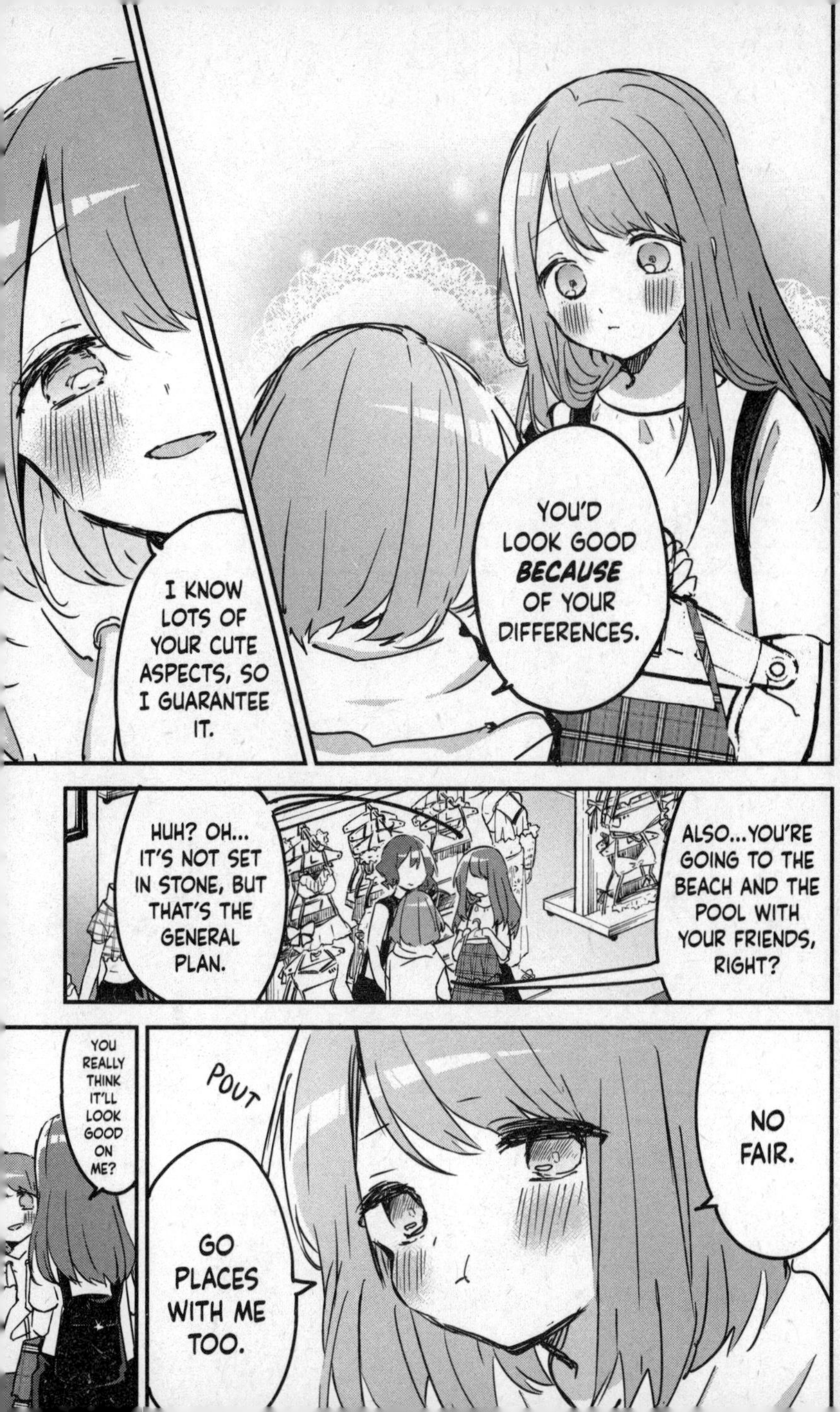
YOU'D LOOK GOOD ***BECAUSE*** OF YOUR DIFFERENCES.
I KNOW LOTS OF YOUR CUTE ASPECTS, SO I GUARANTEE IT.
ALSO...YOU'RE GOING TO THE BEACH AND THE POOL WITH YOUR FRIENDS, RIGHT?
HUH? OH... IT'S NOT SET IN STONE, BUT THAT'S THE GENERAL PLAN.
NO FAIR.
POUT
GO PLACES WITH ME TOO.
YOU REALLY THINK IT'LL LOOK GOOD ON ME?

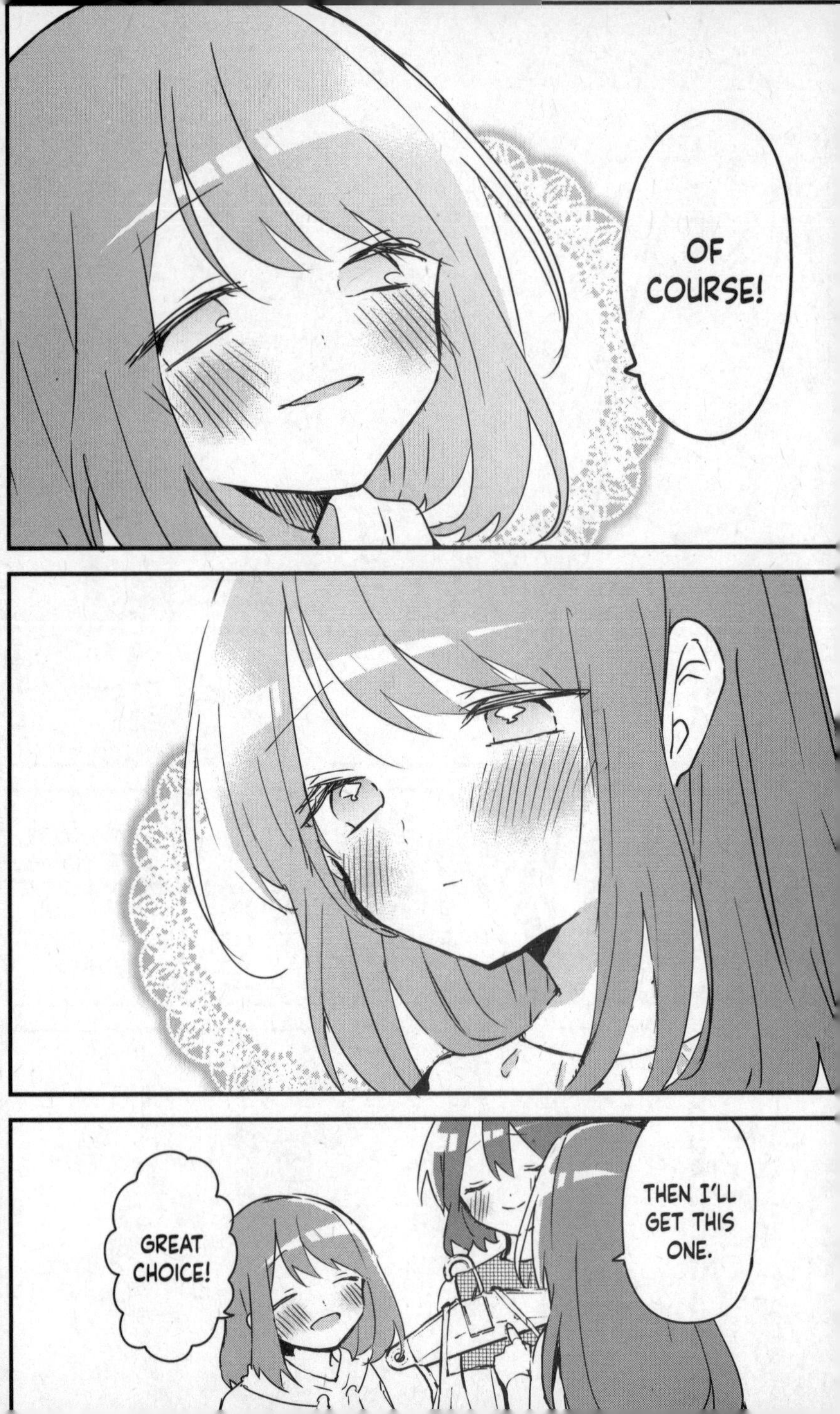
OF COURSE!
THEN I'LL GET THIS ONE.
GREAT CHOICE!

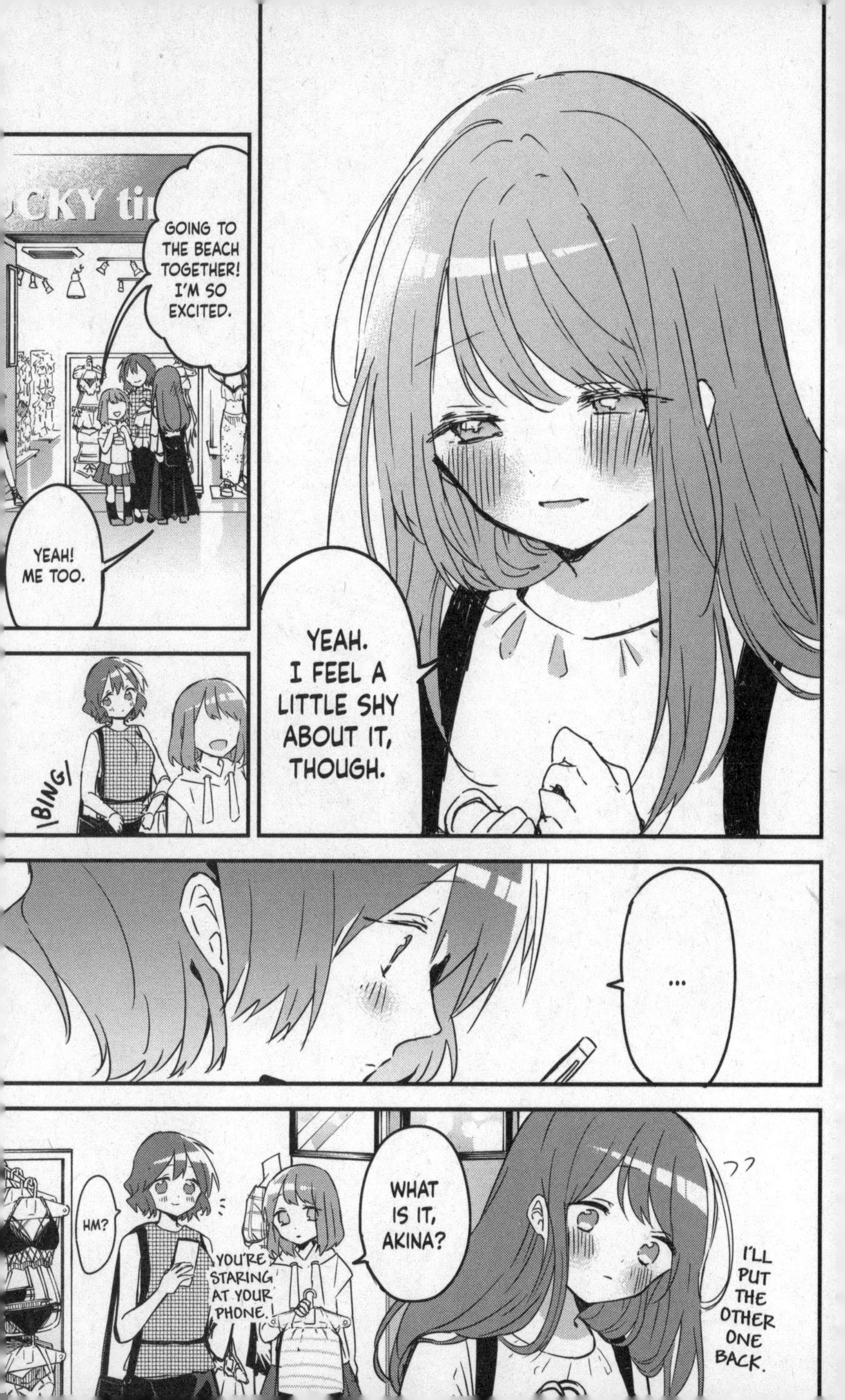
YEAH. I FEEL A LITTLE SHY ABOUT IT, THOUGH.
GOING TO THE BEACH TOGETHER! I'M SO EXCITED.
YEAH! ME TOO.
BING
...
I'LL PUT THE OTHER ONE BACK.
WHAT IS IT, AKINA?
YOU'RE STARING AT YOUR PHONE.
HM?

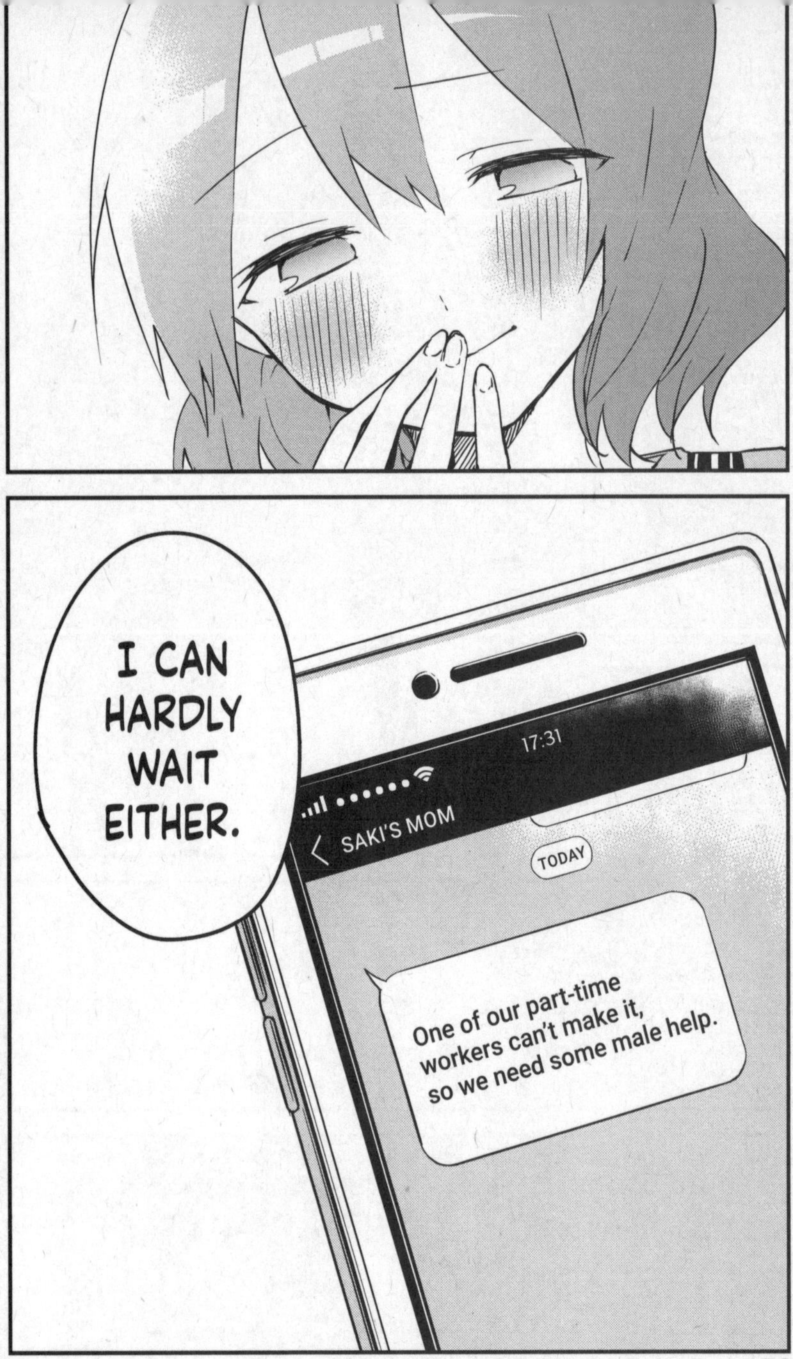
I CAN HARDLY WAIT EITHER.
17:31
SAKI'S MOM
TODAY
One of our part-time workers can't make it, so we need some male help.

episode 083

BEACH SHACK AND THE KUBO PROBLEM

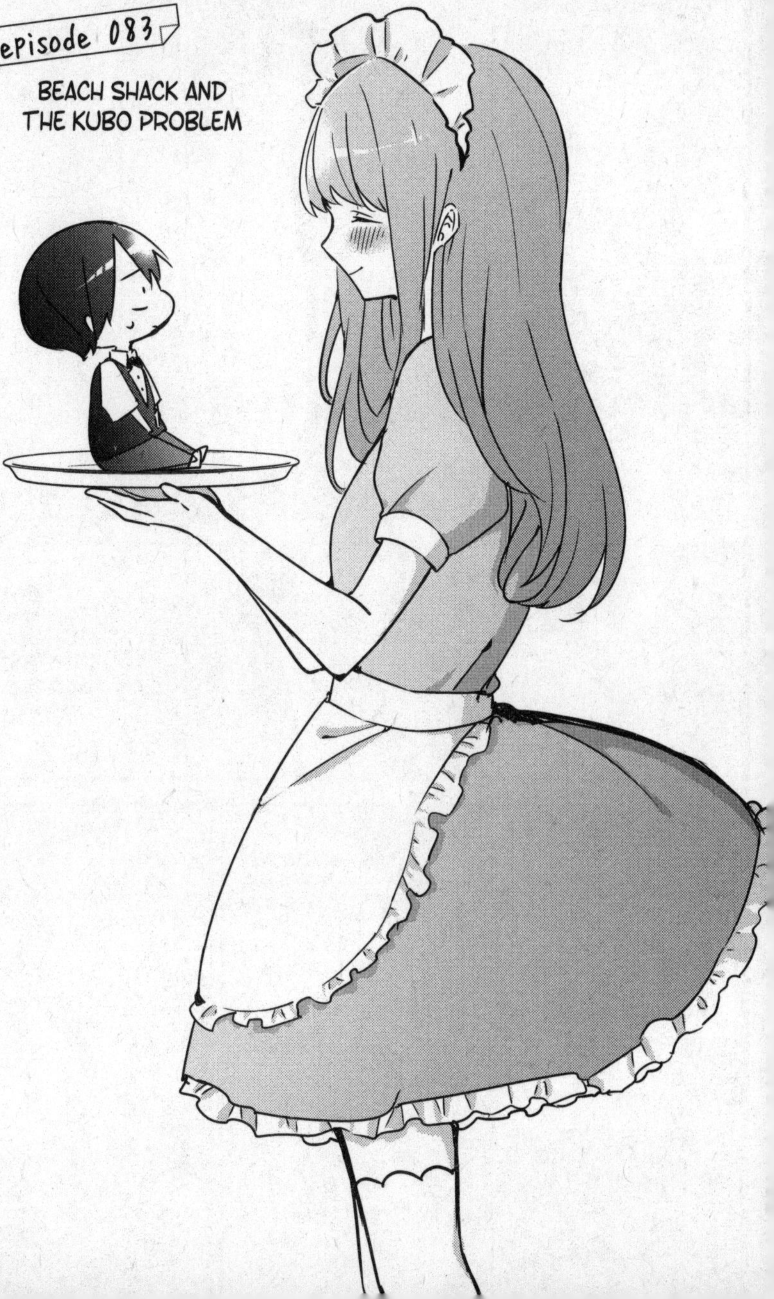

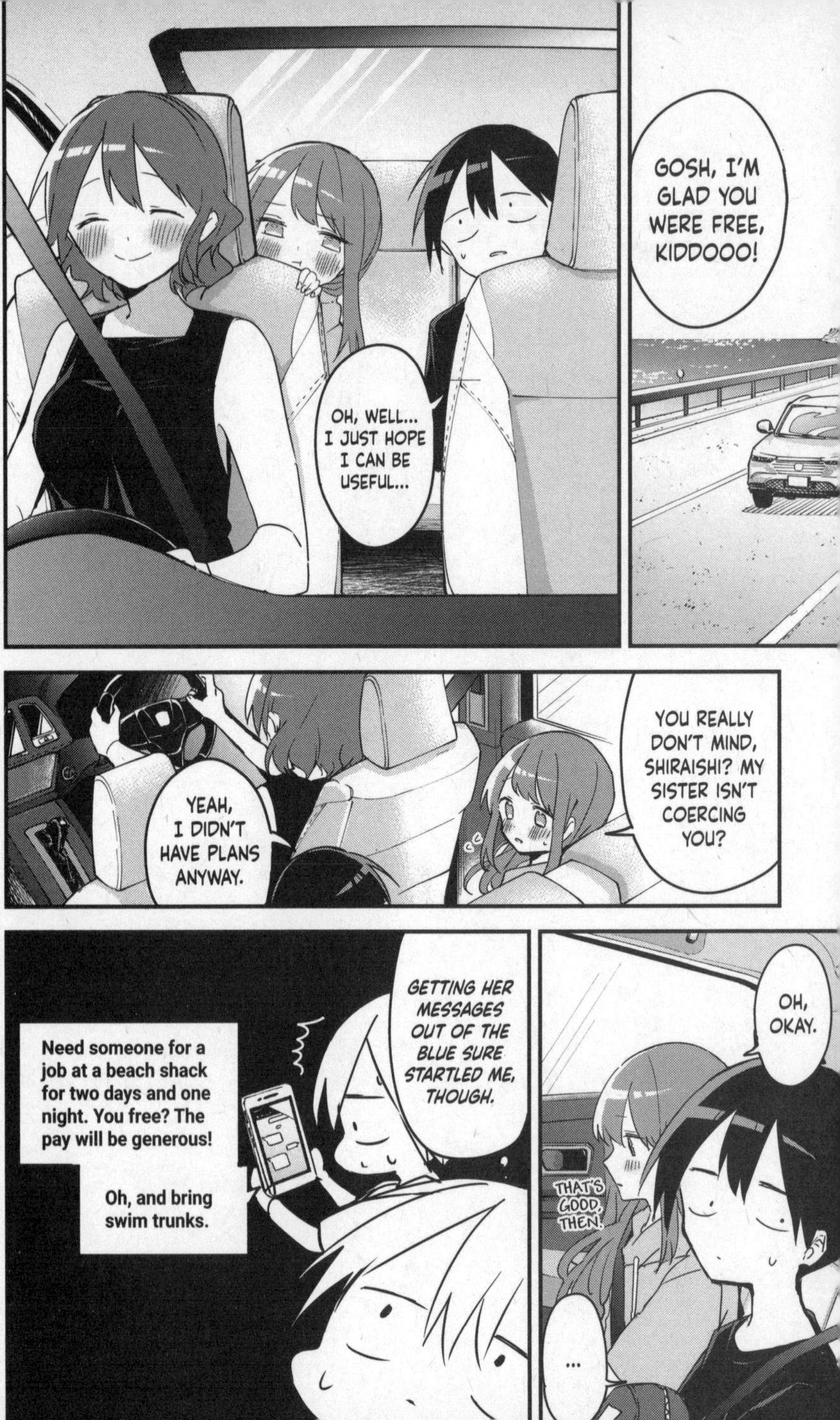
GOSH, I'M GLAD YOU WERE FREE, KIDDOOO!
OH, WELL... I JUST HOPE I CAN BE USEFUL...
YOU REALLY DON'T MIND, SHIRAISHI? MY SISTER ISN'T COERCING YOU?
YEAH, I DIDN'T HAVE PLANS ANYWAY.
OH, OKAY.
THAT'S GOOD, THEN.
...
GETTING HER MESSAGES OUT OF THE BLUE SURE STARTLED ME, THOUGH.
Need someone for a job at a beach shack for two days and one night. You free? The pay will be generous!
Oh, and bring swim trunks.

WELL, HAVING EXTRA MONEY CAN'T HURT.

I'LL GIVE IT MY ALL.

17:02

< August

Sun	M	T	W	Th
	1	2	3	4
		Kubo's birthday		
7	8	9	10	
	15	16	17	

A SUMMER JOB?

AND SO, HERE I AM.

YEAH... CAN'T WAIT...

WAIT, A SWIM-SUIT...

I ASSUMED IT WAS A RANDOM JOB!

NEVER WOULD HAVE GUESSED THE BEACH SHACK BELONGED TO SAKI'S FAMILY...

EEEE, CAN'T WAIT TO PLAY ON THE BEACH AFTER WORK. RIGHT, NAGISA?

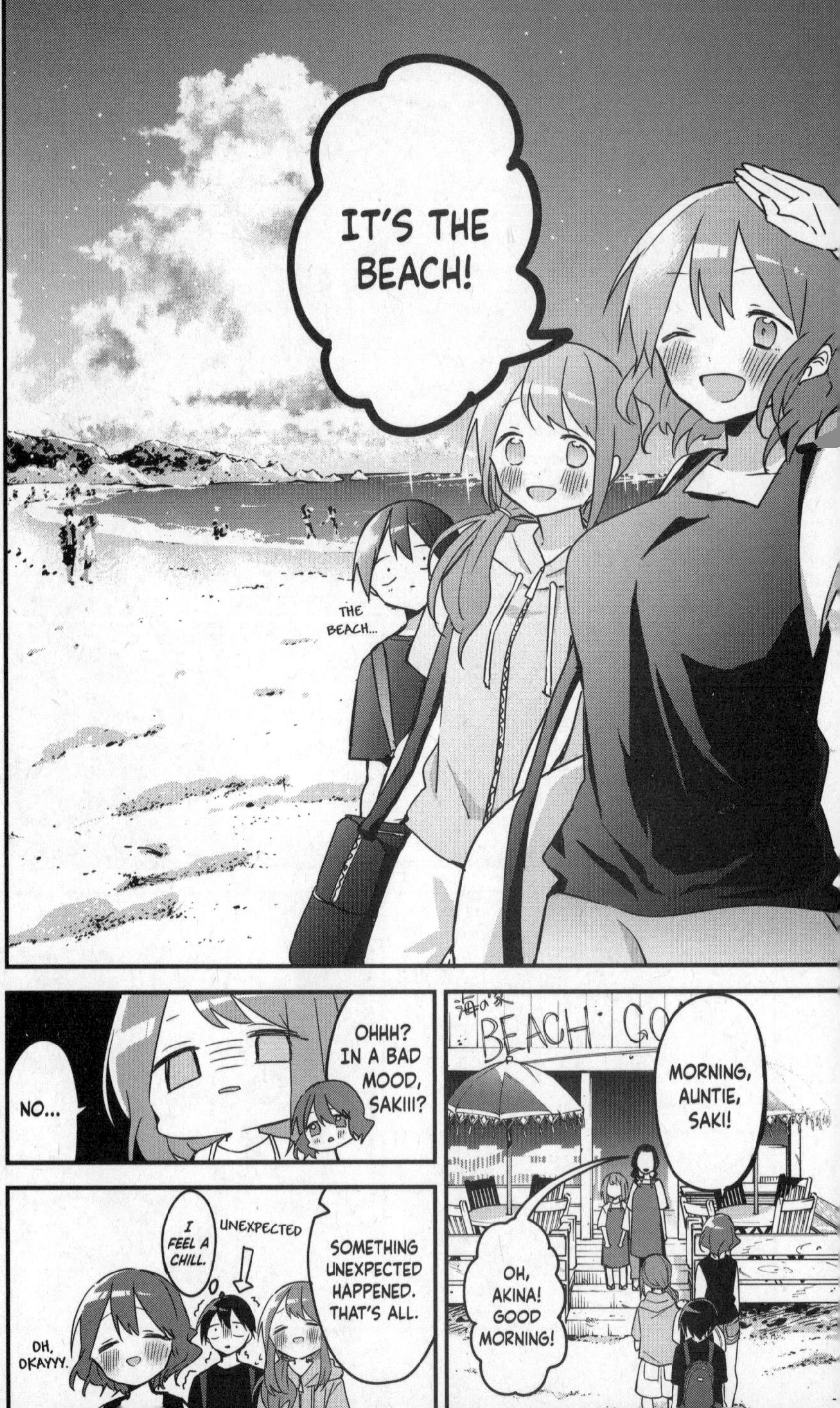
IT'S THE BEACH!
THE BEACH...
BEACH
MORNING, AUNTIE, SAKI!
OH, AKINA! GOOD MORNING!
OHHH? IN A BAD MOOD, SAKIII?
NO...
SOMETHING UNEXPECTED HAPPENED. THAT'S ALL.
UNEXPECTED
I FEEL A CHILL.
OH, OKAYYY.

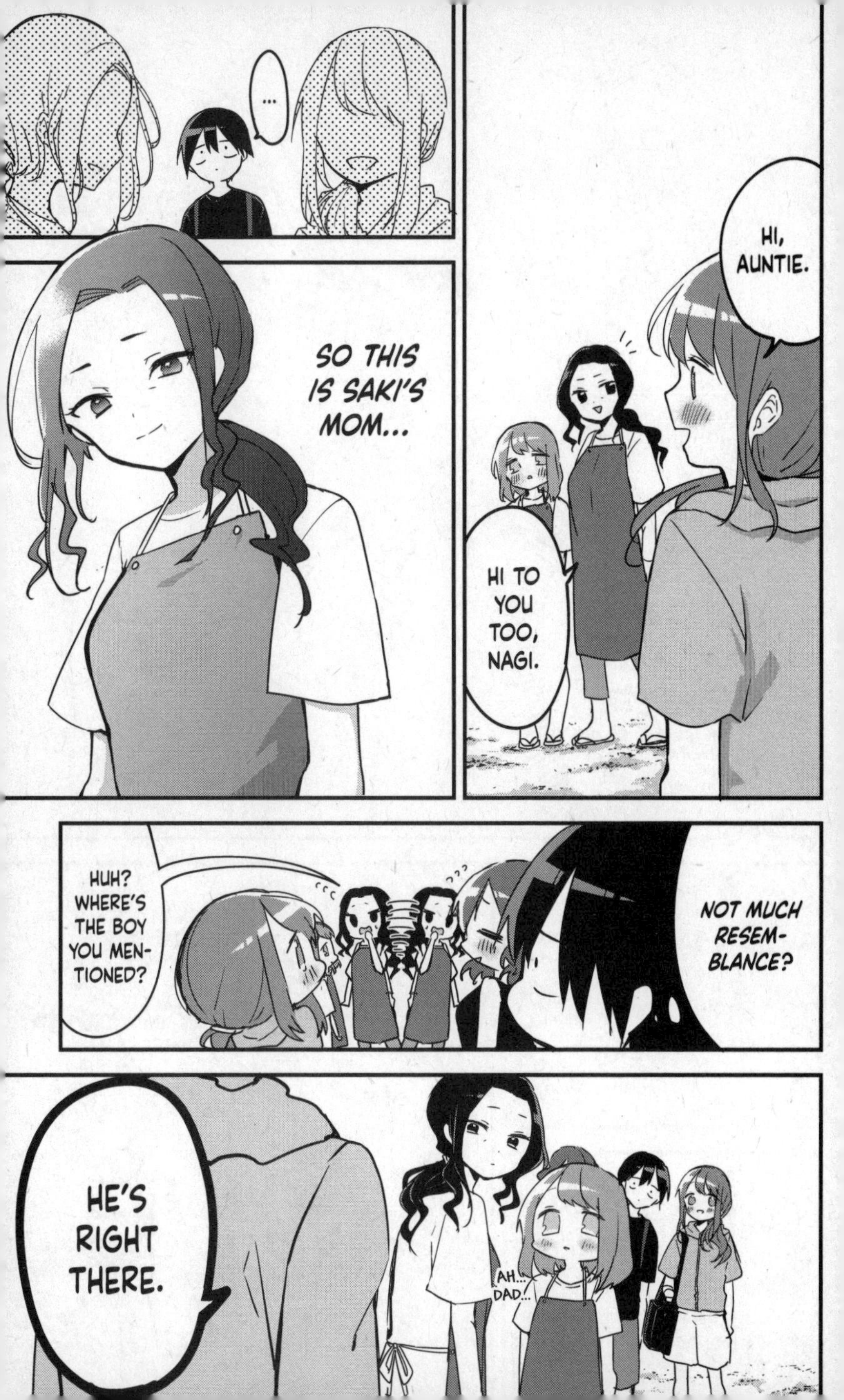
HI, AUNTIE.
HI TO YOU TOO, NAGI.
...
SO THIS IS SAKI'S MOM...
NOT MUCH RESEMBLANCE?
HUH? WHERE'S THE BOY YOU MENTIONED?
HE'S RIGHT THERE.
AH... DAD...

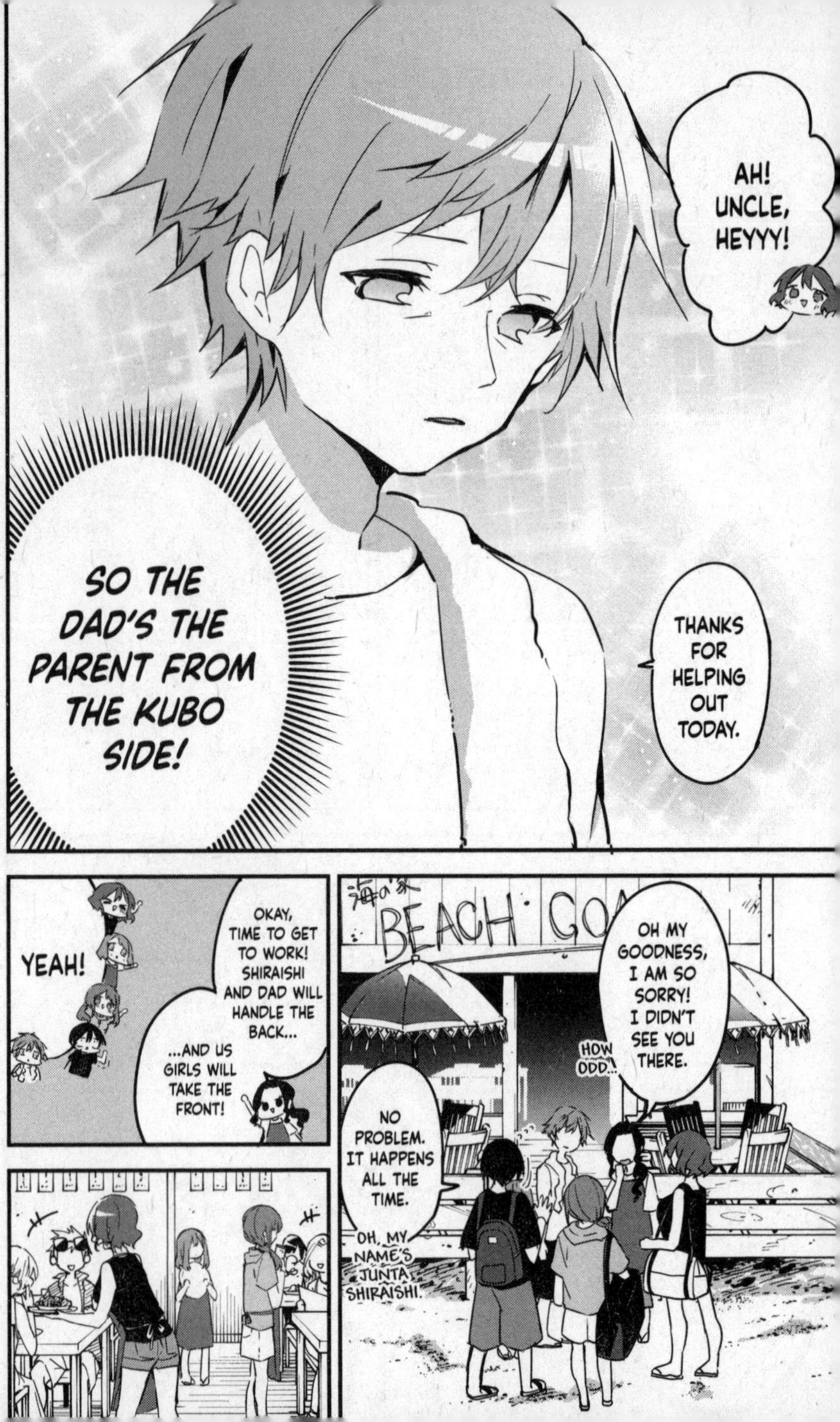
AH! UNCLE, HEYYY!
THANKS FOR HELPING OUT TODAY.
SO THE DAD'S THE PARENT FROM THE KUBO SIDE!
BEACH
OH MY GOODNESS, I AM SO SORRY! I DIDN'T SEE YOU THERE.
HOW ODD...
NO PROBLEM. IT HAPPENS ALL THE TIME.
OH, MY NAME'S JUNTA SHIRAISHI.
OKAY, TIME TO GET TO WORK! SHIRAISHI AND DAD WILL HANDLE THE BACK...
...AND US GIRLS WILL TAKE THE FRONT!
YEAH!

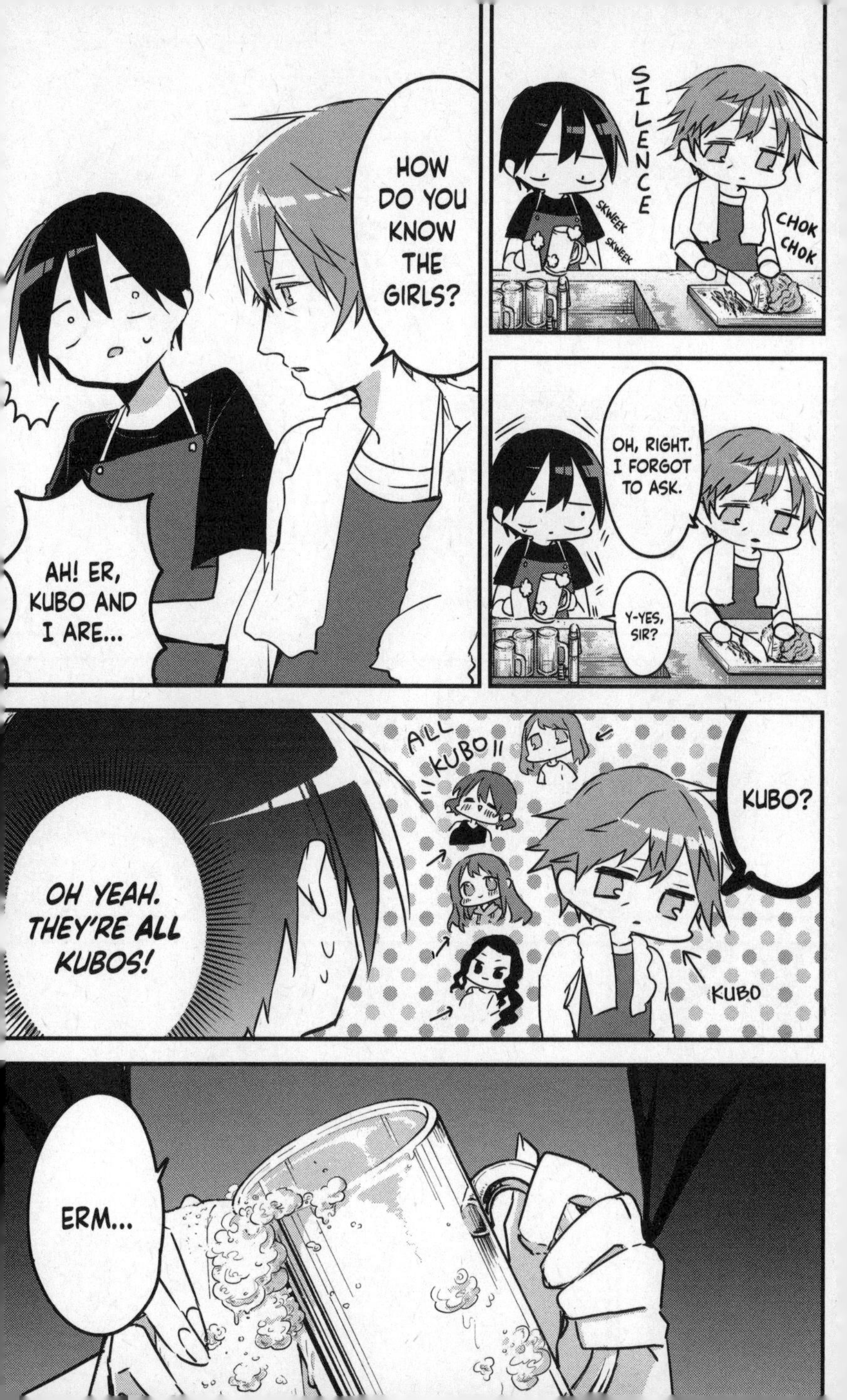
SILENCE
SKWEEK SKWEEK
CHOK CHOK
OH, RIGHT. I FORGOT TO ASK.
Y-YES, SIR?
HOW DO YOU KNOW THE GIRLS?
AH! ER, KUBO AND I ARE...
KUBO?
KUBO
ALL KUBO!!
OH YEAH. THEY'RE ALL KUBOS!
ERM...

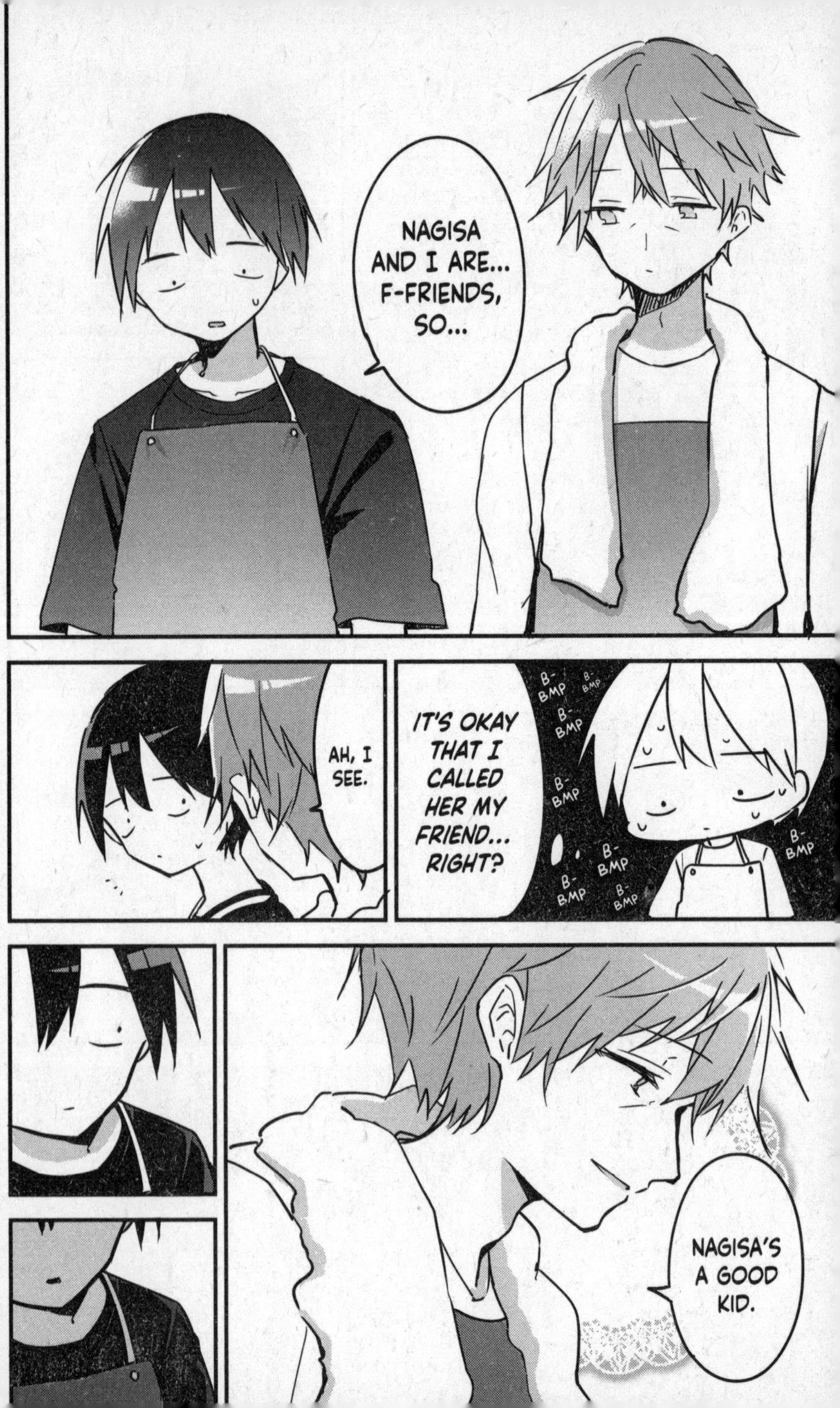
NAGISA AND I ARE... F-FRIENDS, SO...
IT'S OKAY THAT I CALLED HER MY FRIEND... RIGHT?
B-BMP
B-BMP
B-BMP
B-BMP
B-BMP
B-BMP
B-BMP
B-BMP
AH, I SEE.
NAGISA'S A GOOD KID.

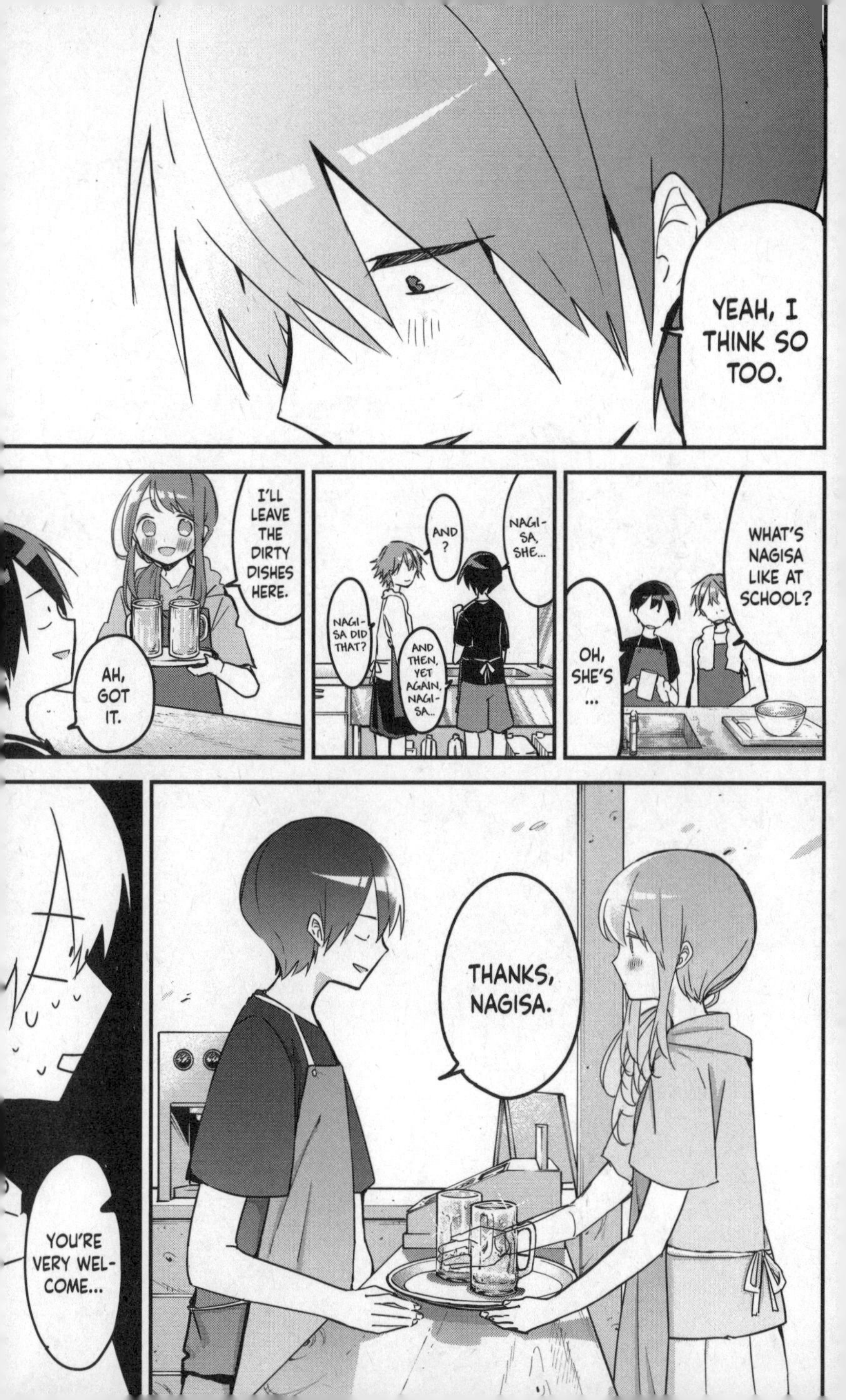
YEAH, I THINK SO TOO.
WHAT'S NAGISA LIKE AT SCHOOL?
OH, SHE'S ...
NAGI-SA, SHE...
AND ?
AND THEN, YET AGAIN, NAGI-SA...
NAGI-SA DID THAT?
I'LL LEAVE THE DIRTY DISHES HERE.
AH, GOT IT.
THANKS, NAGISA.
YOU'RE VERY WEL-COME...

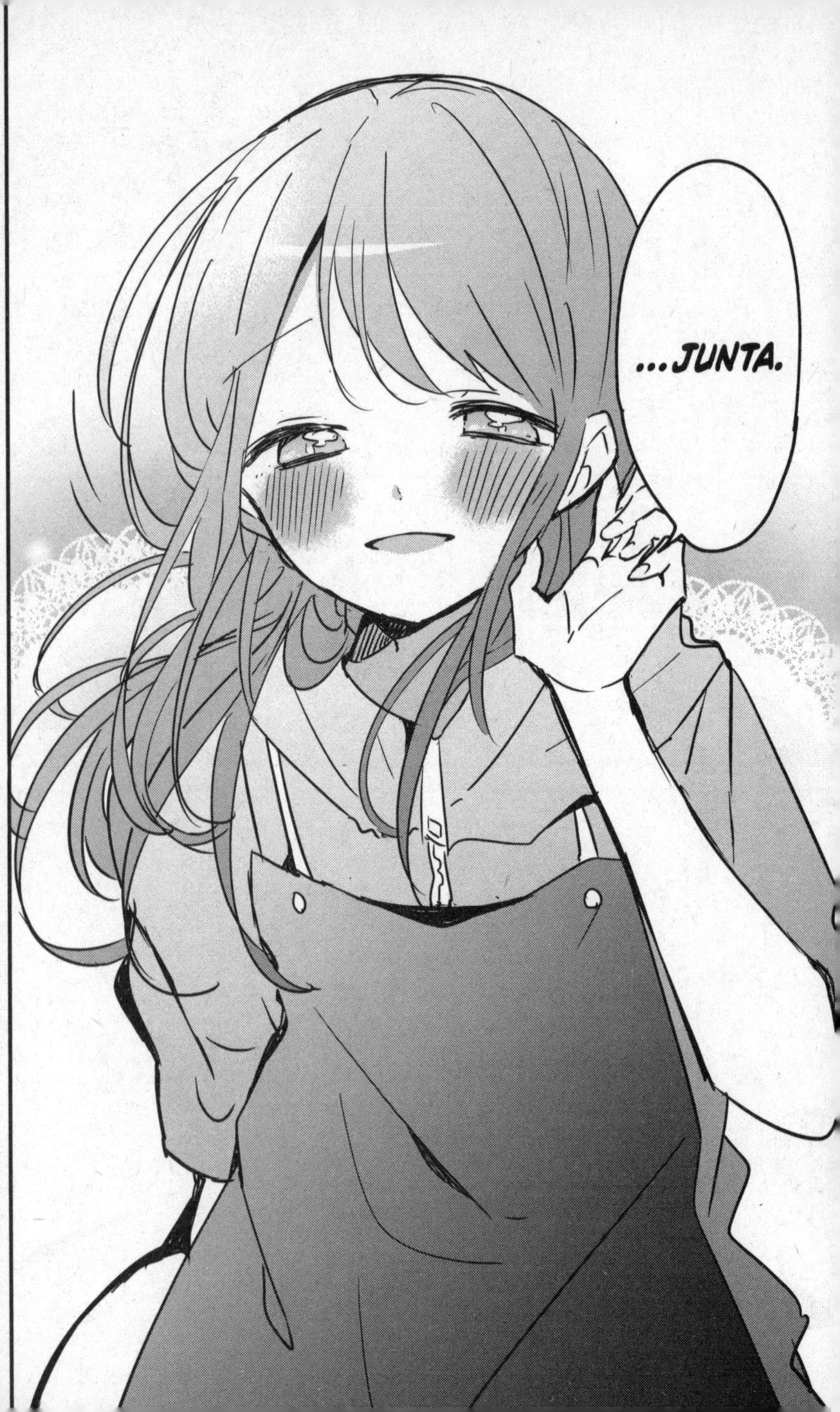
...JUNTA.

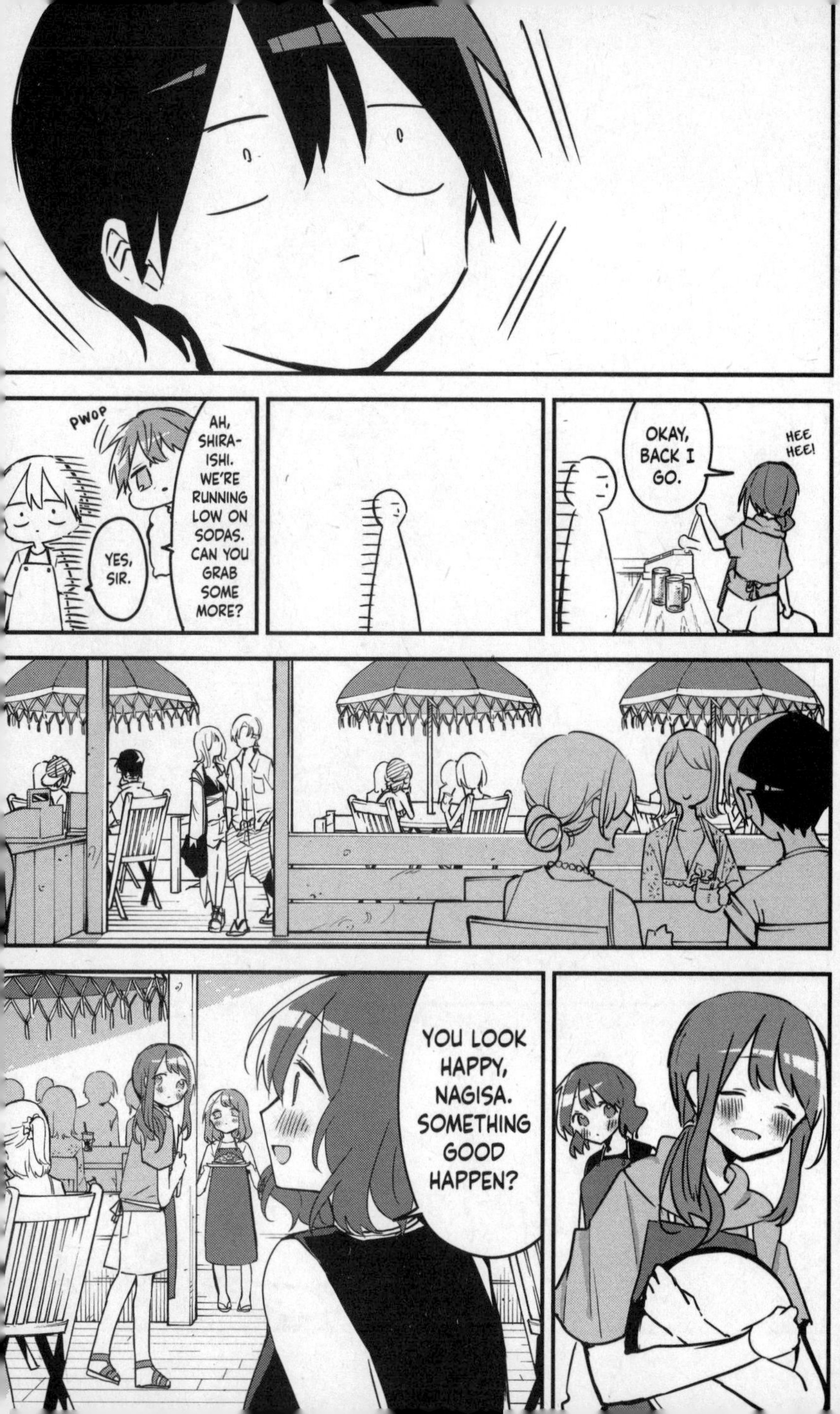
HEE HEE!
OKAY, BACK I GO.
AH, SHIRAISHI. WE'RE RUNNING LOW ON SODAS. CAN YOU GRAB SOME MORE?
PWOP
YES, SIR.
YOU LOOK HAPPY, NAGISA. SOMETHING GOOD HAPPEN?

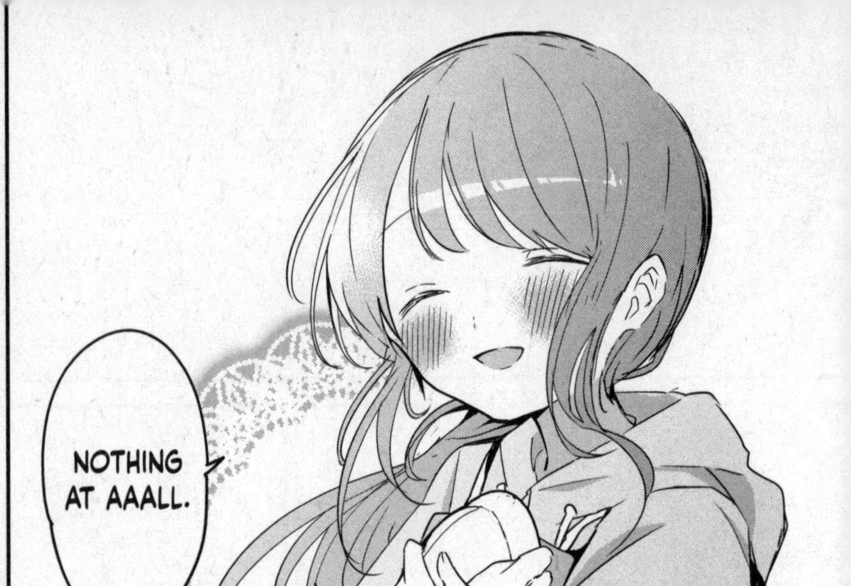
NOTHING AT AAALL.
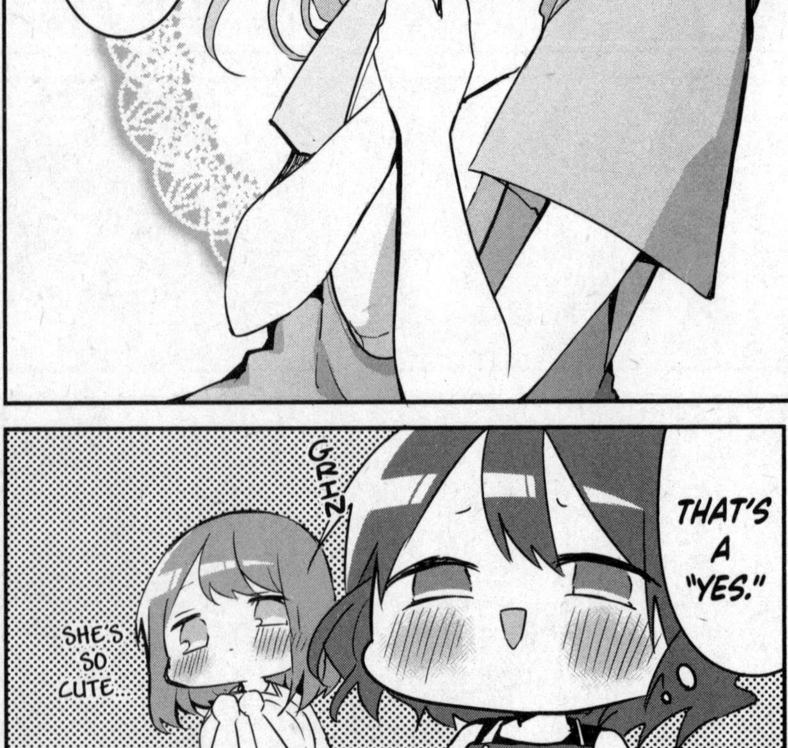
THAT'S A "YES."
GRIN
SHE'S SO CUTE...

episode 084

SANDY BEACH AND SALT WATER

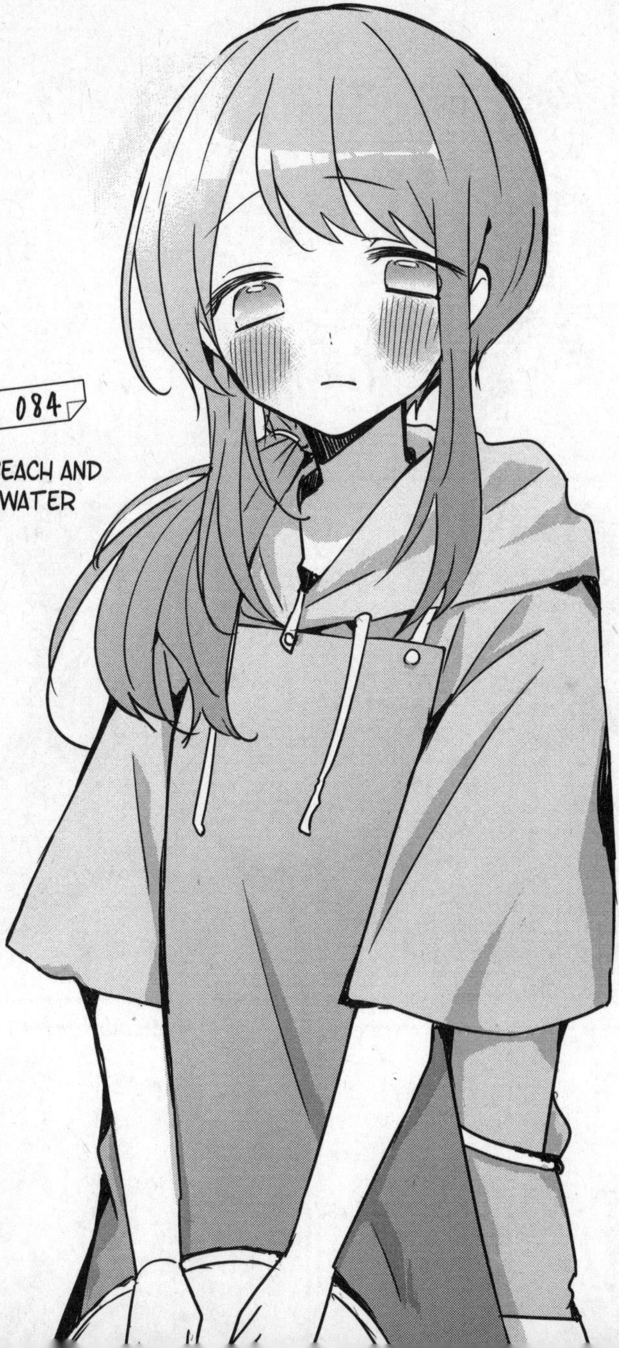

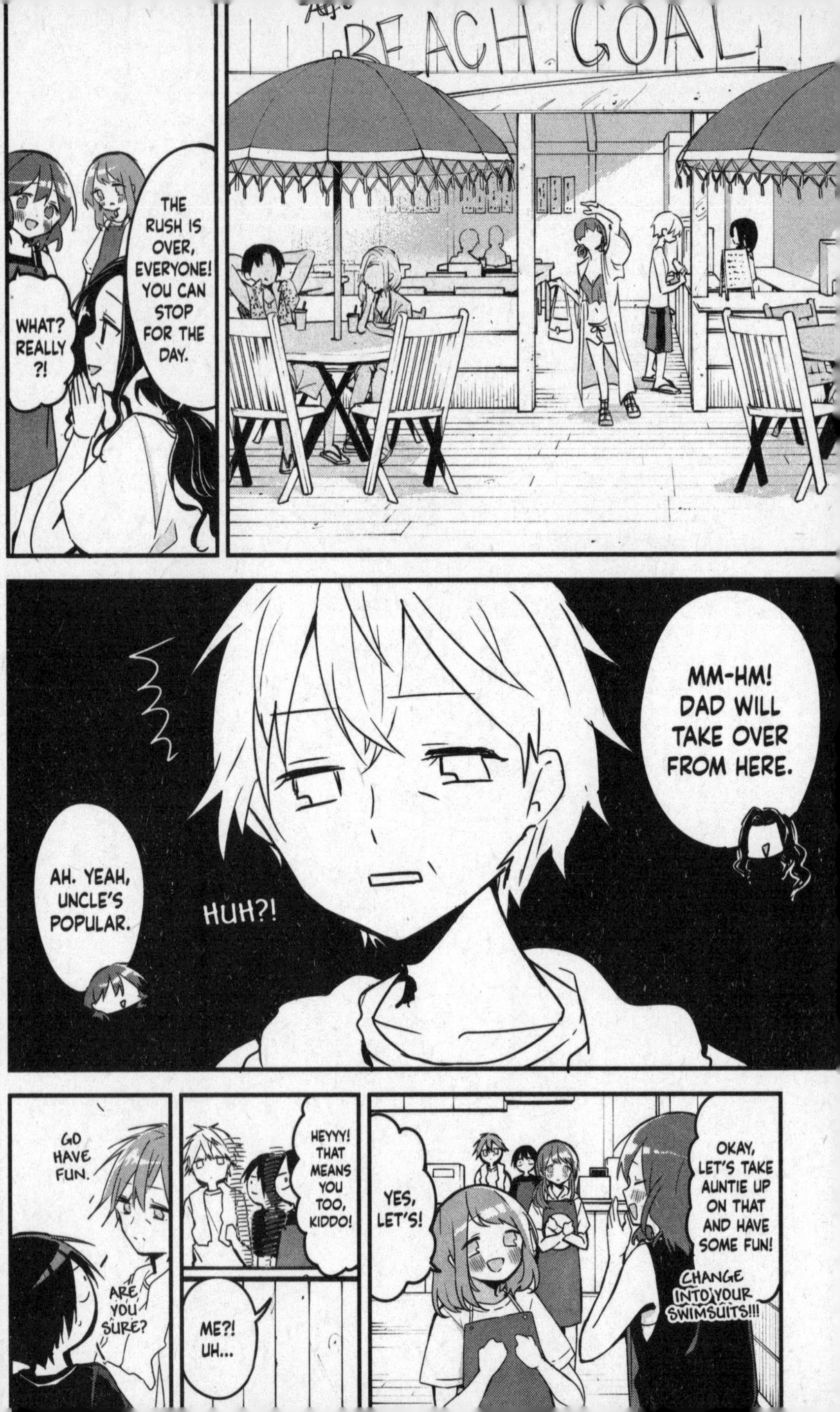
BEACH GOAL
THE RUSH IS OVER, EVERYONE! YOU CAN STOP FOR THE DAY.
WHAT? REALLY?!
MM-HM! DAD WILL TAKE OVER FROM HERE.
HUH?!
AH. YEAH, UNCLE'S POPULAR.
OKAY, LET'S TAKE AUNTIE UP ON THAT AND HAVE SOME FUN!
CHANGE INTO YOUR SWIMSUITS!!!
YES, LET'S!
HEYYY! THAT MEANS YOU TOO, KIDDO!
ME?! UH...
GO HAVE FUN.
ARE YOU SURE?

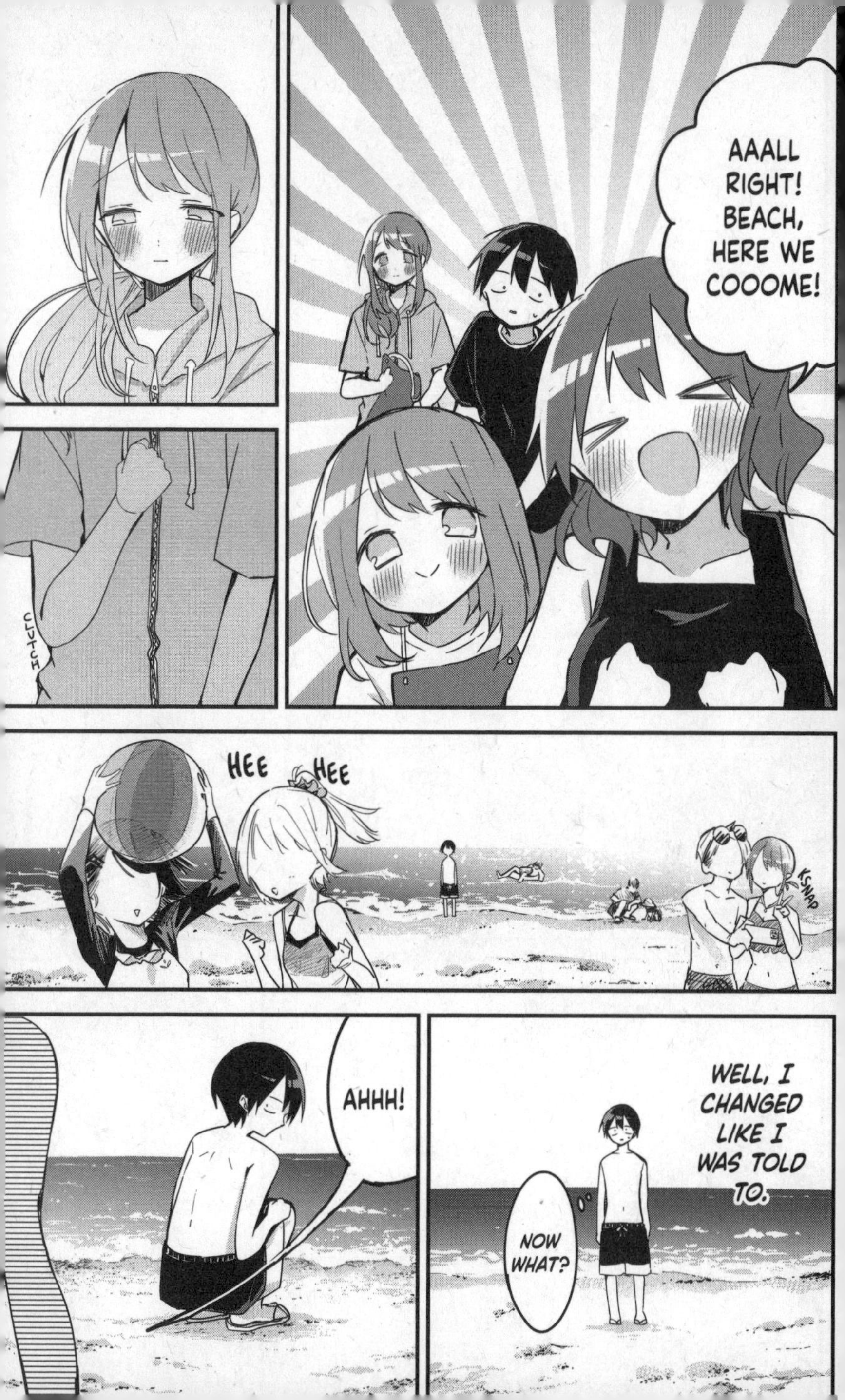
AAALL RIGHT! BEACH, HERE WE COOOME!
CLUTCH
HEE HEE
KSNAP
WELL, I CHANGED LIKE I WAS TOLD TO.
NOW WHAT?
AHHH!

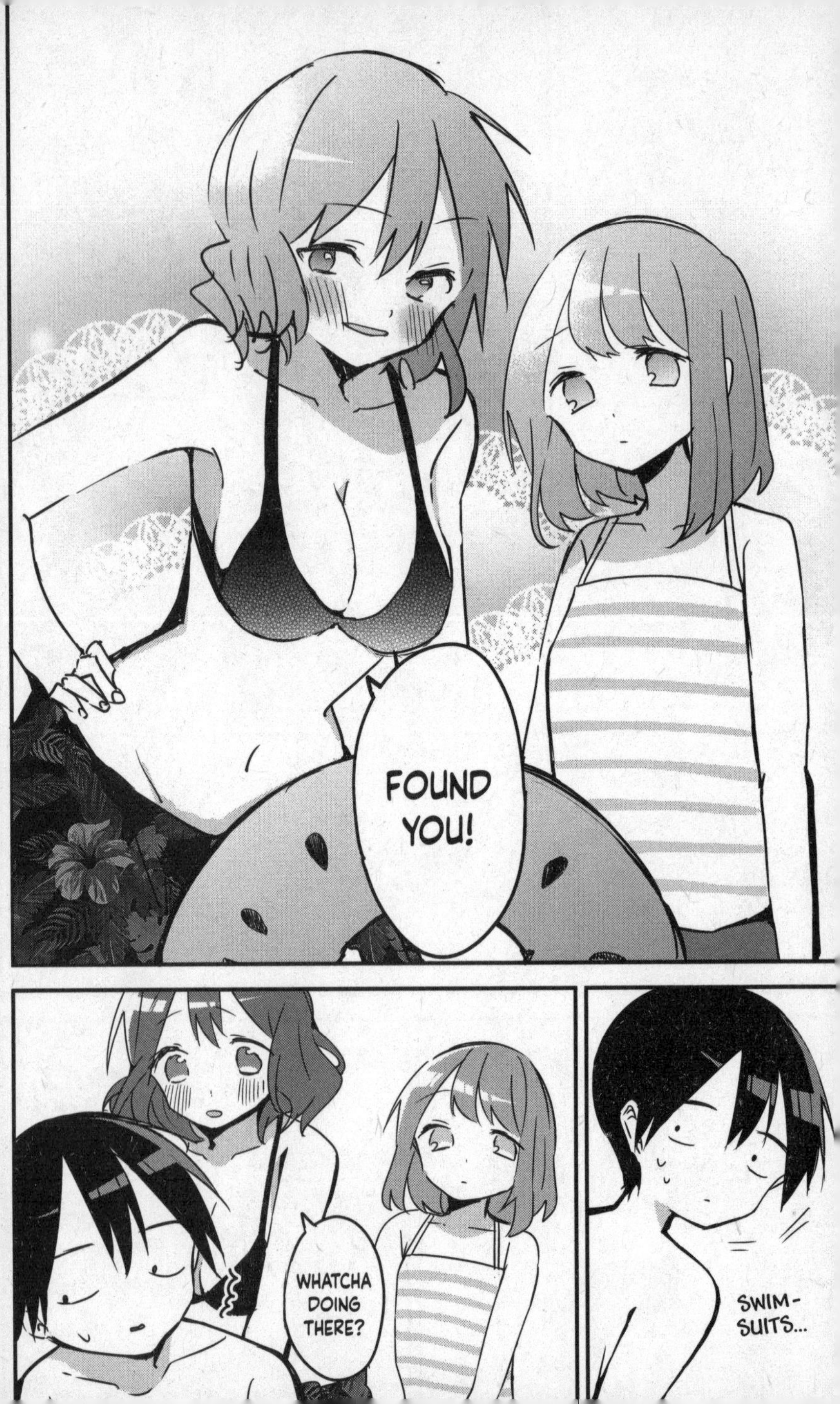
FOUND YOU!
SWIM-SUITS...
WHATCHA DOING THERE?

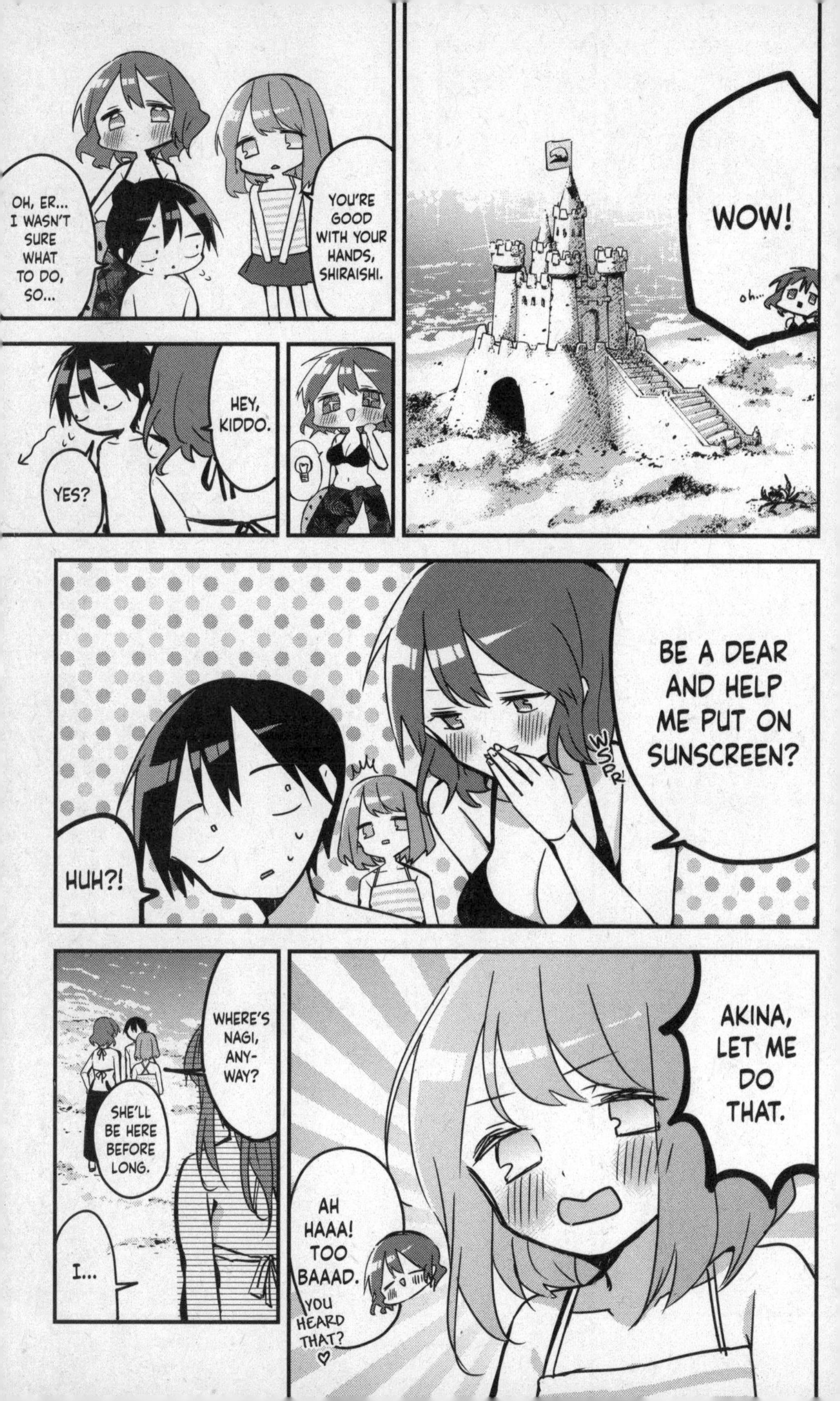
WOW!
oh...
YOU'RE GOOD WITH YOUR HANDS, SHIRAISHI.
OH, ER... I WASN'T SURE WHAT TO DO, SO...
HEY, KIDDO.
YES?
BE A DEAR AND HELP ME PUT ON SUNSCREEN?
WSPR
HUH?!
AKINA, LET ME DO THAT.
AH HAAA! TOO BAAAD.
YOU HEARD THAT? ♡
WHERE'S NAGI, ANYWAY?
SHE'LL BE HERE BEFORE LONG.
I...

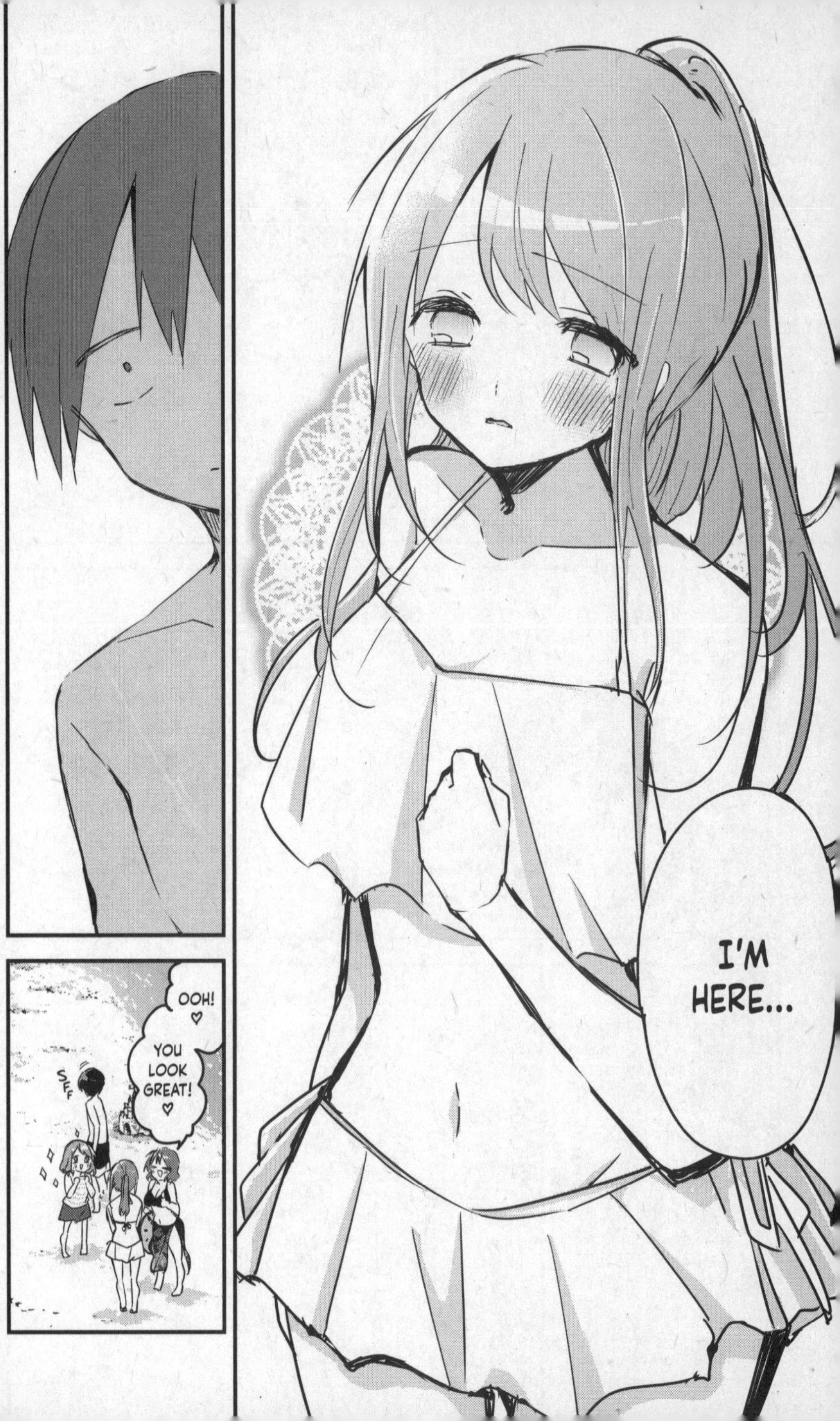
I'M HERE...
OOH! ♡
YOU LOOK GREAT! ♡
SFF

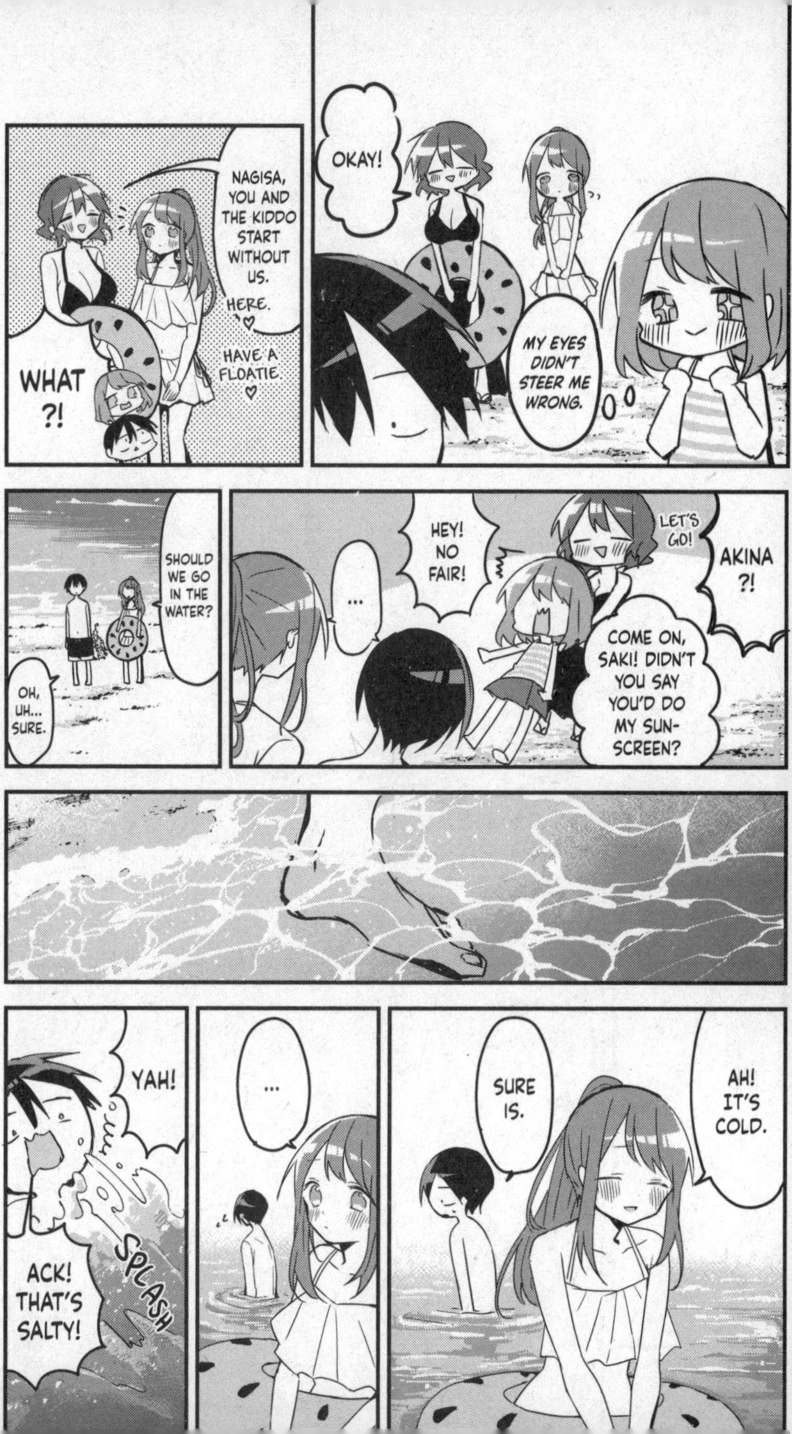
OKAY!
MY EYES DIDN'T STEER ME WRONG.
NAGISA, YOU AND THE KIDDO START WITHOUT US.
HERE.
HAVE A FLOATIE
WHAT ?!
AKINA ?!
LET'S GO!
COME ON, SAKI! DIDN'T YOU SAY YOU'D DO MY SUN-SCREEN?
HEY! NO FAIR!
...
SHOULD WE GO IN THE WATER?
OH, UH... SURE.
AH! IT'S COLD.
SURE IS.
...
YAH!
SPLASH
ACK! THAT'S SALTY!

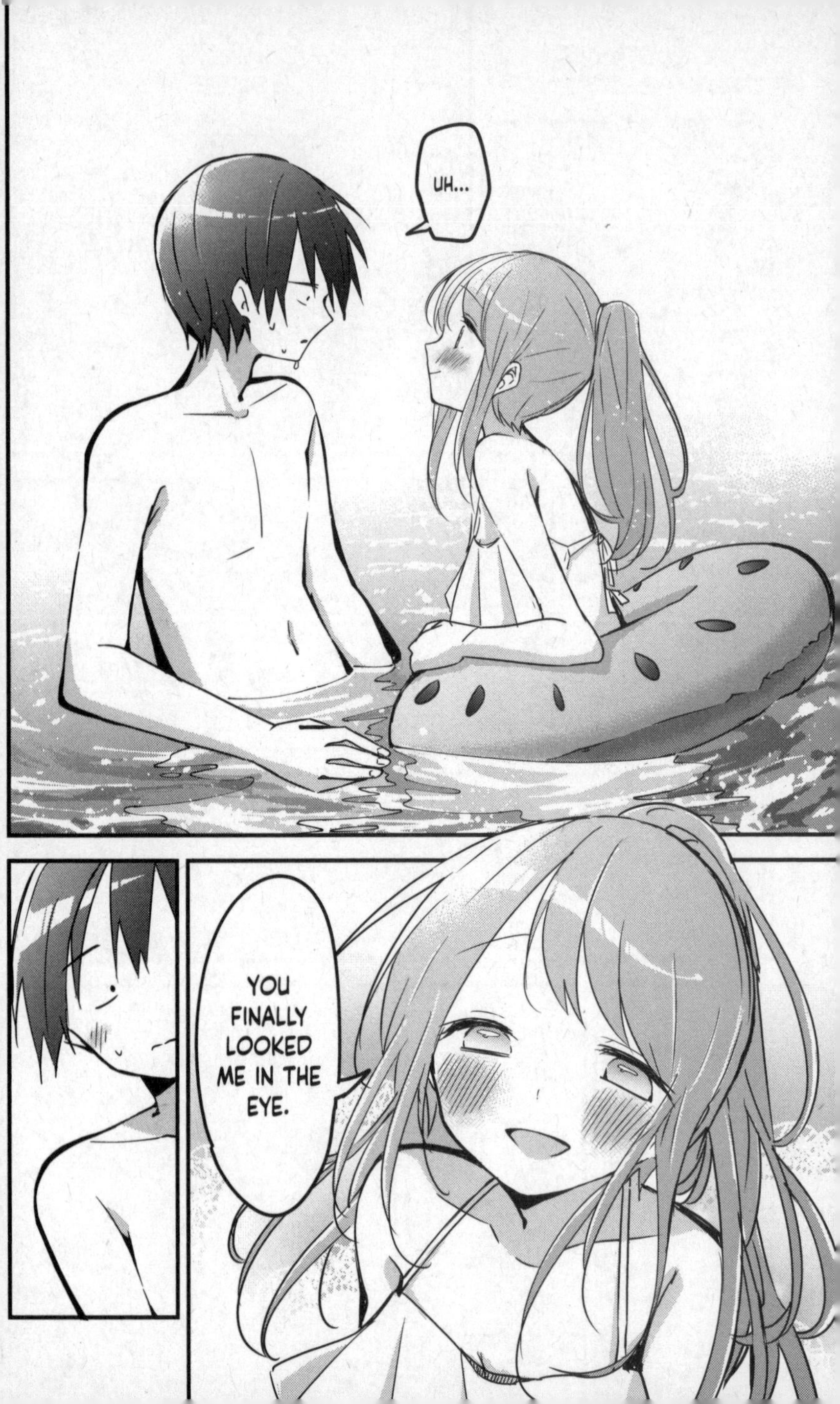
UH...
YOU FINALLY LOOKED ME IN THE EYE.

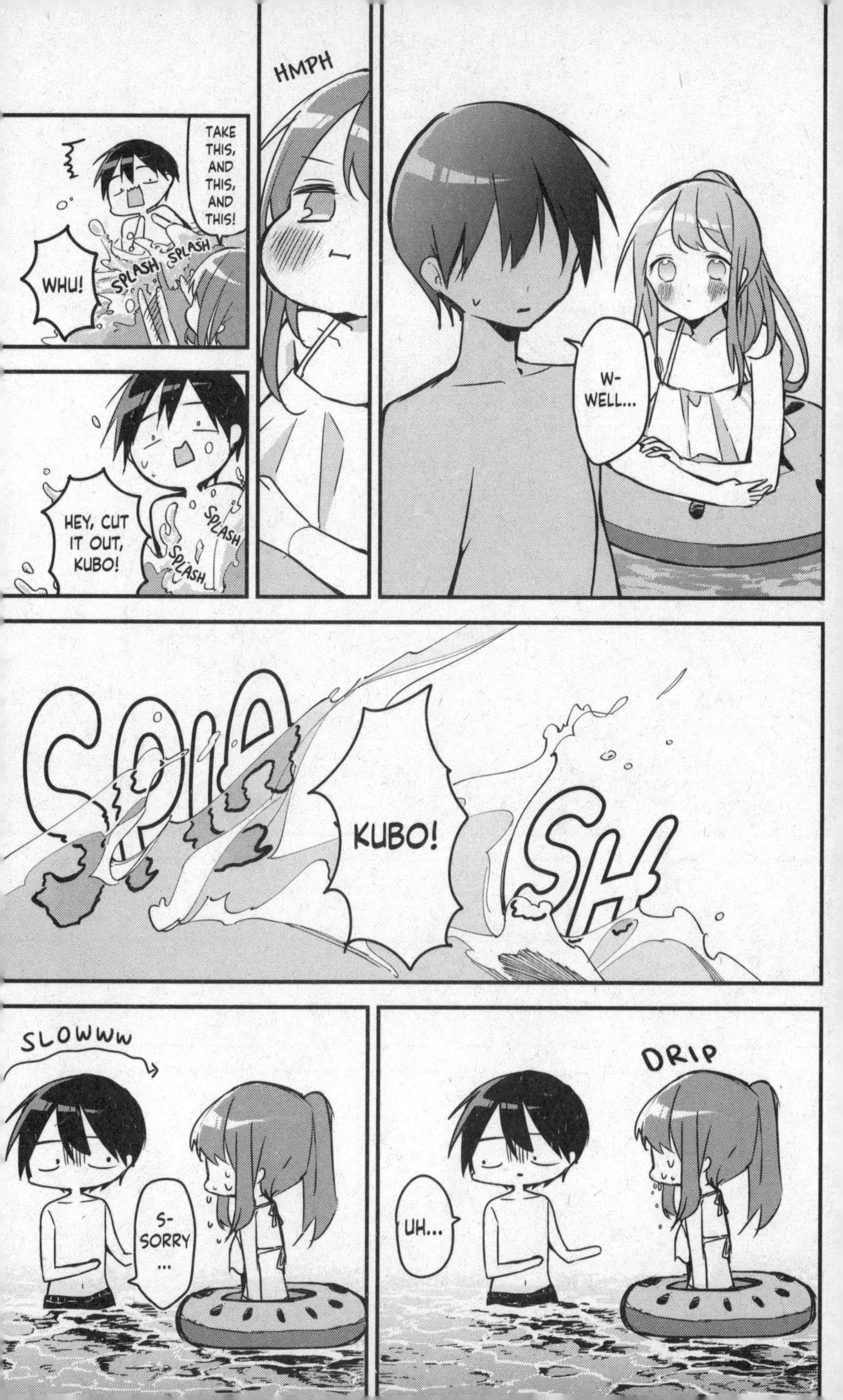
W-WELL...
HMPH
TAKE THIS, AND THIS, AND THIS!
SPLASH
SPLASH
WHU!
SPLASH
SPLASH
HEY, CUT IT OUT, KUBO!
SPLASH
KUBO!
DRIP
UH...
SLOWWW
S-SORRY...

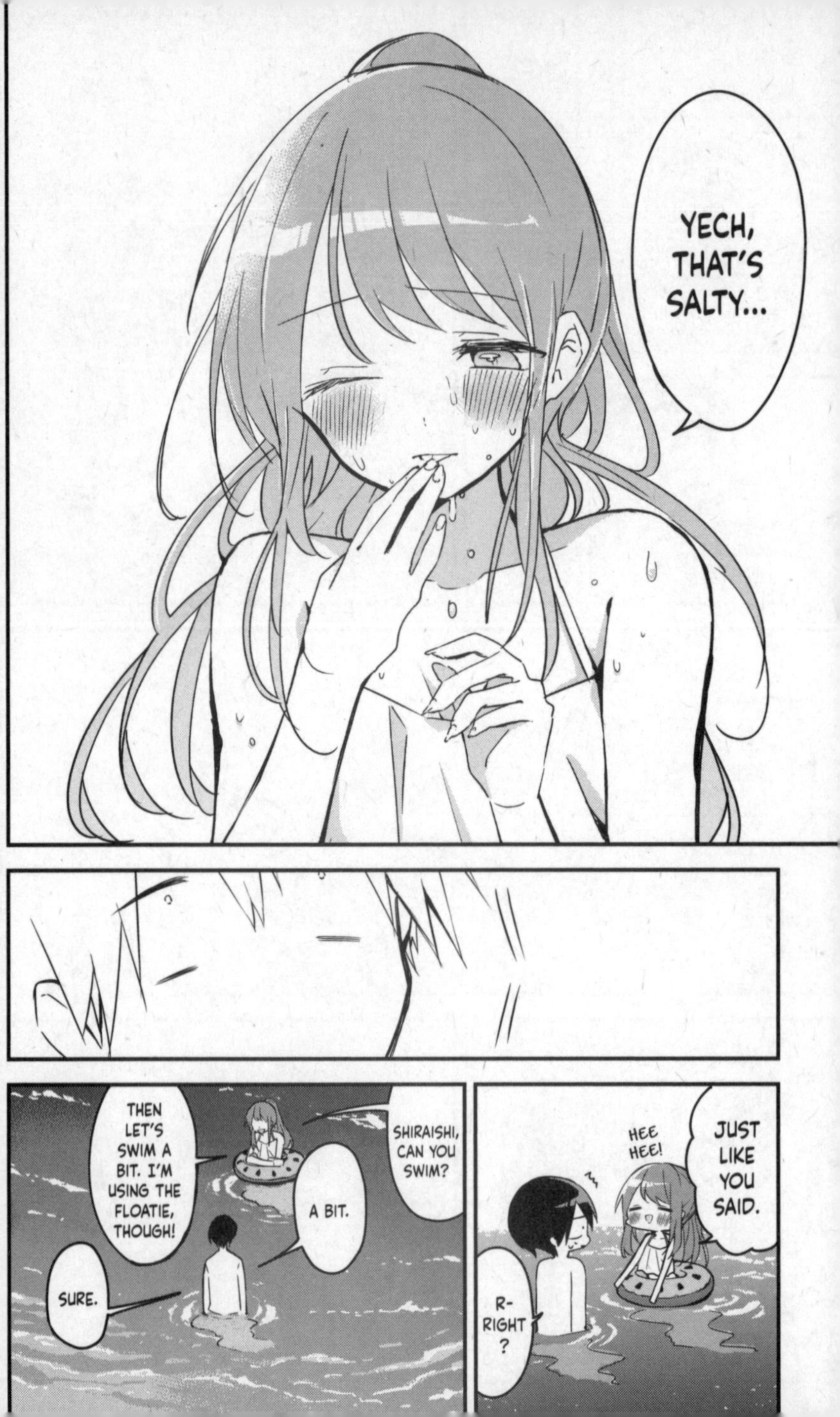
YECH, THAT'S SALTY...
JUST LIKE YOU SAID.
HEE HEE!
R-RIGHT?
SHIRAISHI, CAN YOU SWIM?
A BIT.
THEN LET'S SWIM A BIT. I'M USING THE FLOATIE, THOUGH!
SURE.

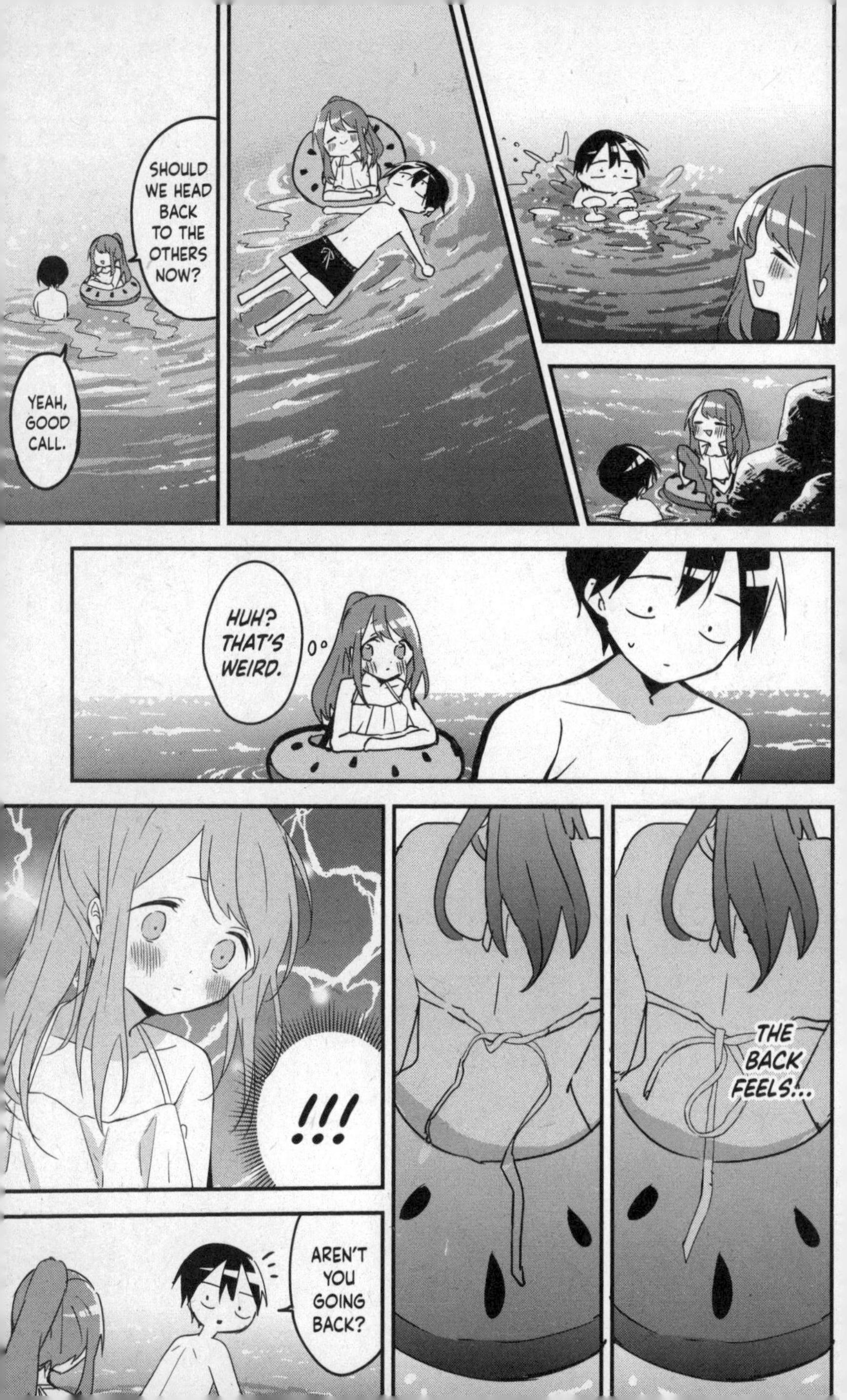
SHOULD WE HEAD BACK TO THE OTHERS NOW?
YEAH, GOOD CALL.
HUH? THAT'S WEIRD.
THE BACK FEELS...
!!!
AREN'T YOU GOING BACK?

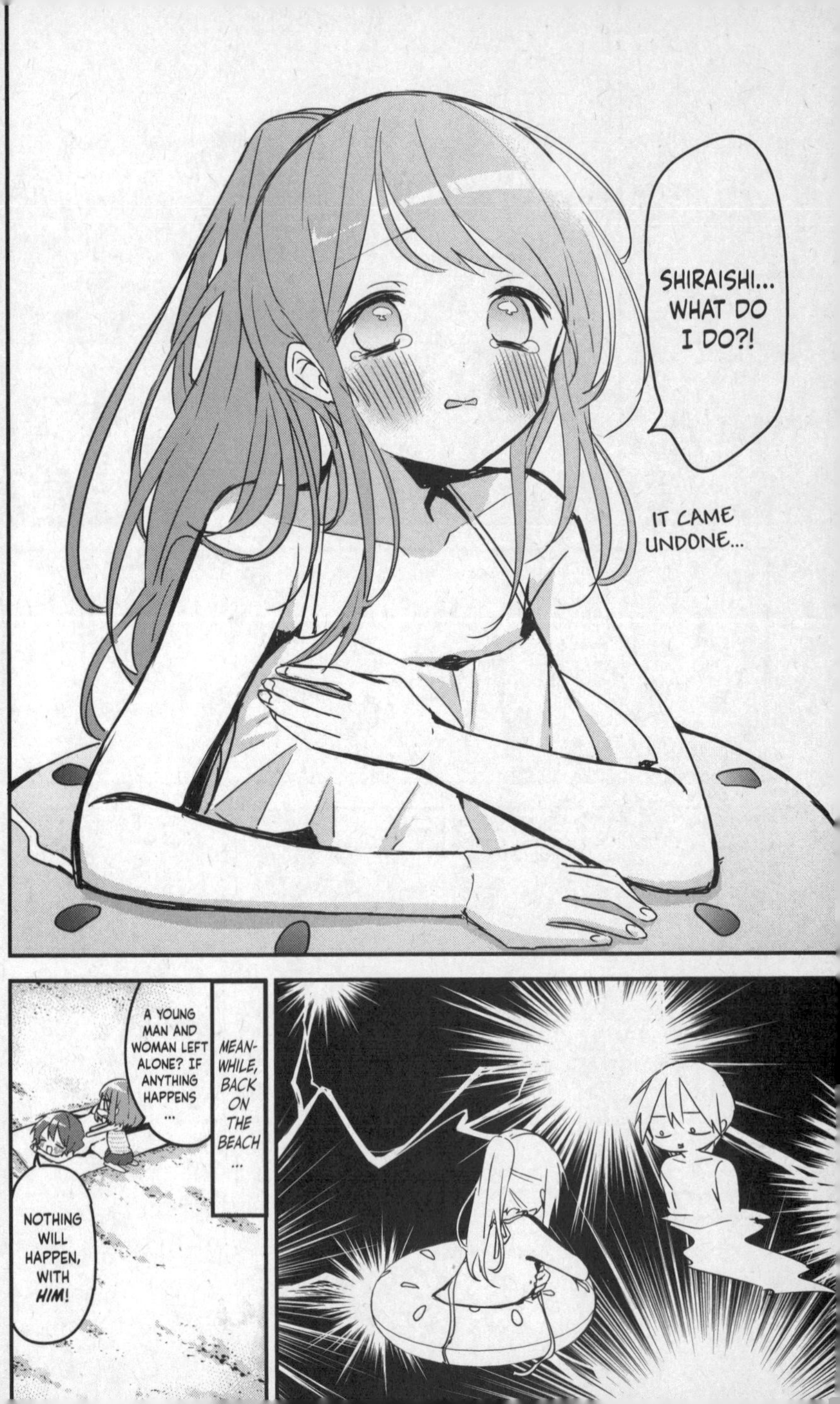
SHIRAISHI... WHAT DO I DO?!
IT CAME UNDONE...
MEAN-WHILE, BACK ON THE BEACH...
A YOUNG MAN AND WOMAN LEFT ALONE? IF ANYTHING HAPPENS...
NOTHING WILL HAPPEN, WITH *HIM*!

KUBO WORKING UP THE
NERVE TO JOIN THE OTHERS.

DOES IT
REALLY
LOOK GOOD
ON ME?

I TRY TO MAKE
AKINA'S CHEST
LOOK SOFT.

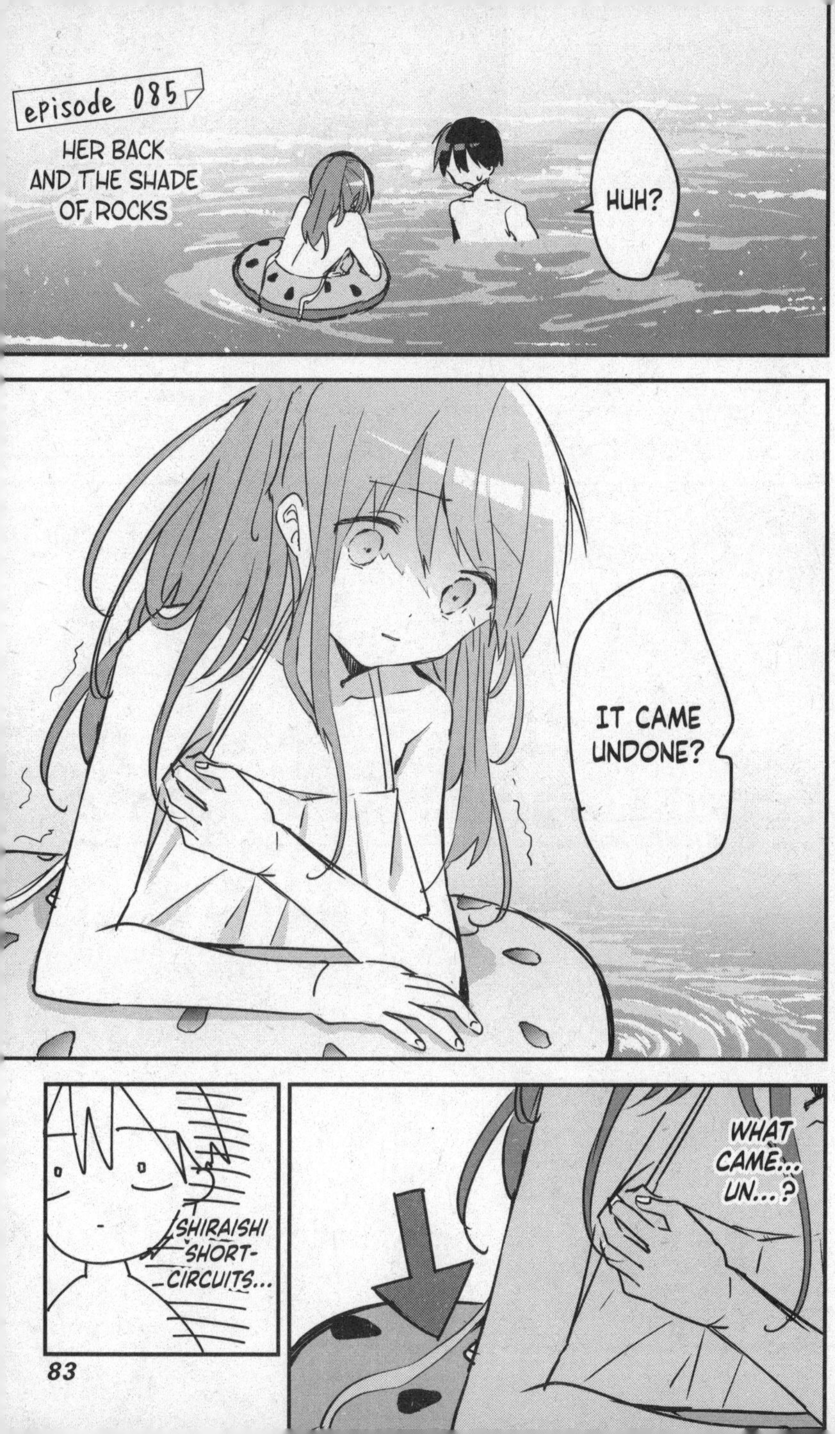
episode 085
HER BACK AND THE SHADE OF ROCKS
HUH?
IT CAME UNDONE?
WHAT CAME... UN...?
SHIRAISHI SHORT-CIRCUITS...

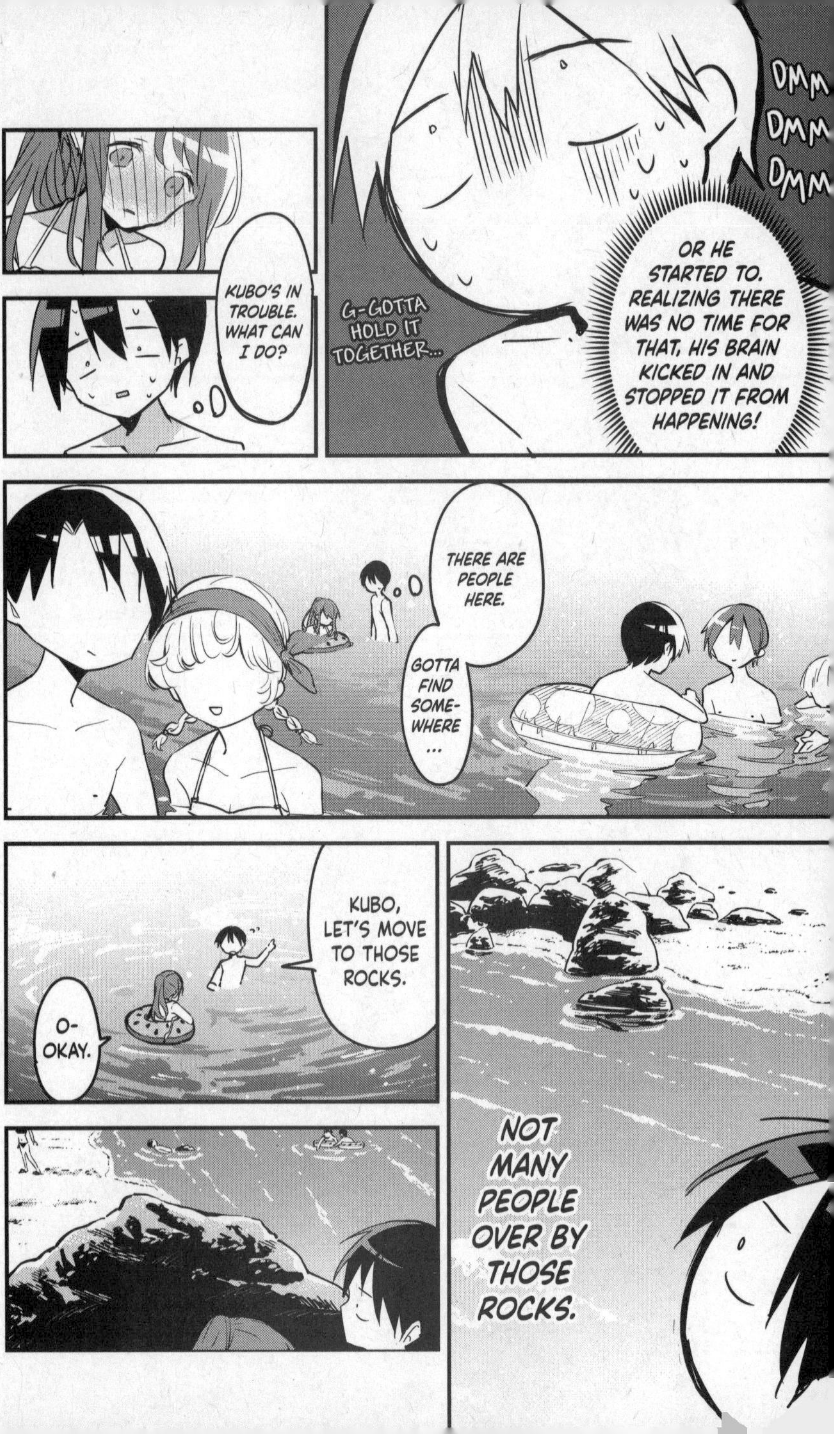
DMM DMM DMM
OR HE STARTED TO. REALIZING THERE WAS NO TIME FOR THAT, HIS BRAIN KICKED IN AND STOPPED IT FROM HAPPENING!
G-GOTTA HOLD IT TOGETHER...
KUBO'S IN TROUBLE. WHAT CAN I DO?
THERE ARE PEOPLE HERE.
GOTTA FIND SOME-WHERE...
NOT MANY PEOPLE OVER BY THOSE ROCKS.
KUBO, LET'S MOVE TO THOSE ROCKS.
O-OKAY.

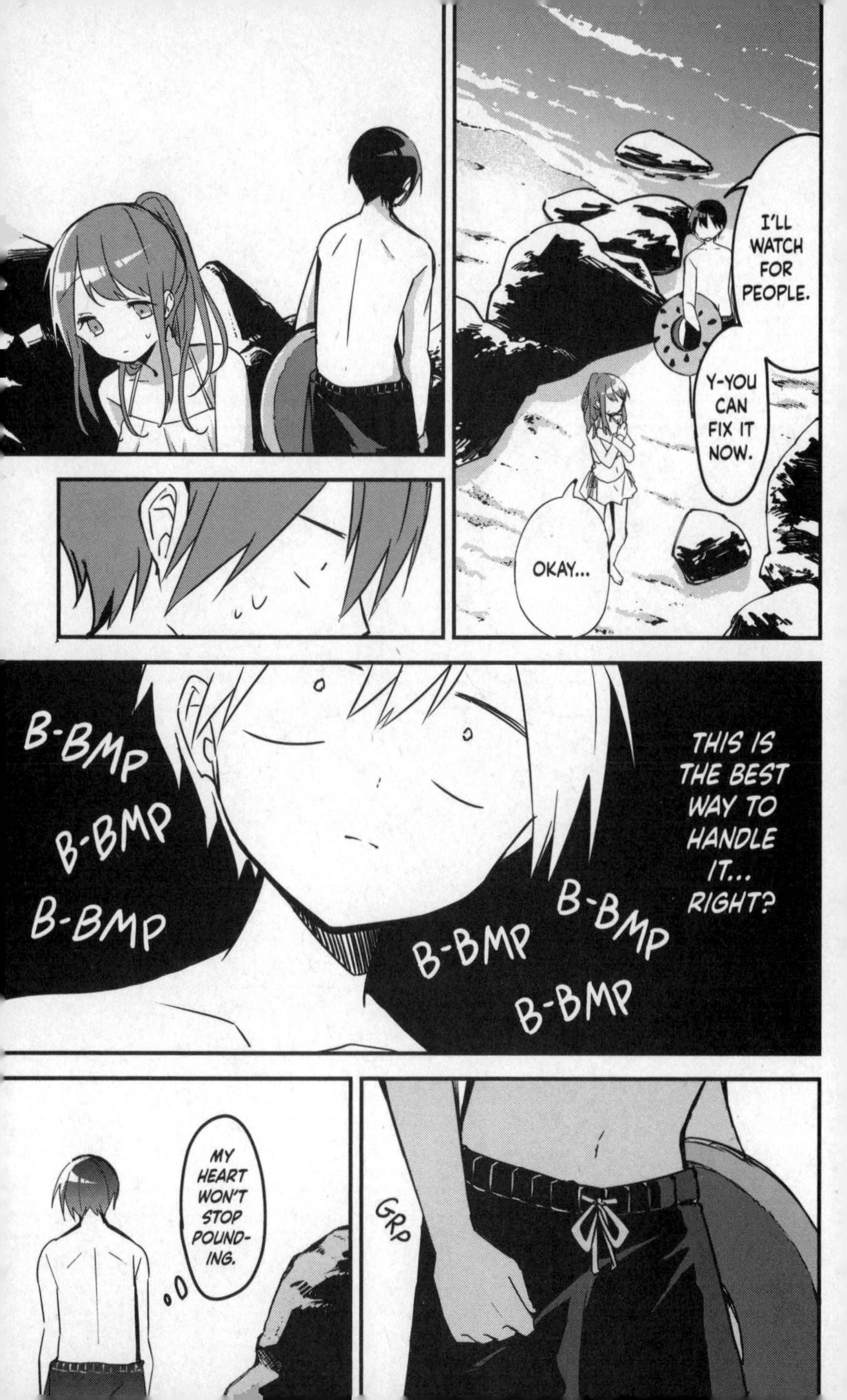
I'LL WATCH FOR PEOPLE.
Y-YOU CAN FIX IT NOW.
OKAY...
THIS IS THE BEST WAY TO HANDLE IT... RIGHT?
B-BMP
B-BMP
B-BMP
B-BMP
B-BMP
B-BMP
GRP
MY HEART WON'T STOP POUNDING.

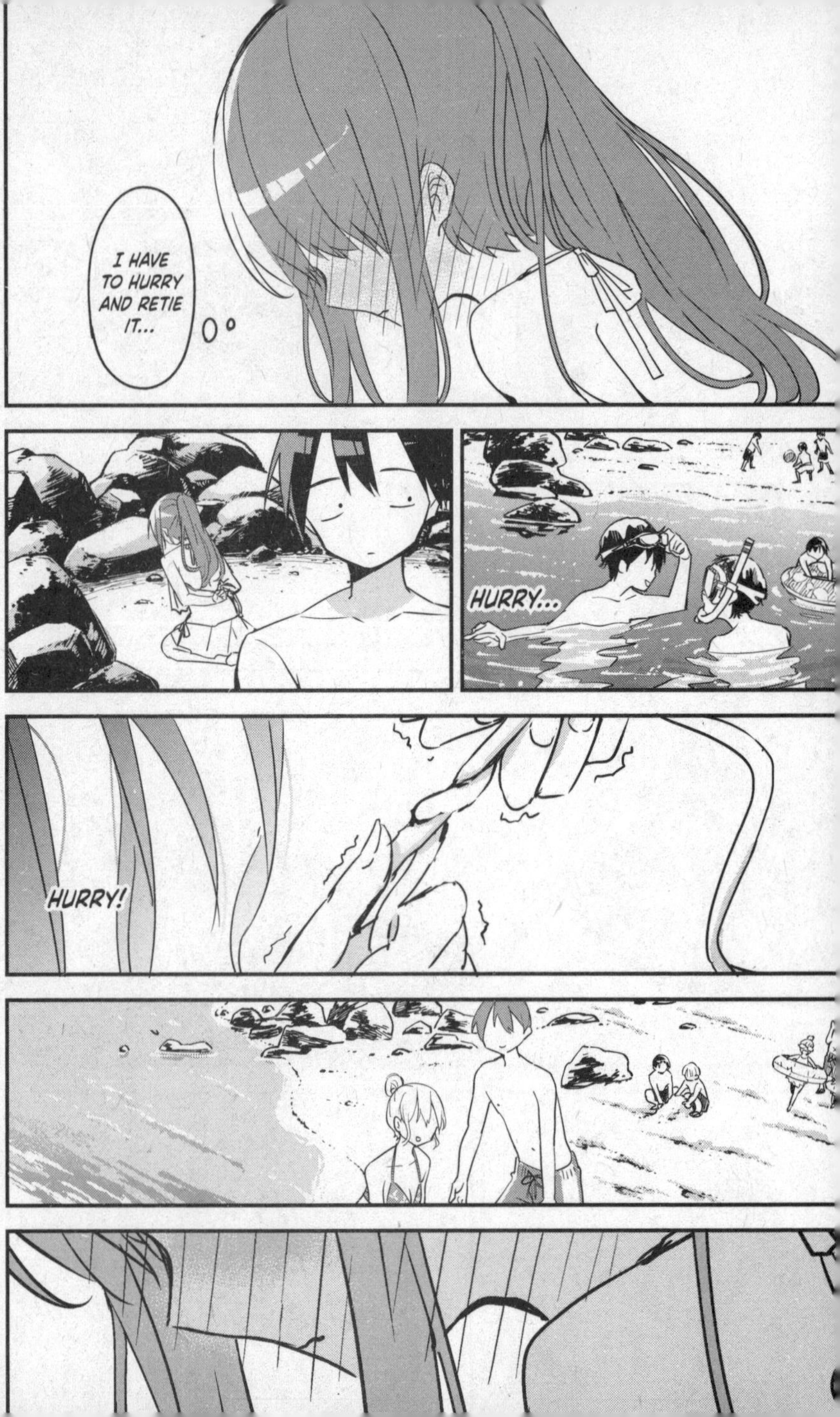
I HAVE TO HURRY AND RETIE IT...
HURRY...
HURRY!

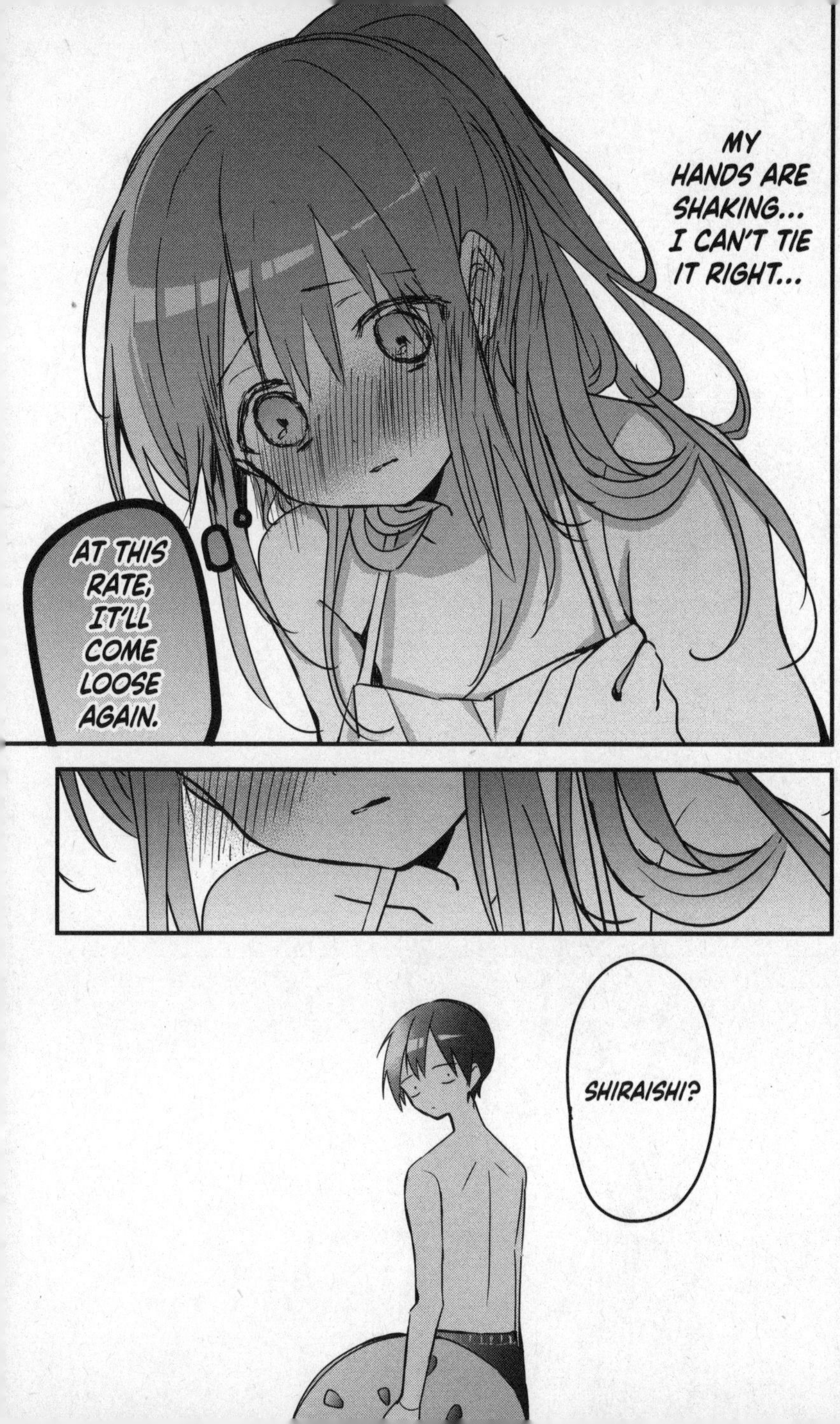
MY HANDS ARE SHAKING... I CAN'T TIE IT RIGHT...
AT THIS RATE, IT'LL COME LOOSE AGAIN.
SHIRAISHI?

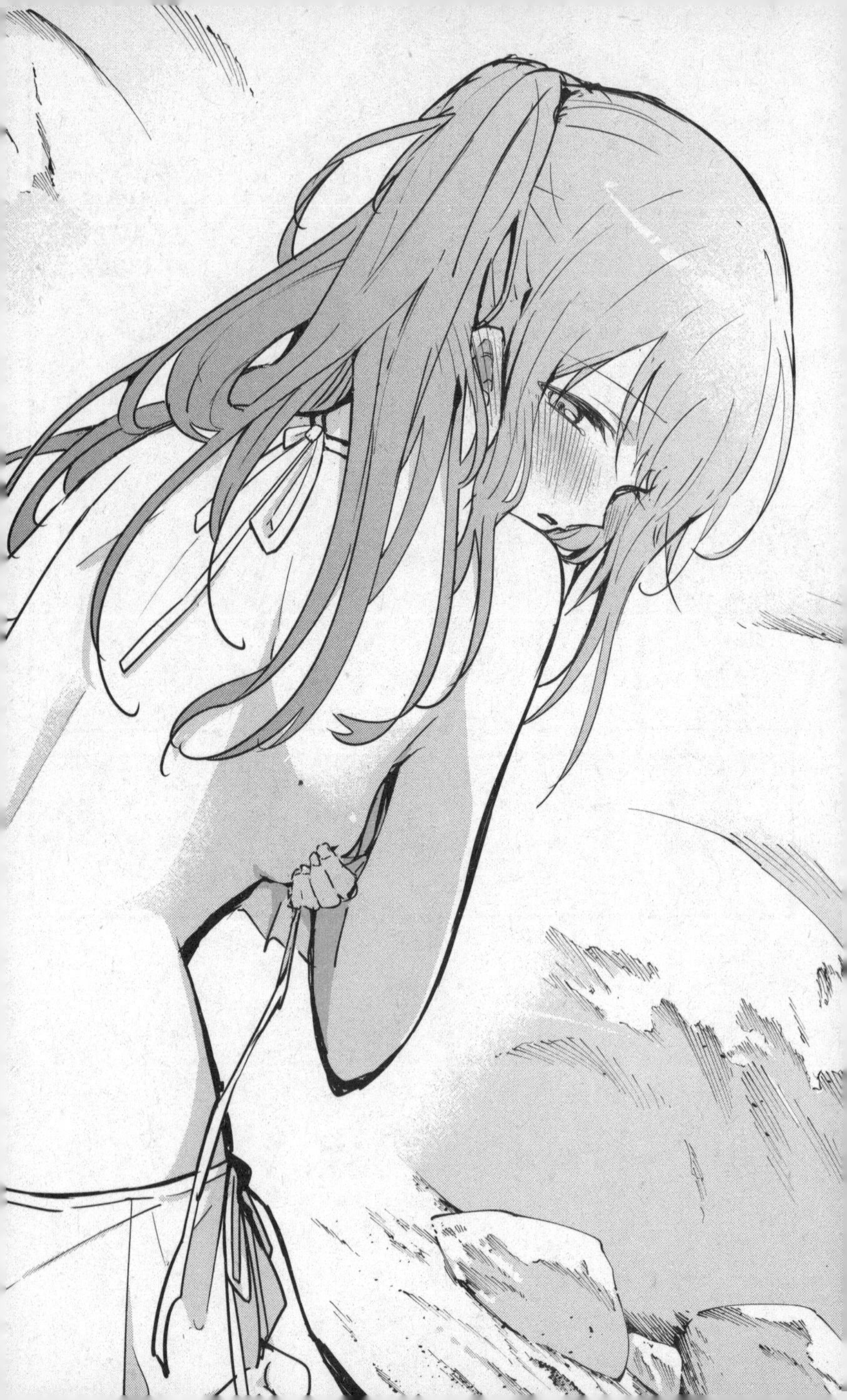

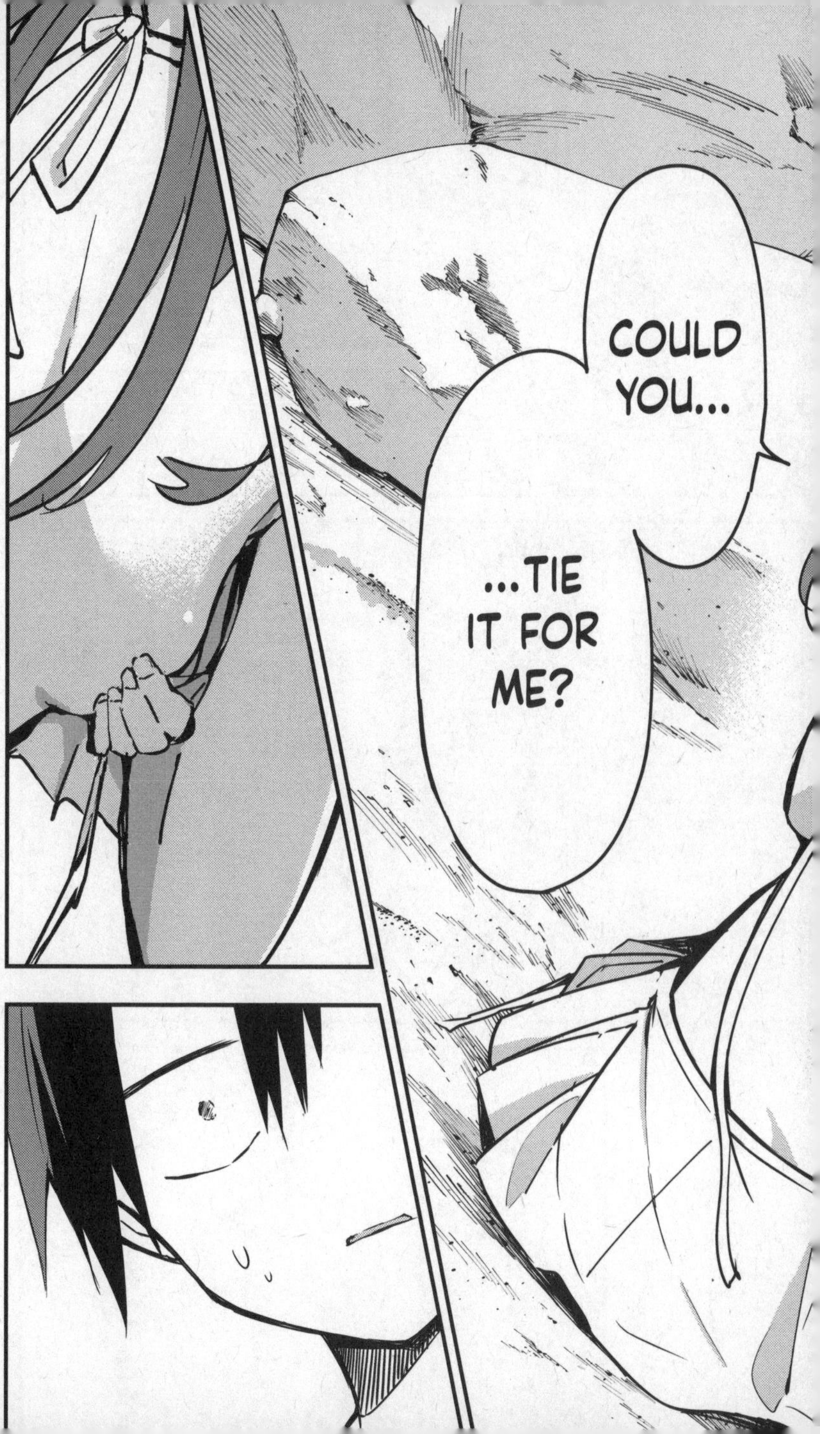
COULD YOU...
...TIE IT FOR ME?

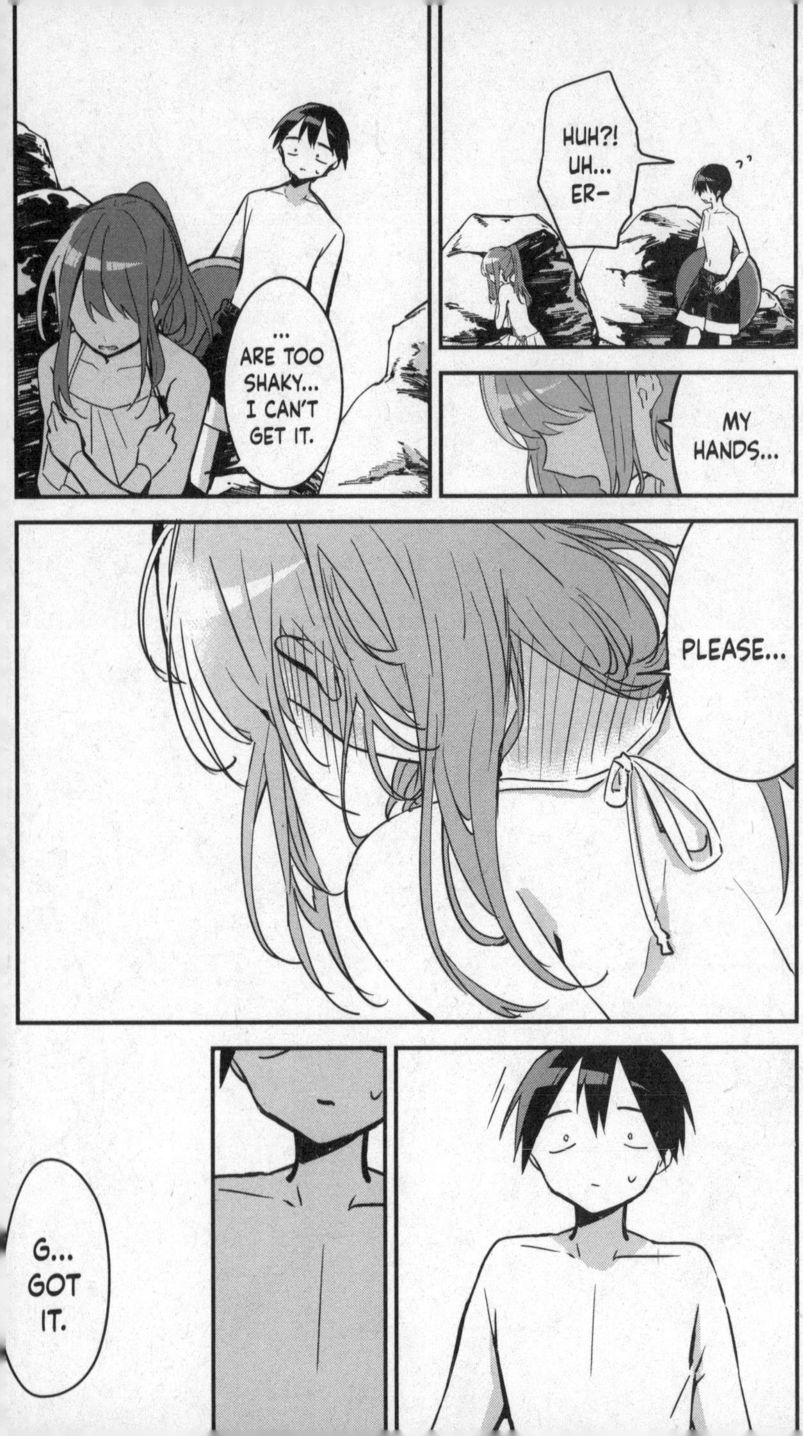
HUH?! UH... ER-
MY HANDS...
... ARE TOO SHAKY... I CAN'T GET IT.
PLEASE...
G... GOT IT.

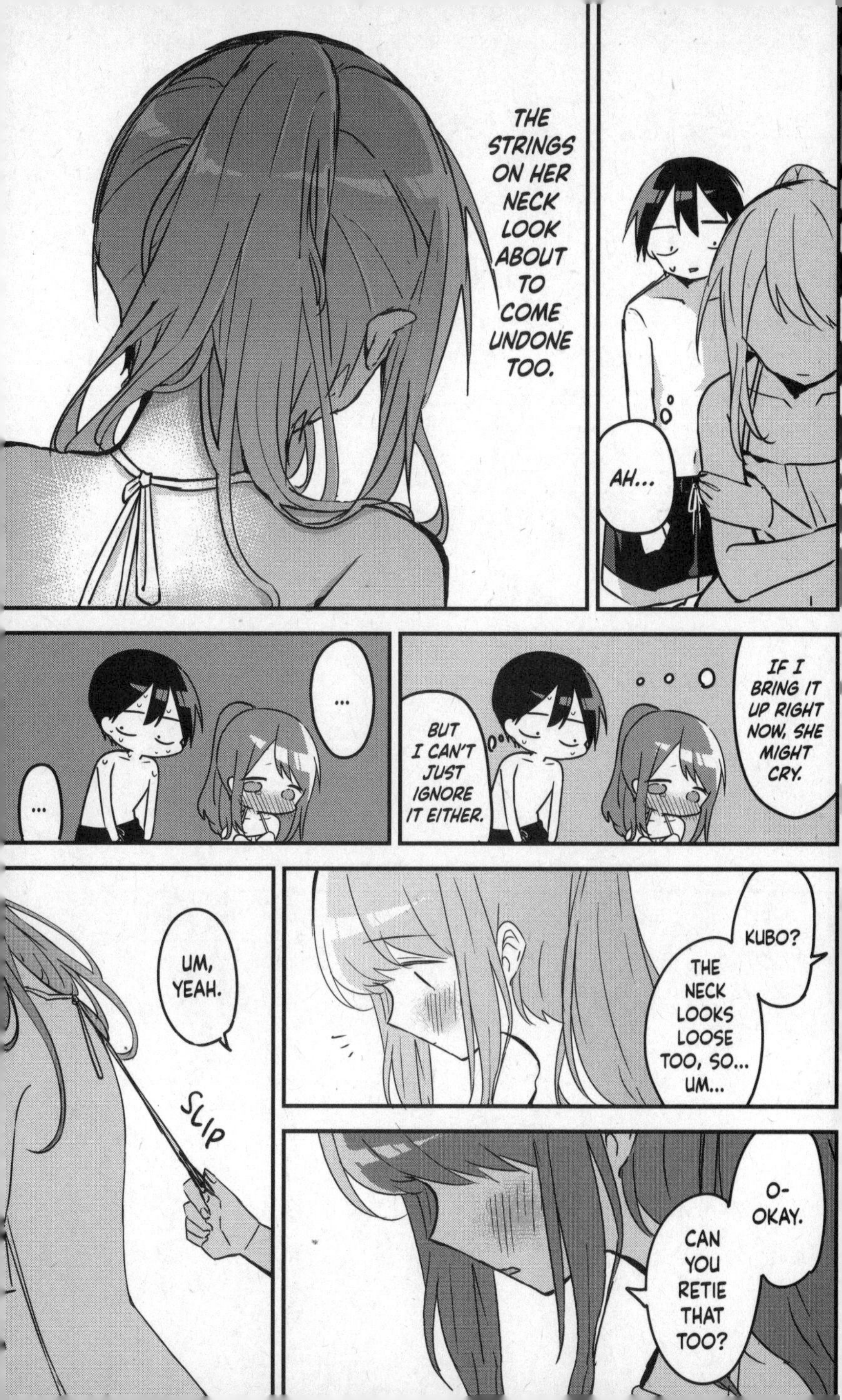
AH...
THE STRINGS ON HER NECK LOOK ABOUT TO COME UNDONE TOO.
IF I BRING IT UP RIGHT NOW, SHE MIGHT CRY.
BUT I CAN'T JUST IGNORE IT EITHER.
...
...
KUBO?
THE NECK LOOKS LOOSE TOO, SO... UM...
O-OKAY.
CAN YOU RETIE THAT TOO?
UM, YEAH.
SLIP

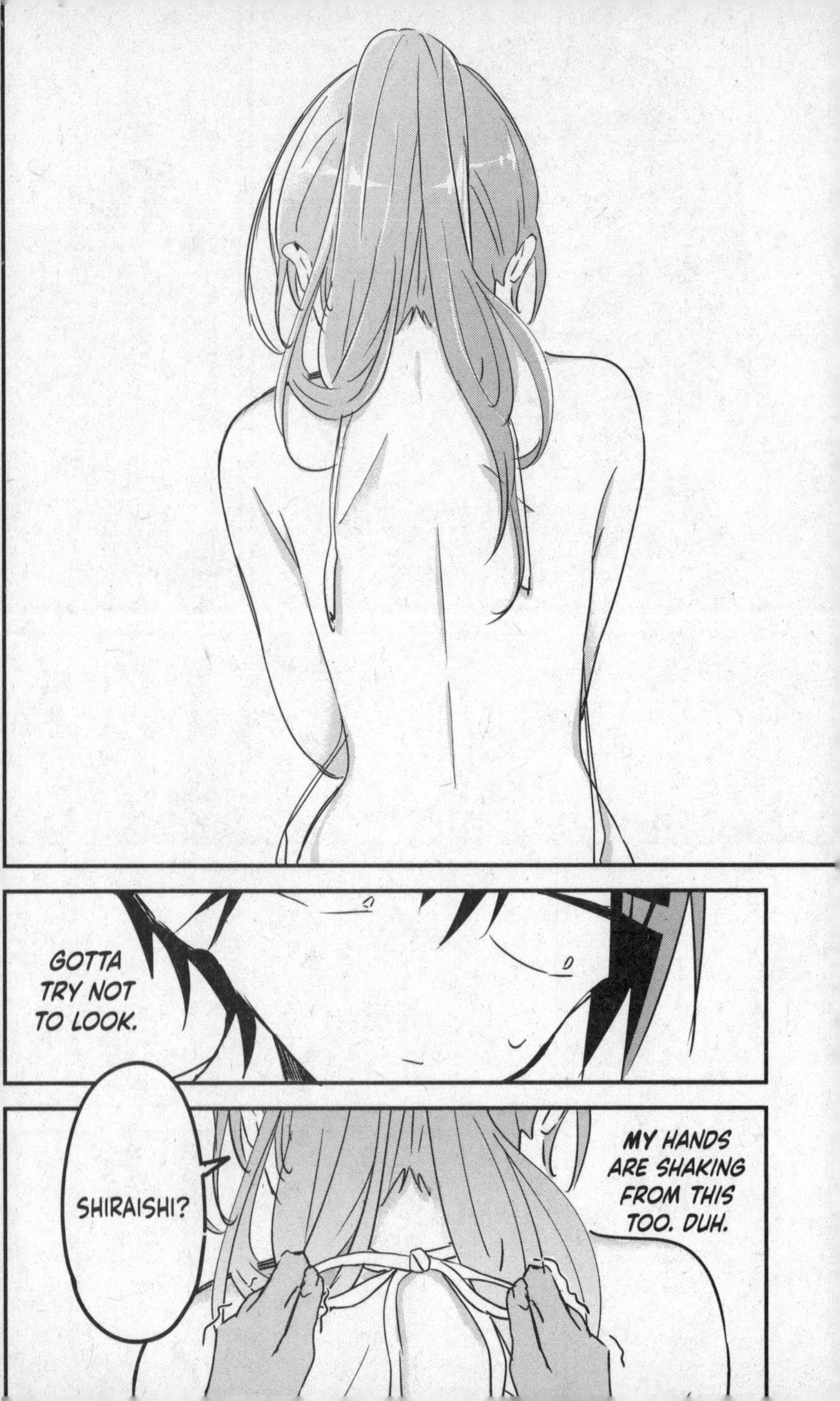
GOTTA TRY NOT TO LOOK.
MY HANDS ARE SHAKING FROM THIS TOO. DUH.
SHIRAISHI?

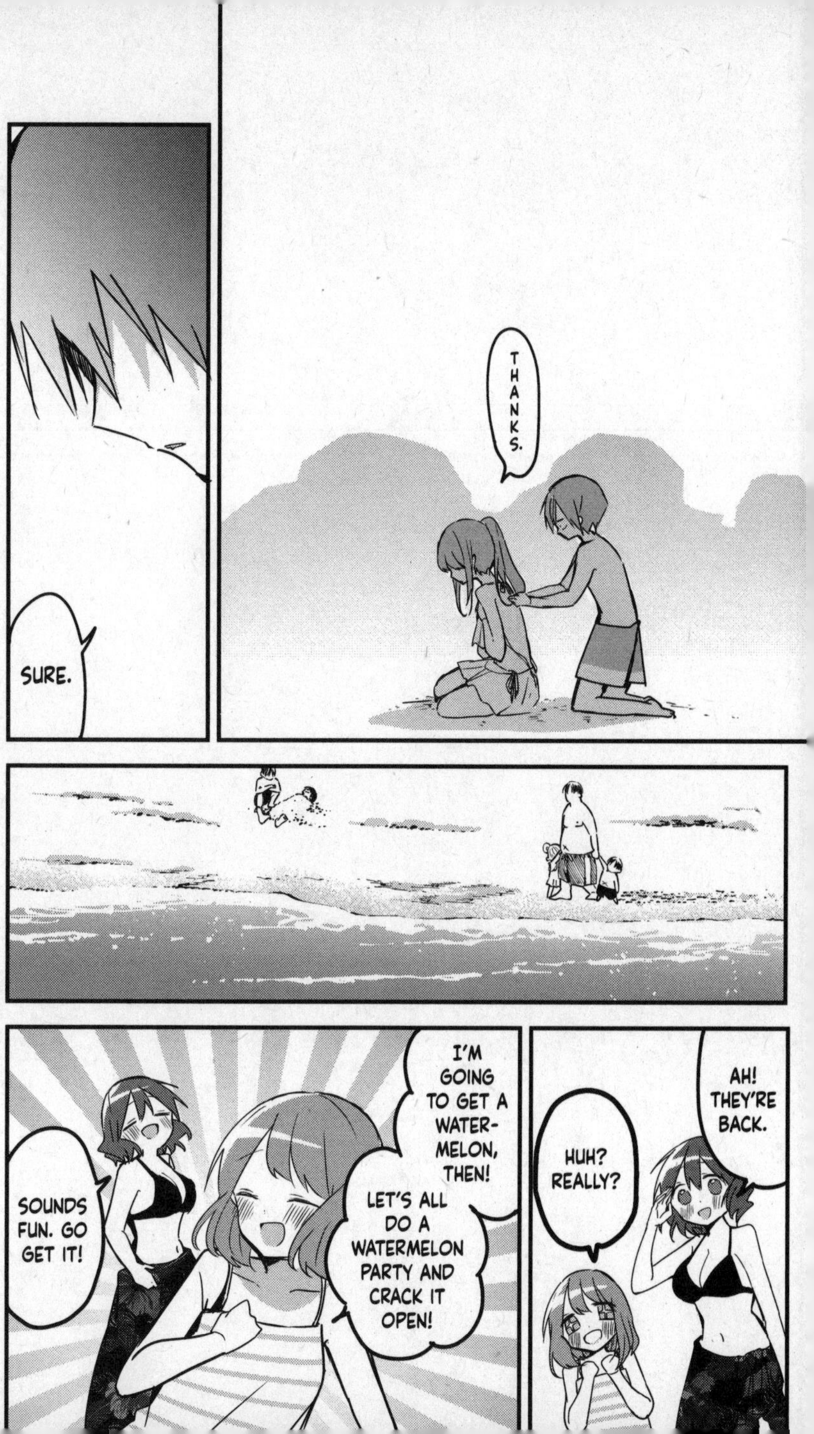
THANKS.
SURE.
AH! THEY'RE BACK.
HUH? REALLY?
I'M GOING TO GET A WATER-MELON, THEN!
LET'S ALL DO A WATERMELON PARTY AND CRACK IT OPEN!
SOUNDS FUN. GO GET IT!

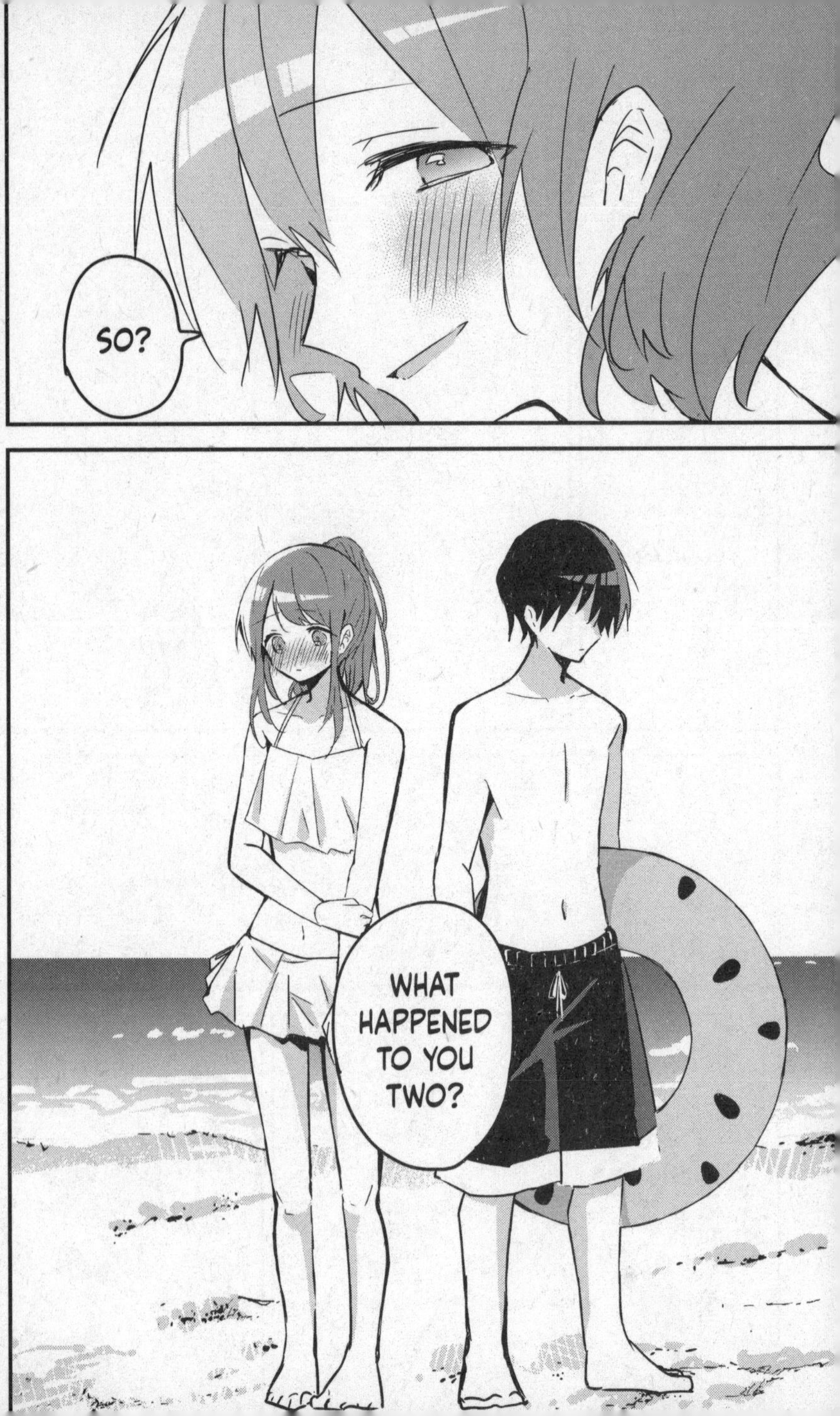
SO?
WHAT HAPPENED TO YOU TWO?

episode 086

CHOCOLATE AND BEDROOM

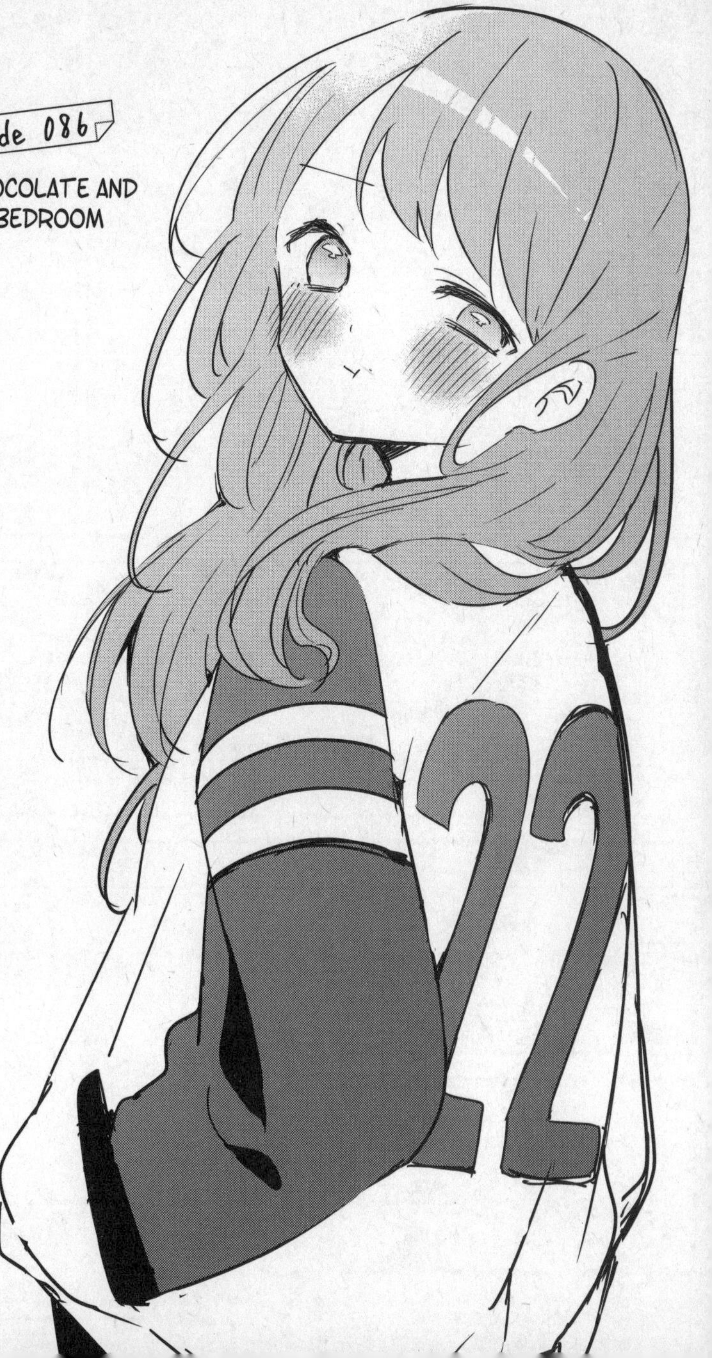

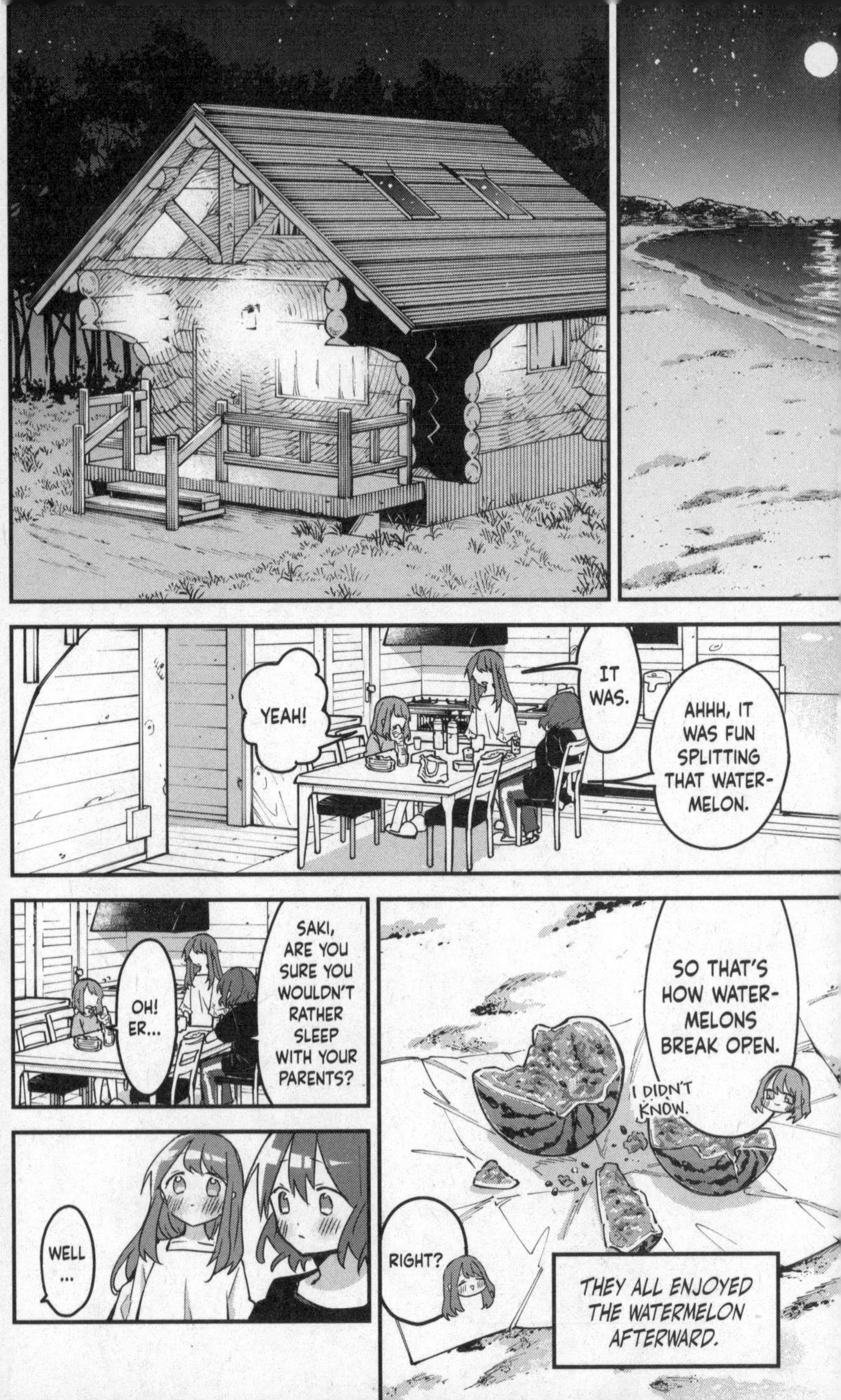
AHHH, IT WAS FUN SPLITTING THAT WATER-MELON.
IT WAS.
YEAH!
SO THAT'S HOW WATER-MELONS BREAK OPEN.
I DIDN'T KNOW.
RIGHT?
THEY ALL ENJOYED THE WATERMELON AFTERWARD.
SAKI, ARE YOU SURE YOU WOULDN'T RATHER SLEEP WITH YOUR PARENTS?
OH! ER...
WELL ...

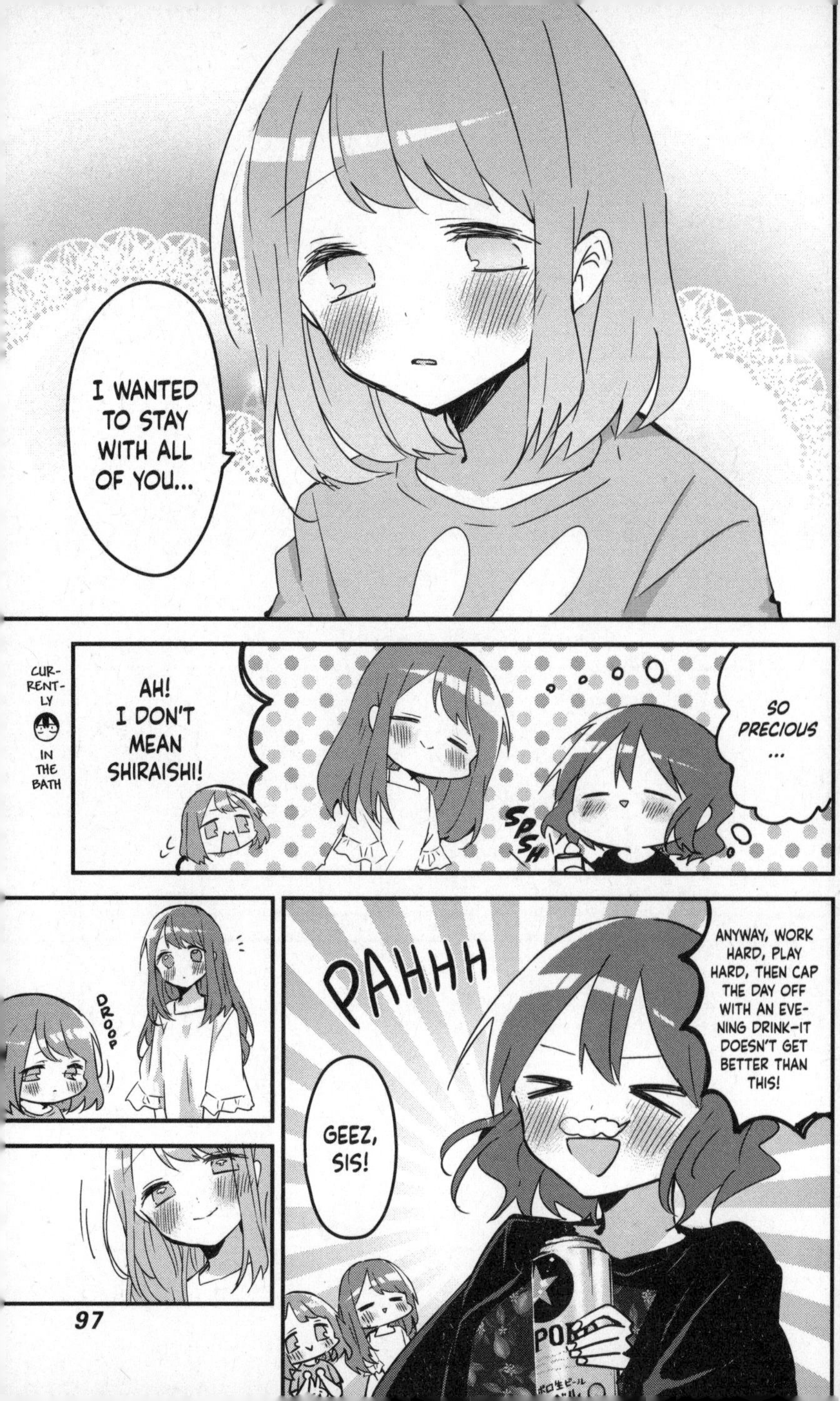
I WANTED TO STAY WITH ALL OF YOU...
SO PRECIOUS ...
SPSH
AH! I DON'T MEAN SHIRAISHI!
CUR-RENT-LY IN THE BATH
ANYWAY, WORK HARD, PLAY HARD, THEN CAP THE DAY OFF WITH AN EVE-NING DRINK—IT DOESN'T GET BETTER THAN THIS!
PAHHH
GEEZ, SIS!
DROOP

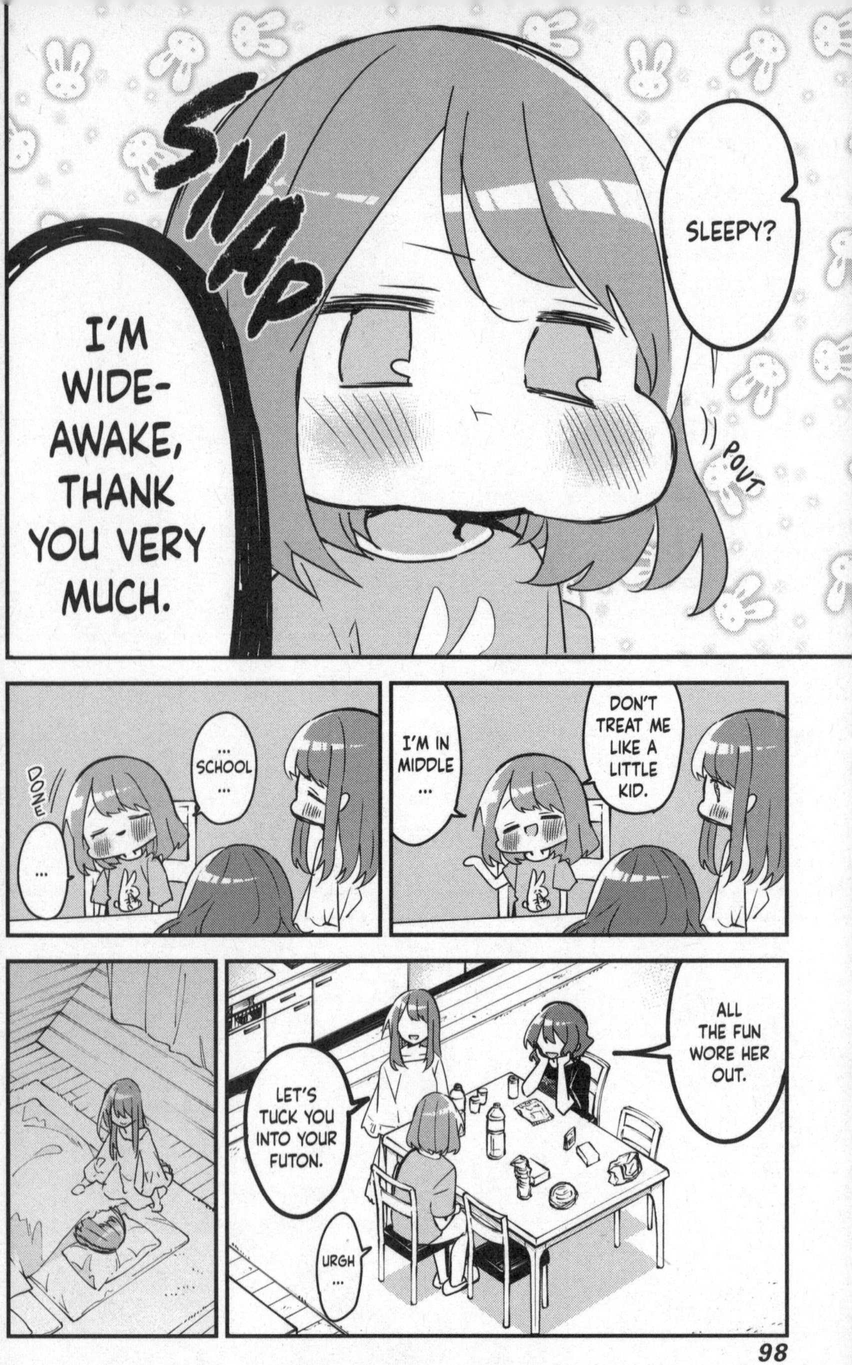
SLEEPY?
POUT
SNAP
I'M WIDE-AWAKE, THANK YOU VERY MUCH.
DON'T TREAT ME LIKE A LITTLE KID.
I'M IN MIDDLE ...
... SCHOOL ...
DOZE
...
ALL THE FUN WORE HER OUT.
LET'S TUCK YOU INTO YOUR FUTON.
URGH ...
......

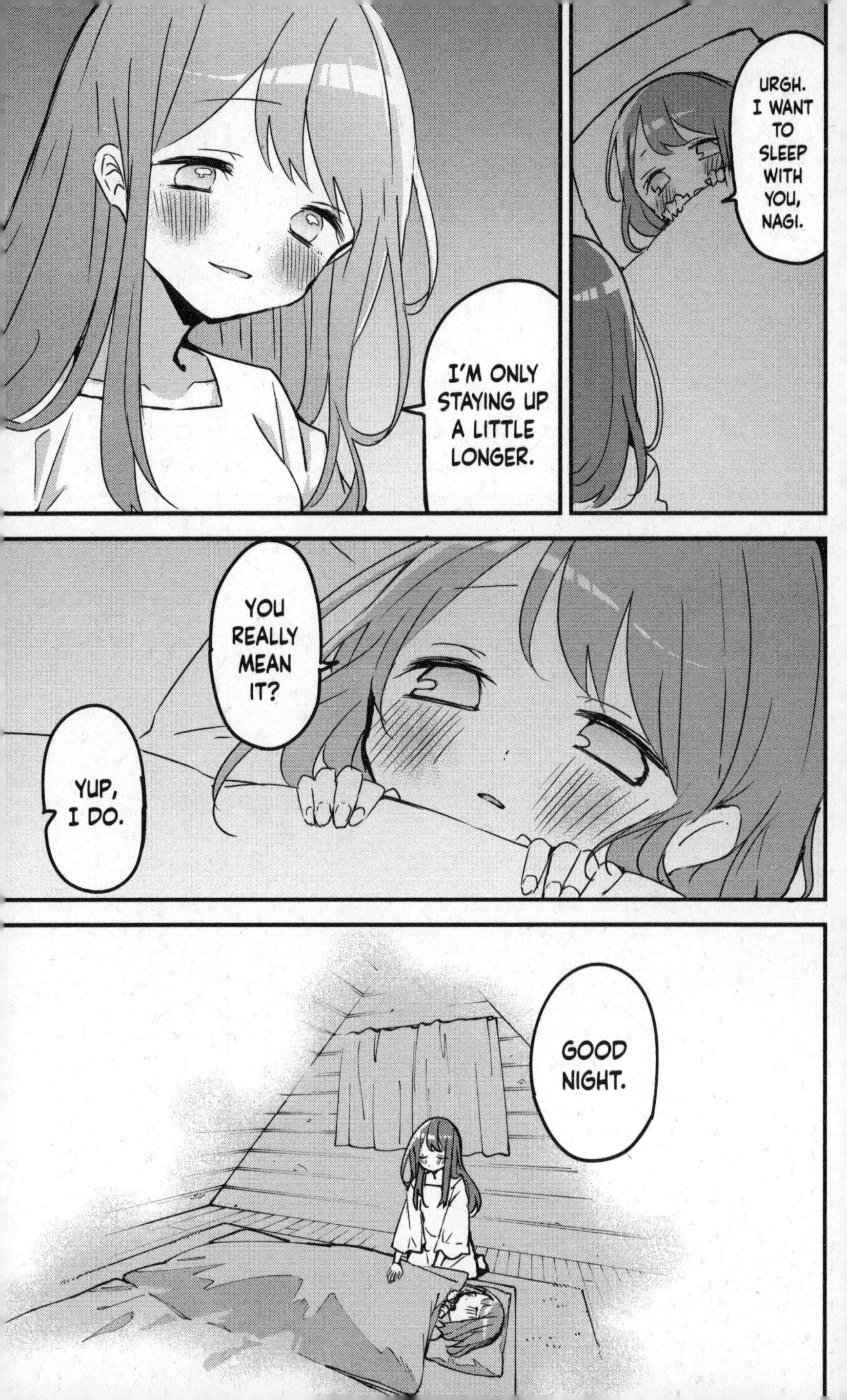
URGH. I WANT TO SLEEP WITH YOU, NAGI.
I'M ONLY STAYING UP A LITTLE LONGER.
YOU REALLY MEAN IT?
YUP, I DO.
GOOD NIGHT.

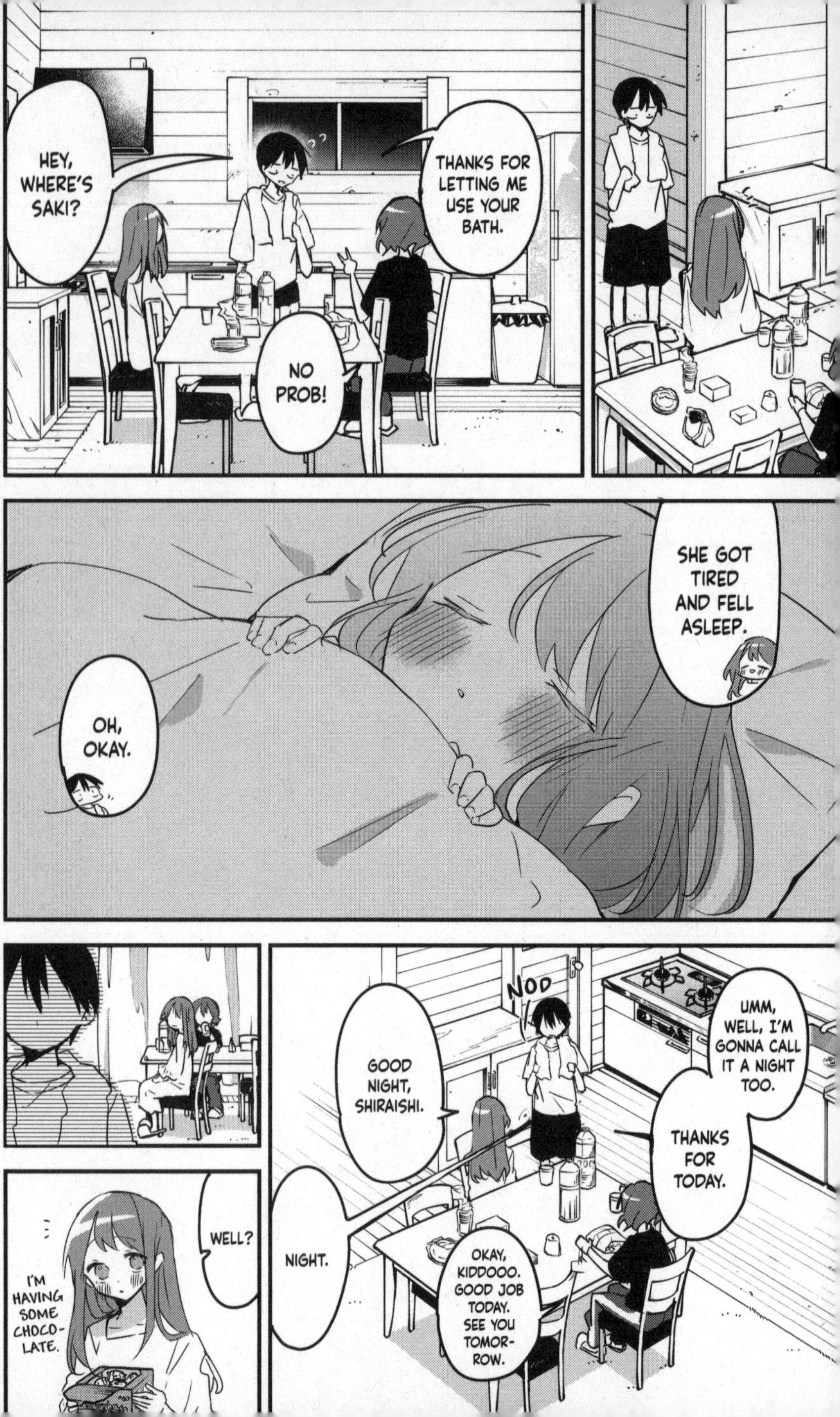
THANKS FOR LETTING ME USE YOUR BATH.
HEY, WHERE'S SAKI?
NO PROB!
SHE GOT TIRED AND FELL ASLEEP.
OH, OKAY.
UMM, WELL, I'M GONNA CALL IT A NIGHT TOO.
THANKS FOR TODAY.
NOD
GOOD NIGHT, SHIRAISHI.
OKAY, KIDDOOO. GOOD JOB TODAY. SEE YOU TOMOR-ROW.
NIGHT.
WELL?
I'M HAVING SOME CHOCO-LATE.

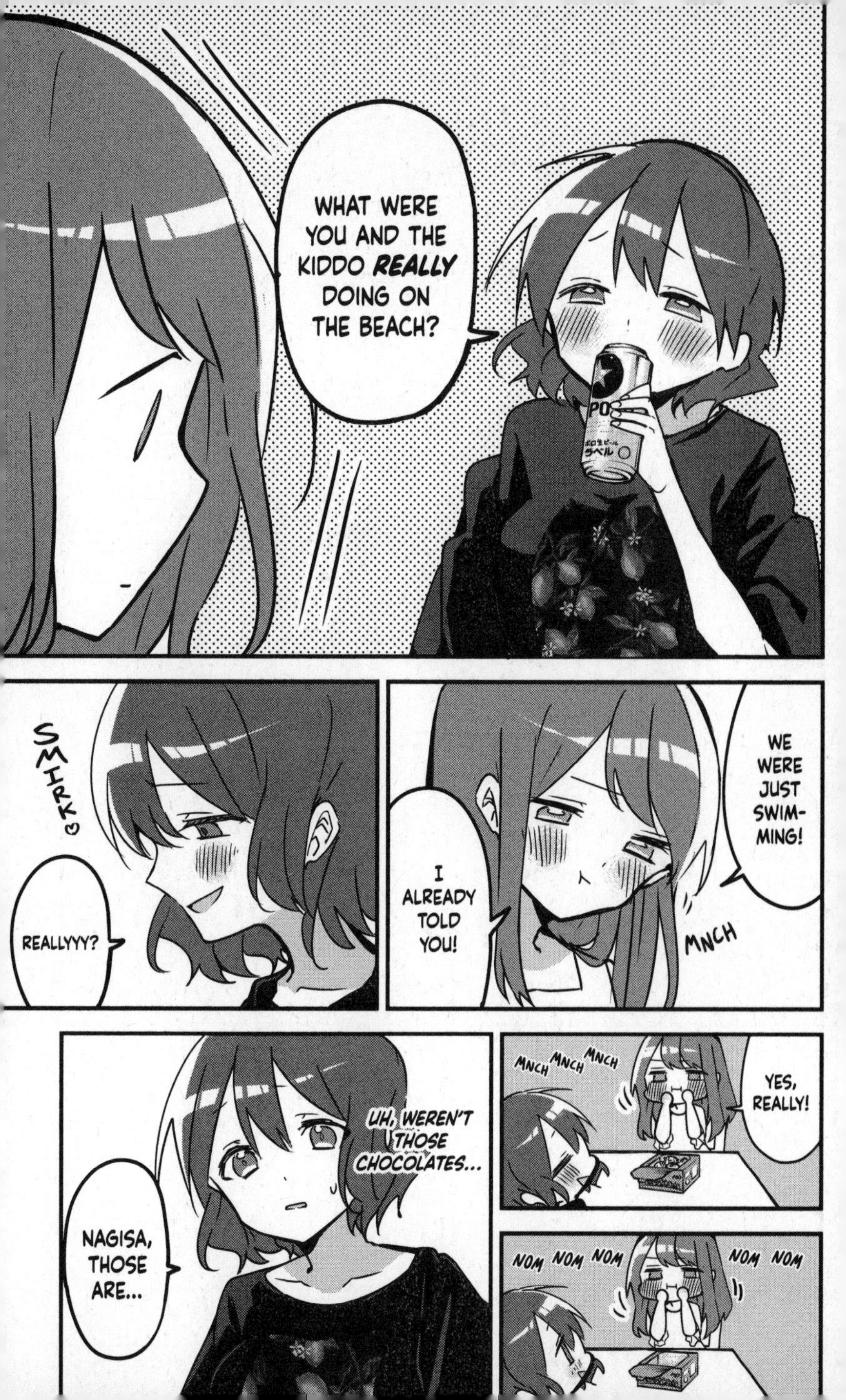
WHAT WERE YOU AND THE KIDDO REALLY DOING ON THE BEACH?
WE WERE JUST SWIMMING!
I ALREADY TOLD YOU!
MNCH
SMIRK
REALLYYY?
MNCH MNCH MNCH
YES, REALLY!
NOM NOM NOM NOM NOM
UH, WEREN'T THOSE CHOCOLATES...
NAGISA, THOSE ARE...

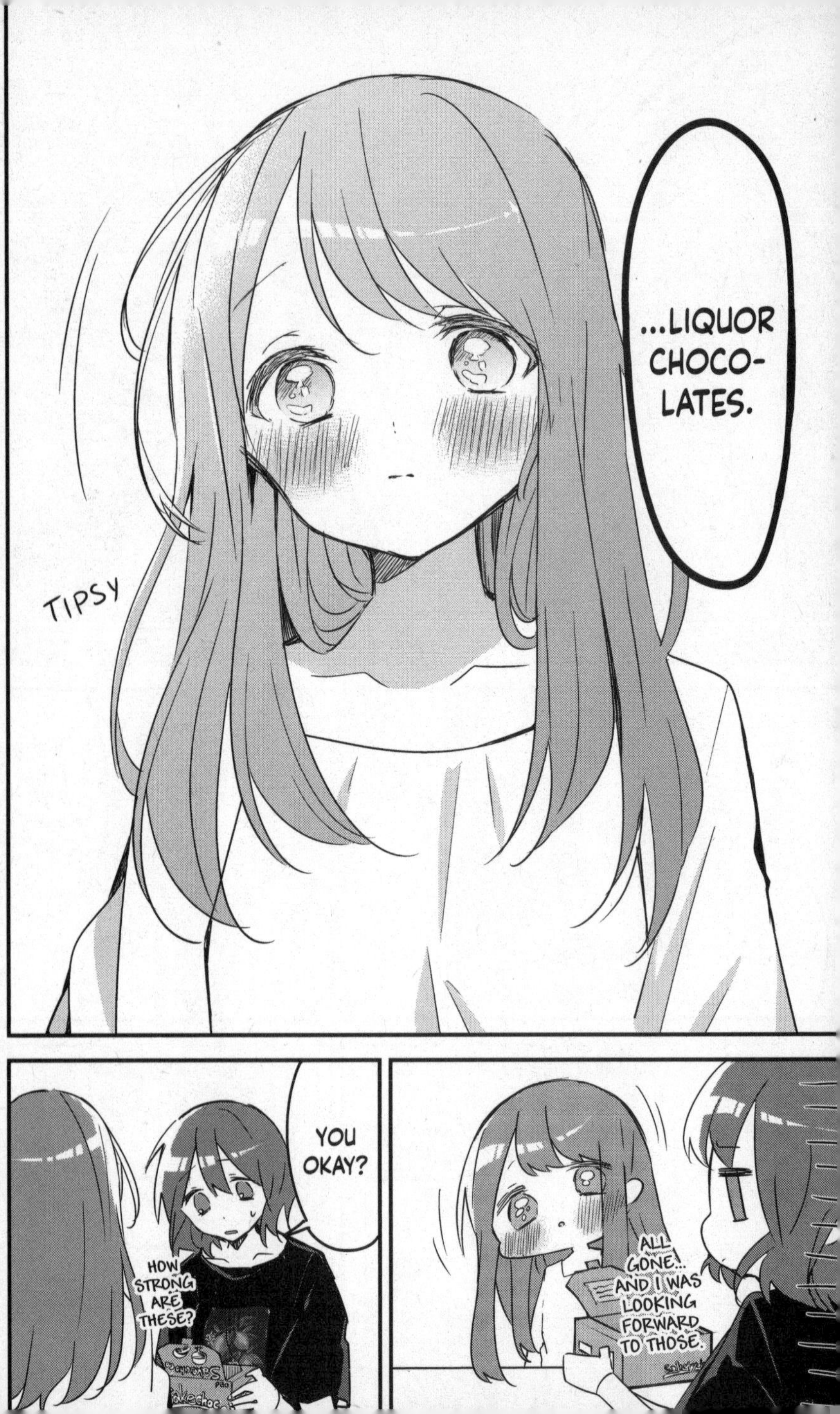
...LIQUOR CHOCO-LATES.
TIPSY
ALL GONE... AND I WAS LOOKING FORWARD TO THOSE.
YOU OKAY?
HOW STRONG ARE THESE?

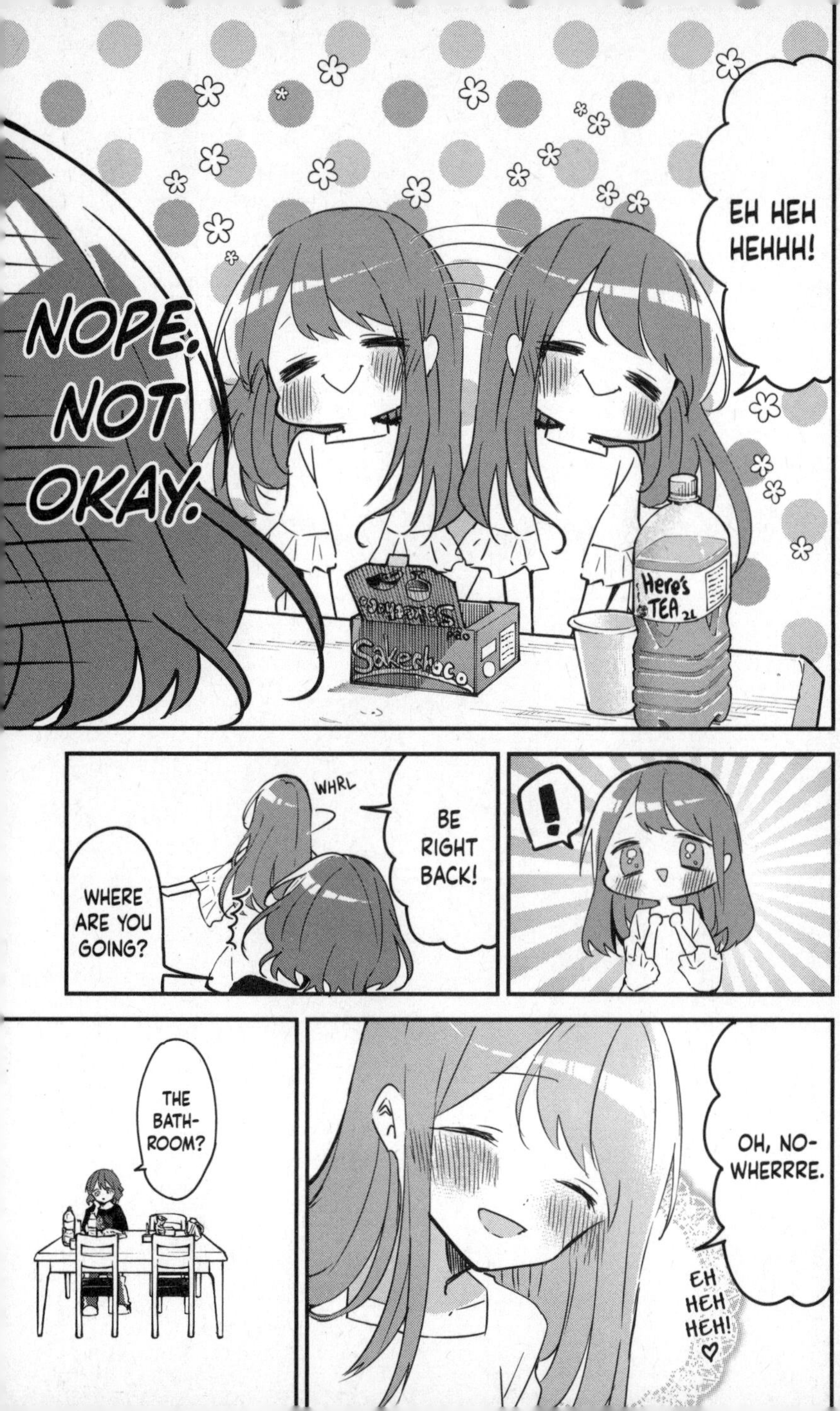
EH HEH HEHHH!
Here's TEA 2L
Sakechoco
NOPE. NOT OKAY.
!
BE RIGHT BACK!
WHRL
WHERE ARE YOU GOING?
OH, NO-WHERRRE.
EH HEH HEH! ♥
THE BATH-ROOM?

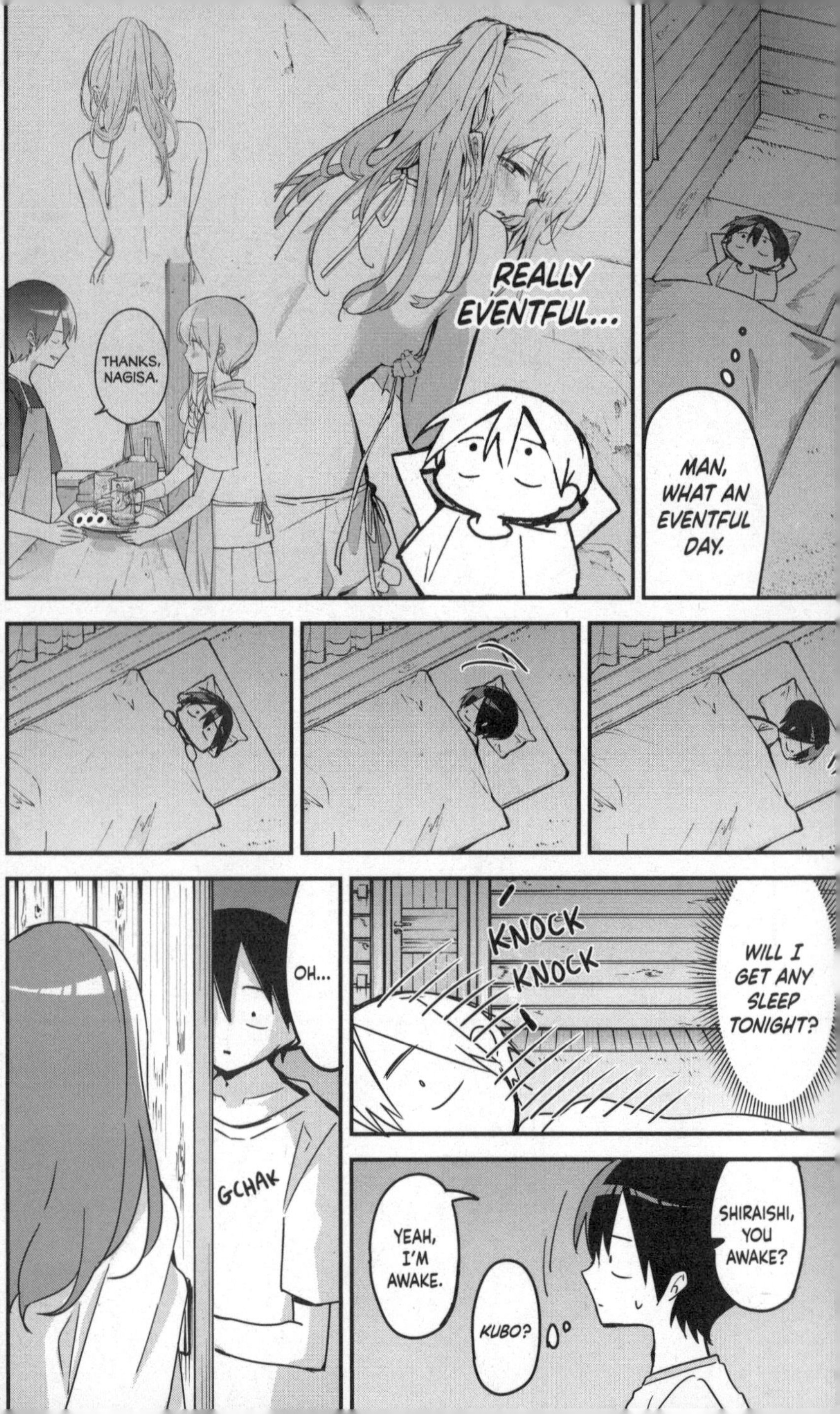
MAN, WHAT AN EVENTFUL DAY.
REALLY EVENTFUL...
THANKS, NAGISA.
WILL I GET ANY SLEEP TONIGHT?
KNOCK KNOCK
SHIRAISHI, YOU AWAKE?
YEAH, I'M AWAKE.
KUBO?
OH...
GCHAK

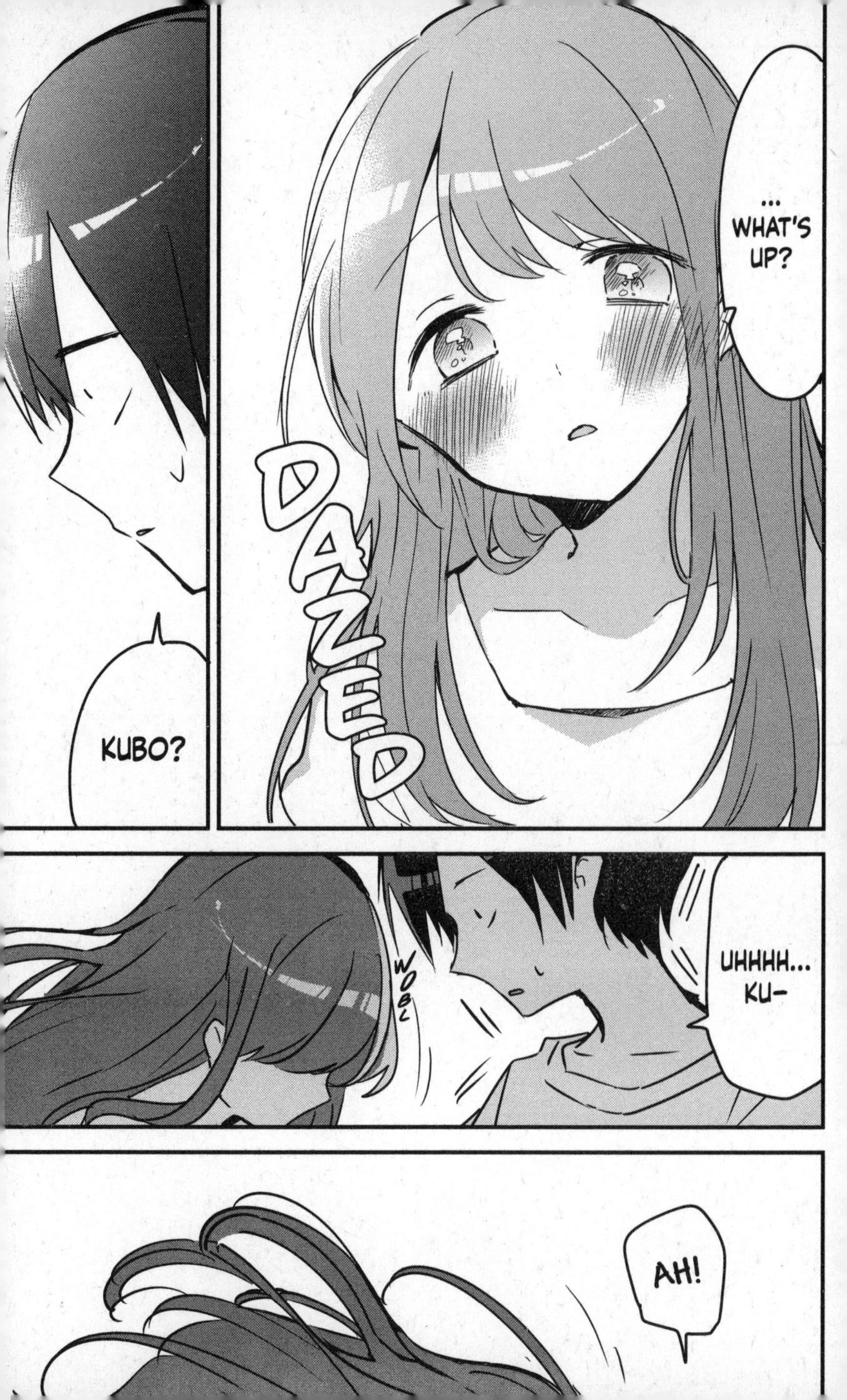
... WHAT'S UP?
DAZED
KUBO?
UHHHH... KU-
WOBL
AH!

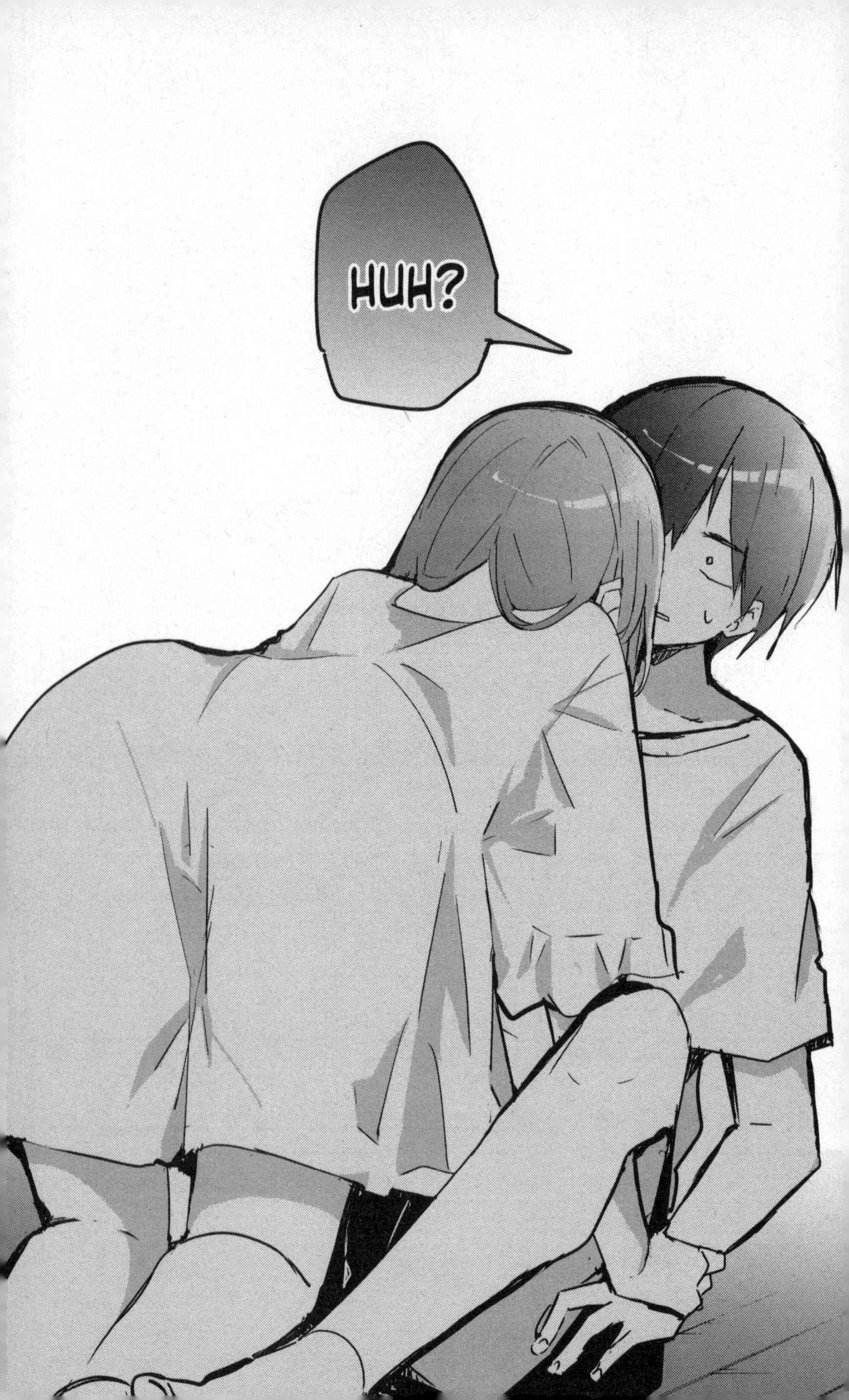
HUH?

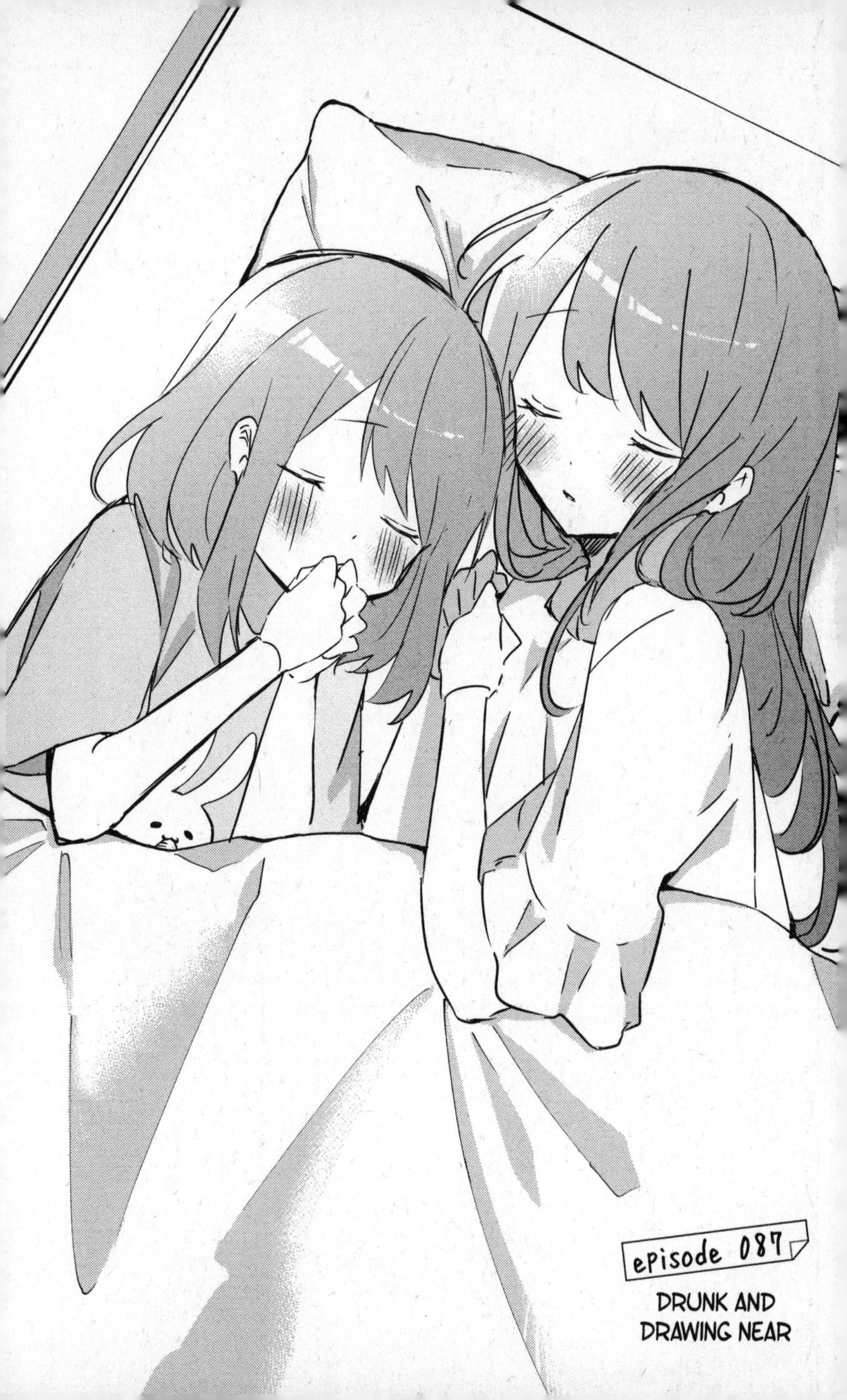
episode 087
DRUNK AND DRAWING NEAR

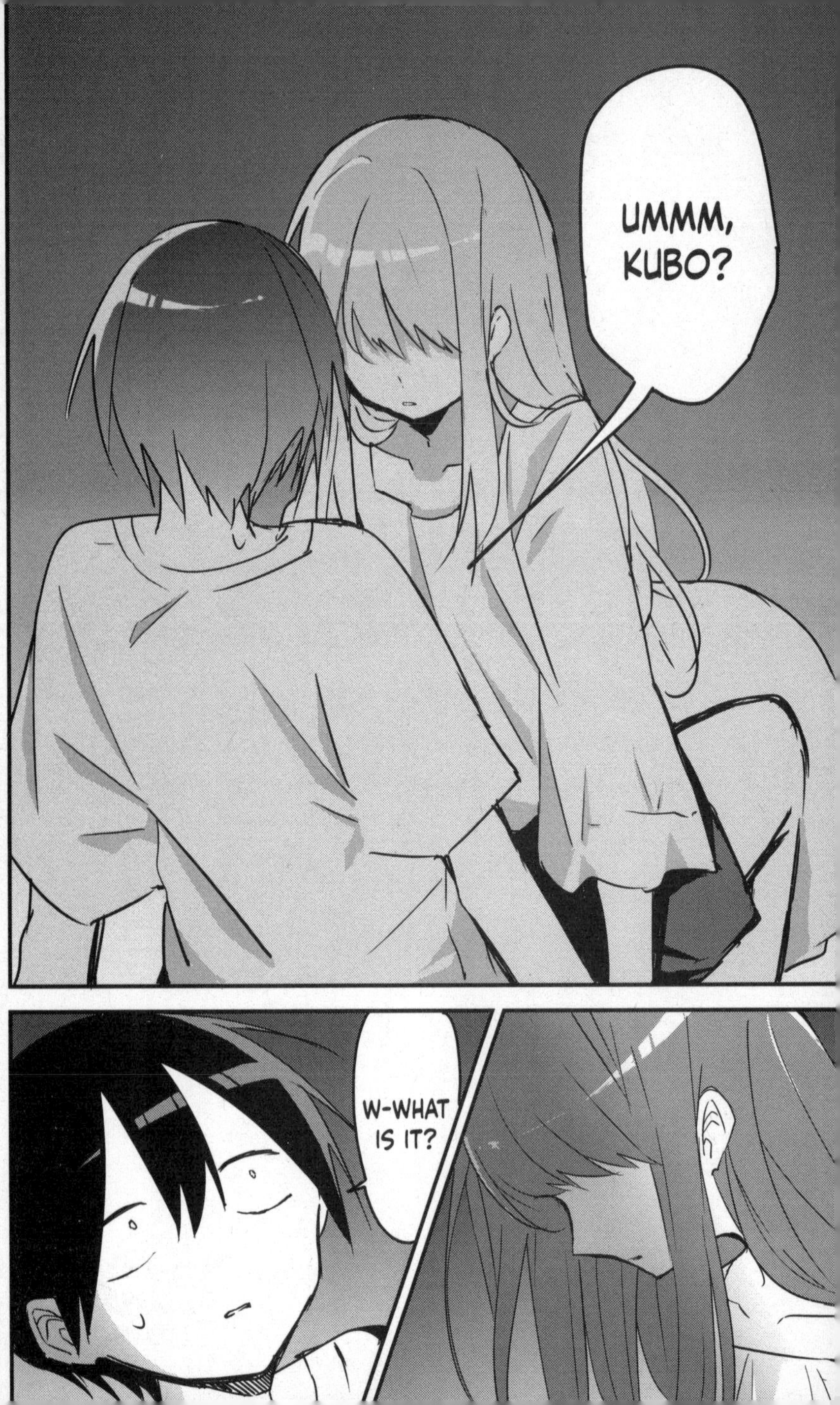
UMMM, KUBO?
W-WHAT IS IT?

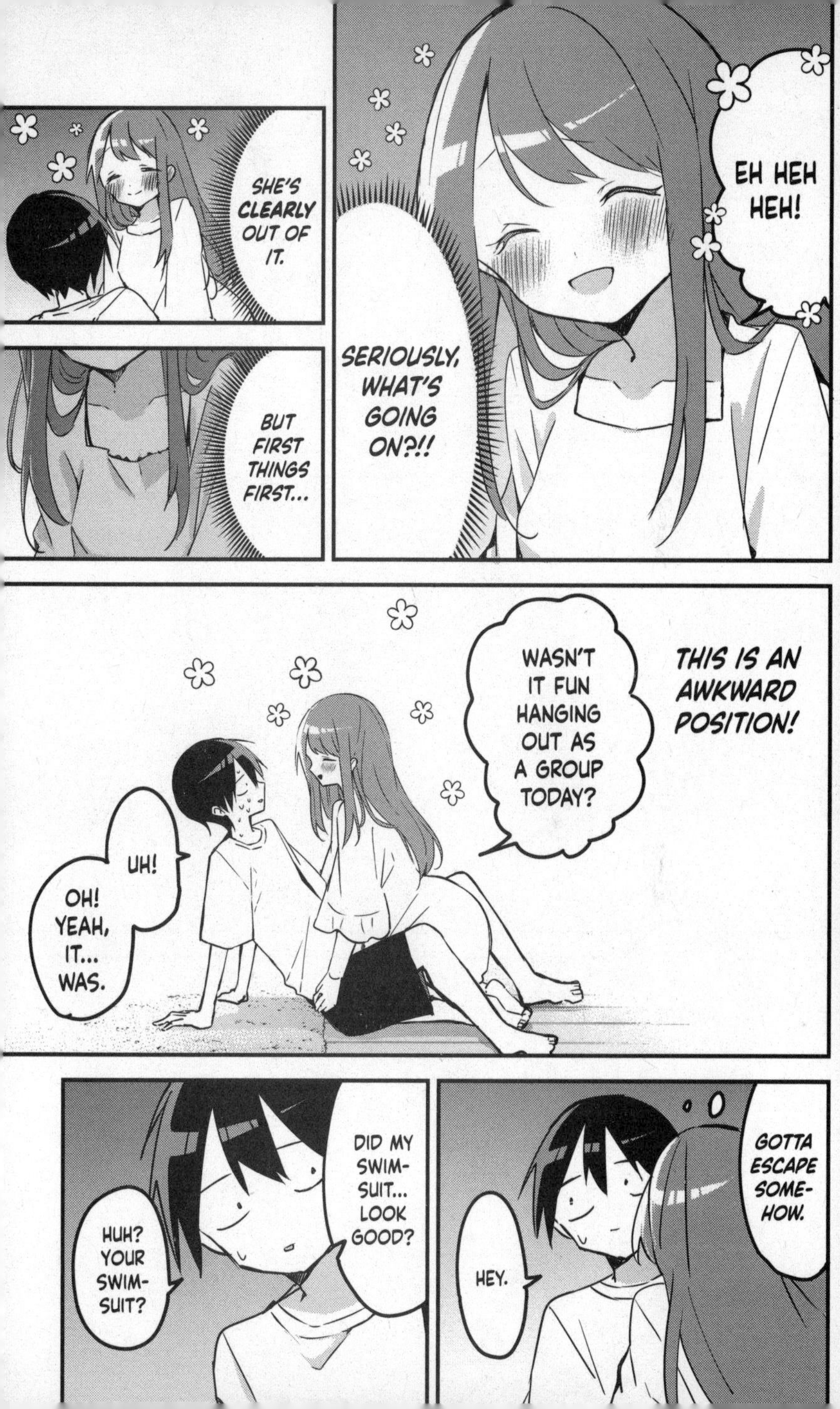
EH HEH HEH!
SERIOUSLY, WHAT'S GOING ON?!!
SHE'S CLEARLY OUT OF IT.
BUT FIRST THINGS FIRST...
THIS IS AN AWKWARD POSITION!
WASN'T IT FUN HANGING OUT AS A GROUP TODAY?
UH!
OH! YEAH, IT... WAS.
GOTTA ESCAPE SOMEHOW.
HEY.
DID MY SWIMSUIT... LOOK GOOD?
HUH? YOUR SWIMSUIT?

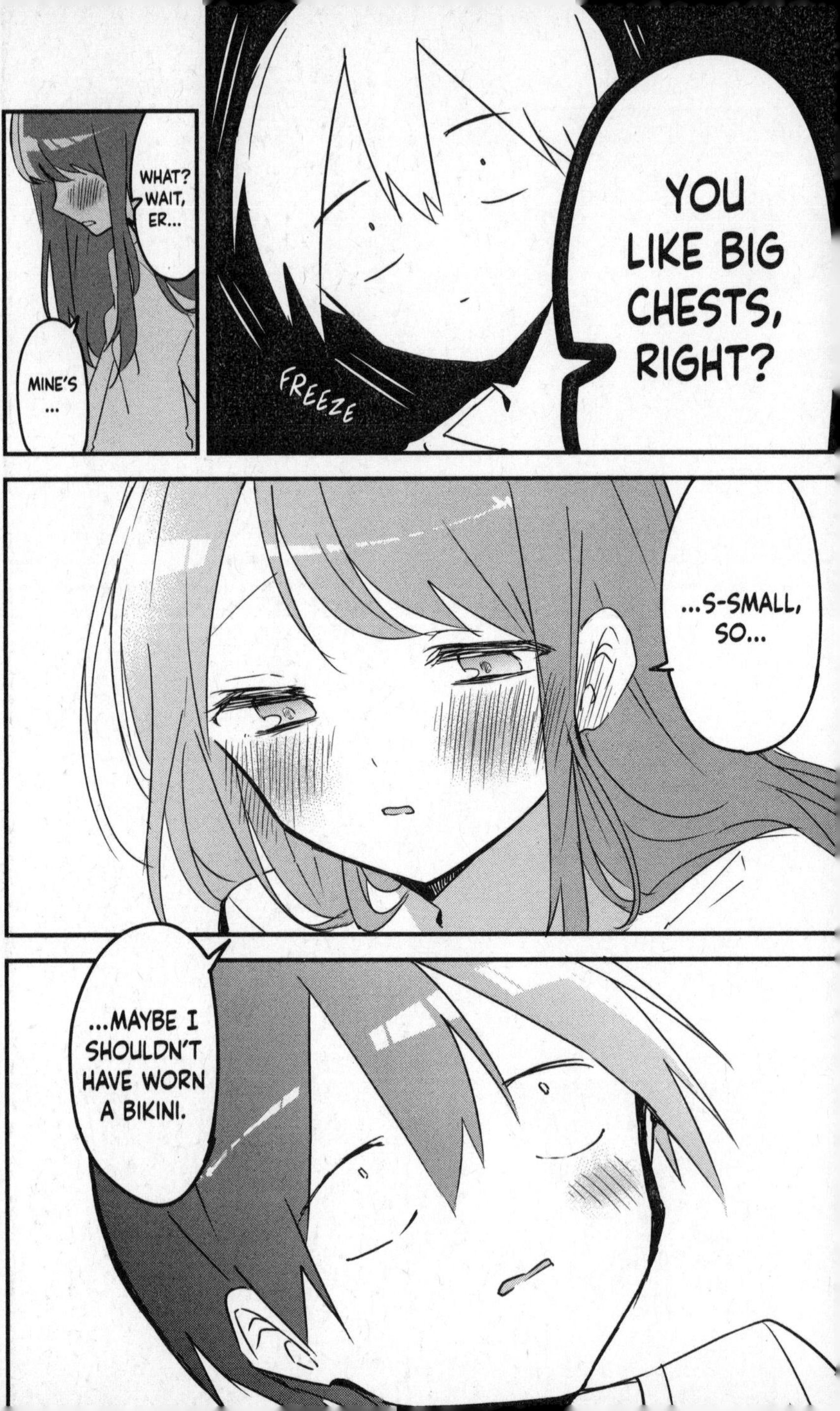
YOU LIKE BIG CHESTS, RIGHT?
FREEZE
WHAT? WAIT, ER...
MINE'S ...
...S-SMALL, SO...
...MAYBE I SHOULDN'T HAVE WORN A BIKINI.

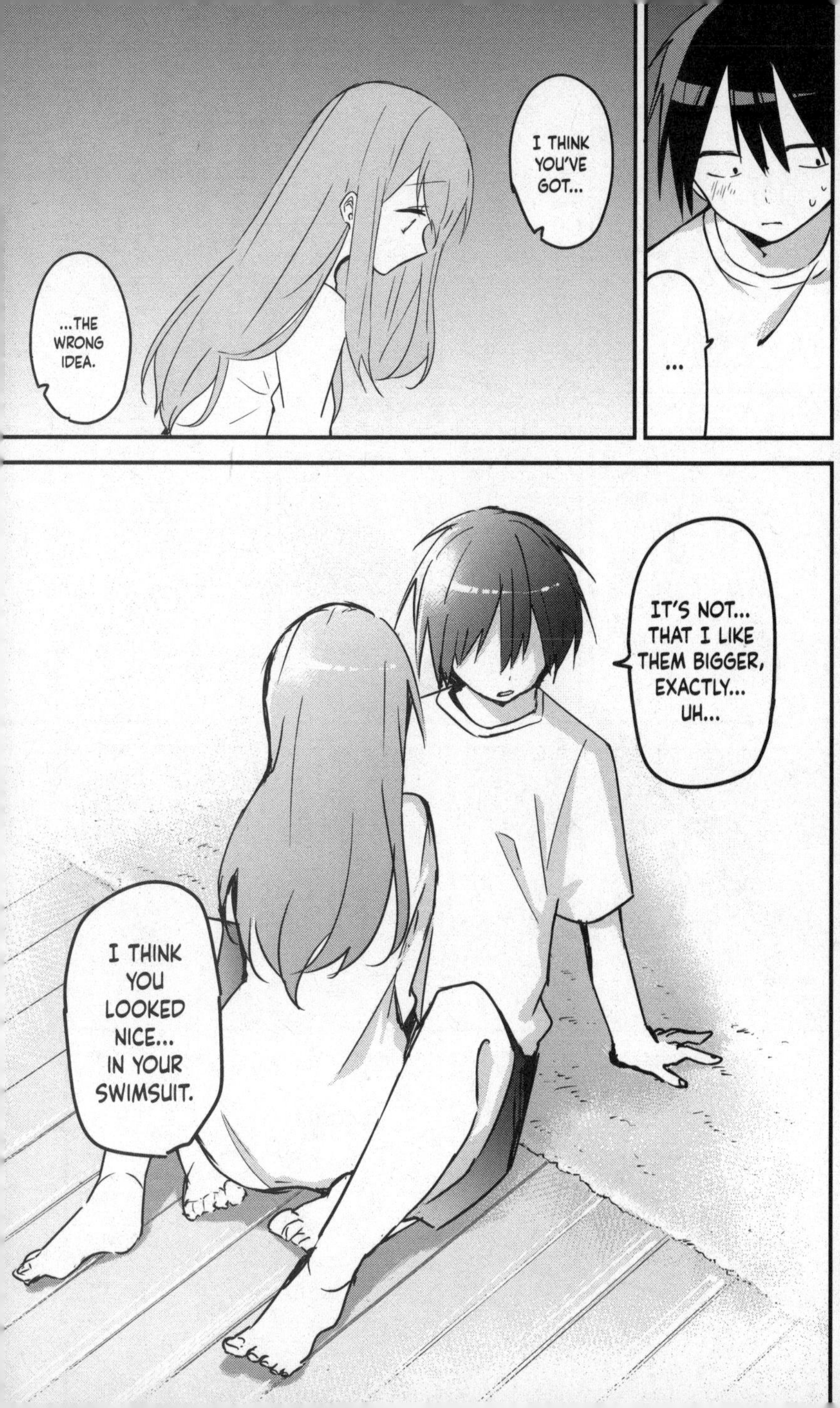
...
I THINK YOU'VE GOT...
...THE WRONG IDEA.
IT'S NOT... THAT I LIKE THEM BIGGER, EXACTLY... UH...
I THINK YOU LOOKED NICE... IN YOUR SWIMSUIT.

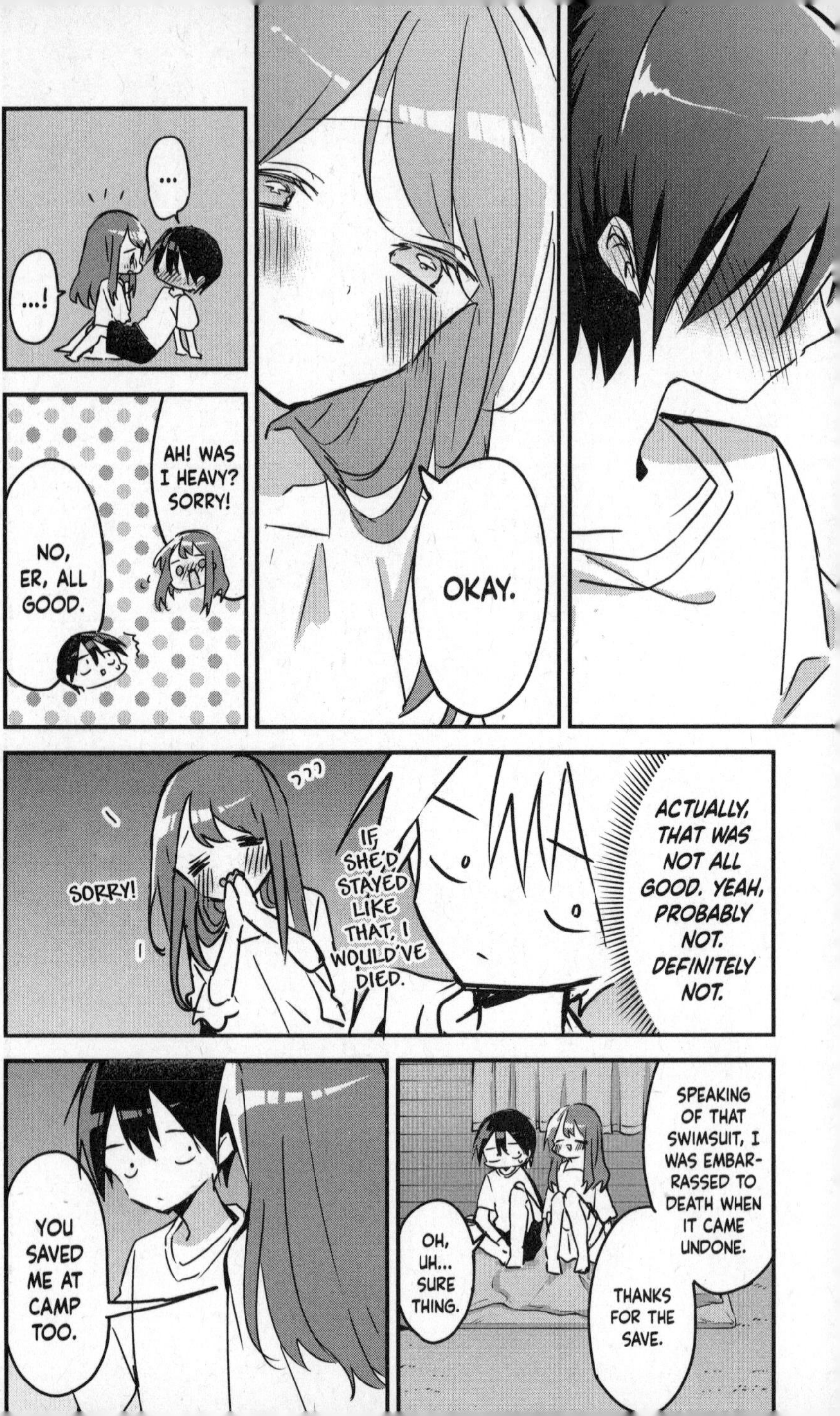
OKAY.
...
...!
AH! WAS I HEAVY? SORRY!
NO, ER, ALL GOOD.
ACTUALLY, THAT WAS NOT ALL GOOD. YEAH, PROBABLY NOT. DEFINITELY NOT.
IF SHE'D STAYED LIKE THAT, I WOULD'VE DIED.
SORRY!
SPEAKING OF THAT SWIMSUIT, I WAS EMBARRASSED TO DEATH WHEN IT CAME UNDONE.
THANKS FOR THE SAVE.
OH, UH... SURE THING.
YOU SAVED ME AT CAMP TOO.

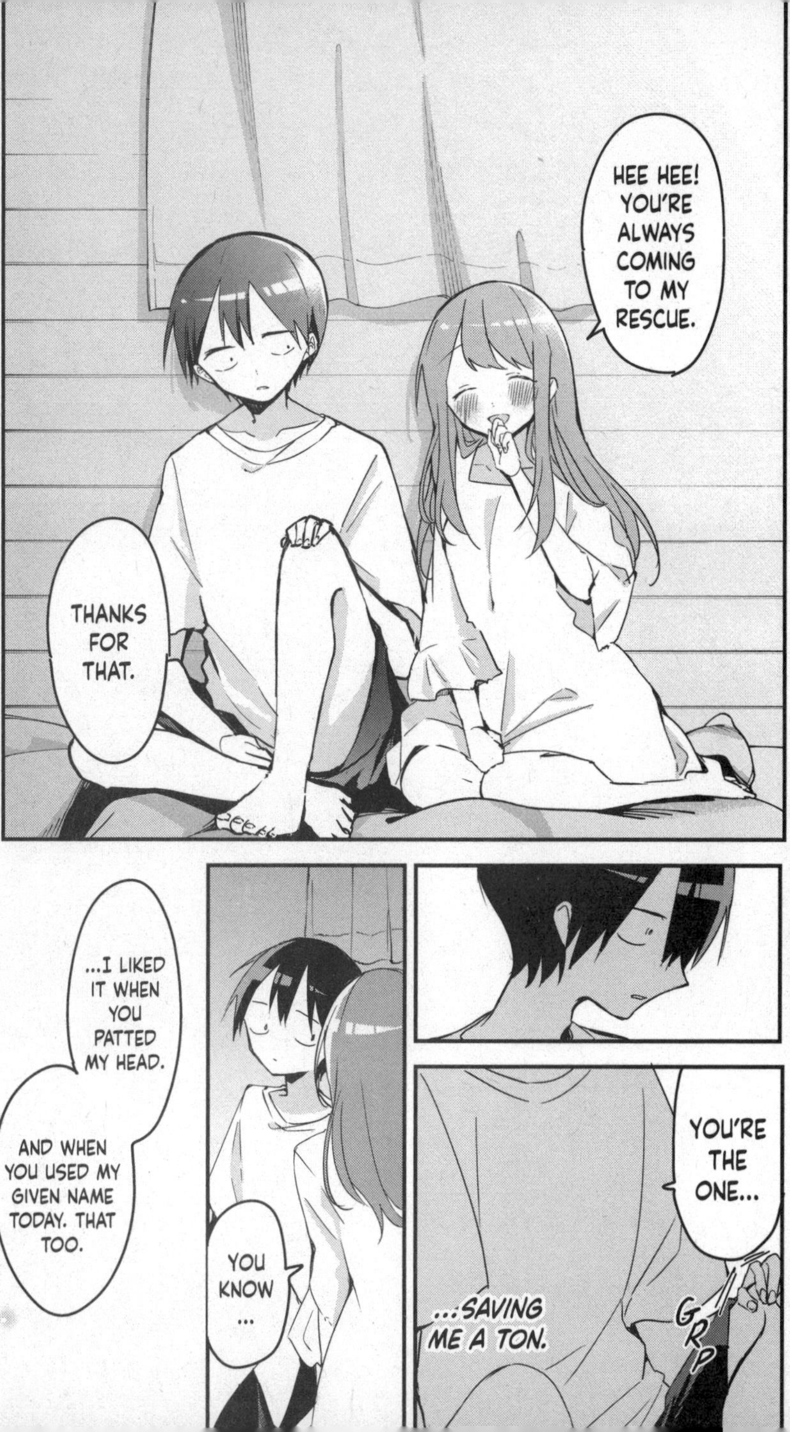
HEE HEE! YOU'RE ALWAYS COMING TO MY RESCUE.
THANKS FOR THAT.
YOU'RE THE ONE...
...SAVING ME A TON.
GRP
YOU KNOW...
...I LIKED IT WHEN YOU PATTED MY HEAD.
AND WHEN YOU USED MY GIVEN NAME TODAY. THAT TOO.

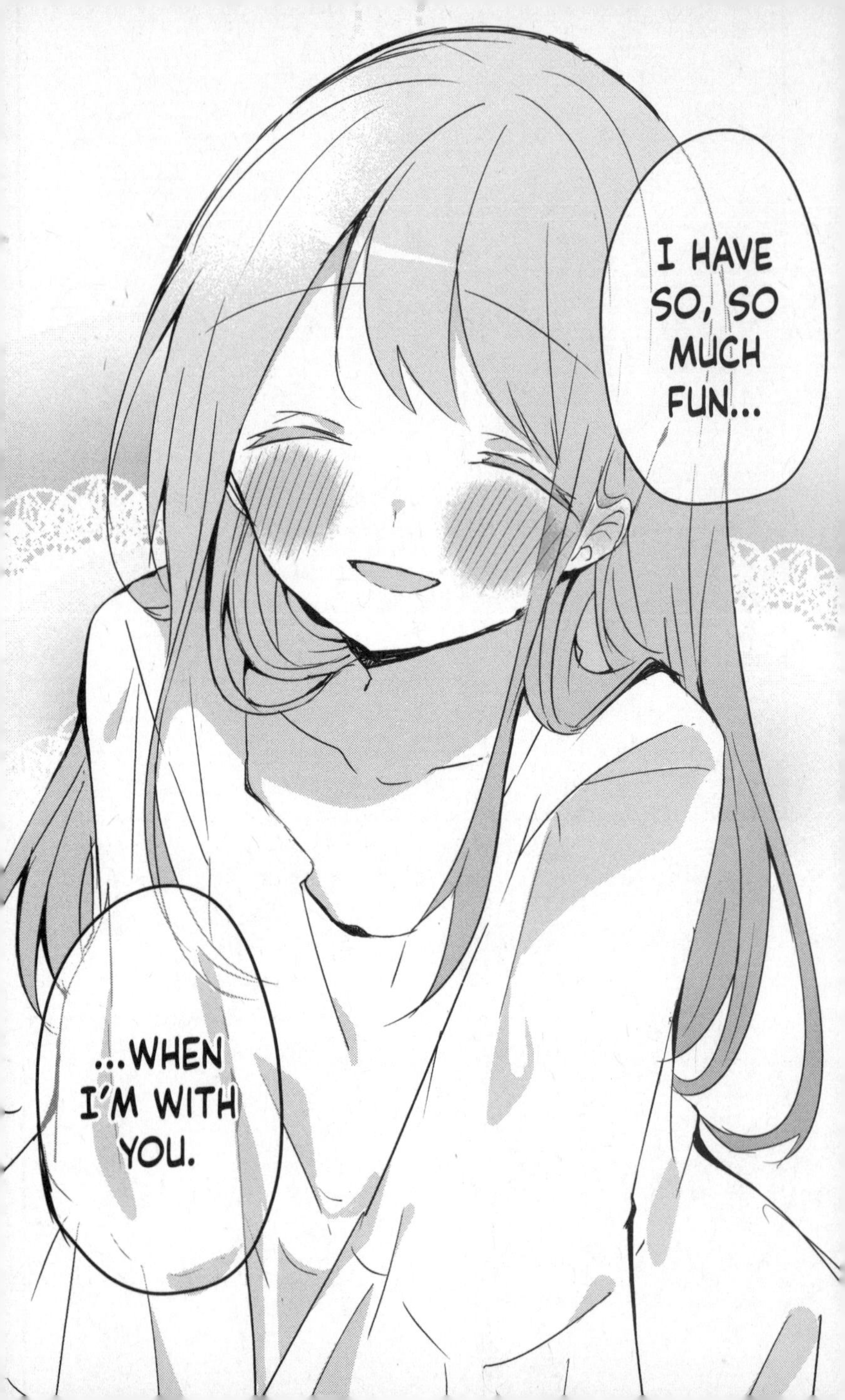
I HAVE SO, SO MUCH FUN...
...WHEN I'M WITH YOU.

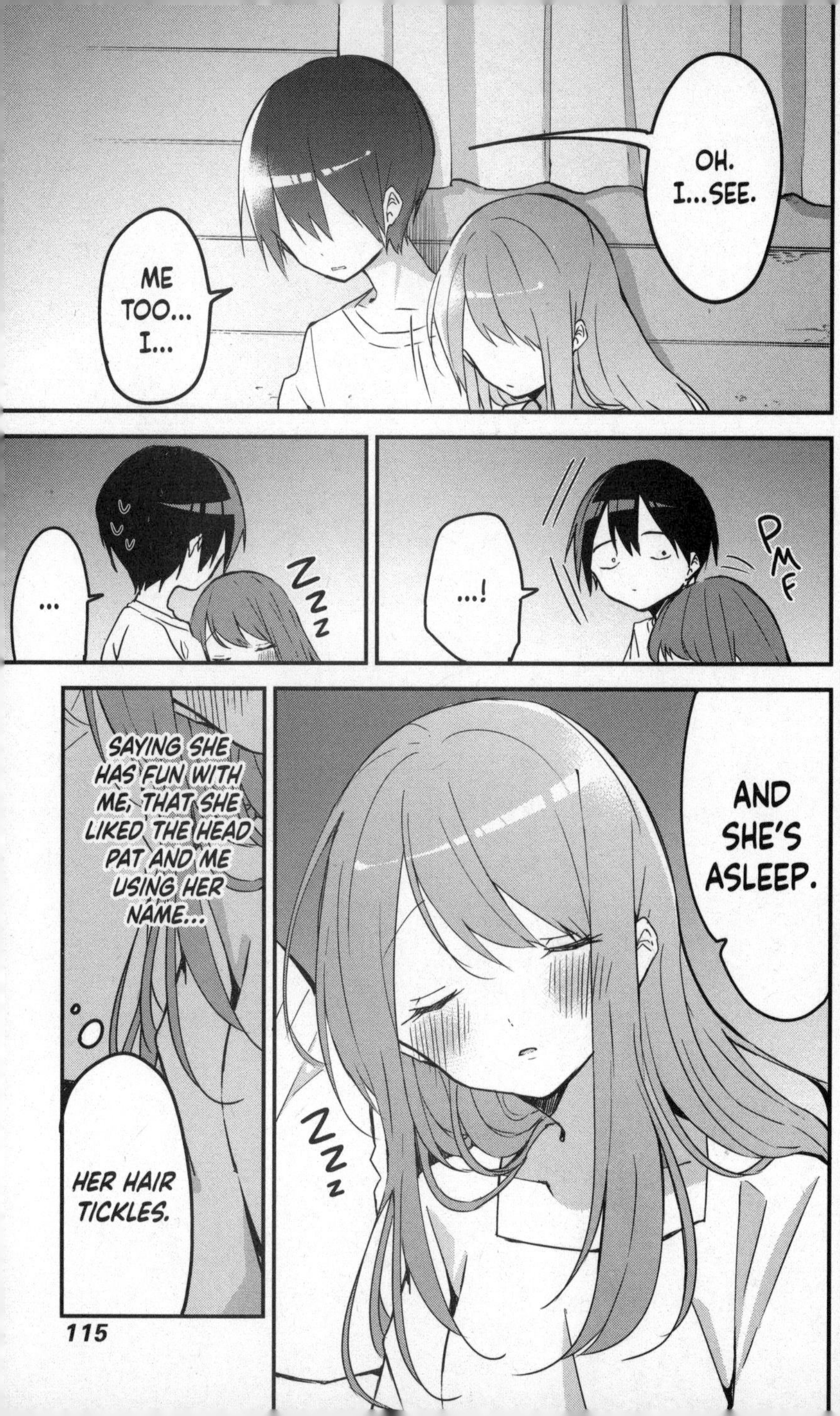
OH. I...SEE.
ME TOO... I...
PMF
...!
ZZZ
...
AND SHE'S ASLEEP.
ZZZ
SAYING SHE HAS FUN WITH ME, THAT SHE LIKED THE HEAD PAT AND ME USING HER NAME...
HER HAIR TICKLES.

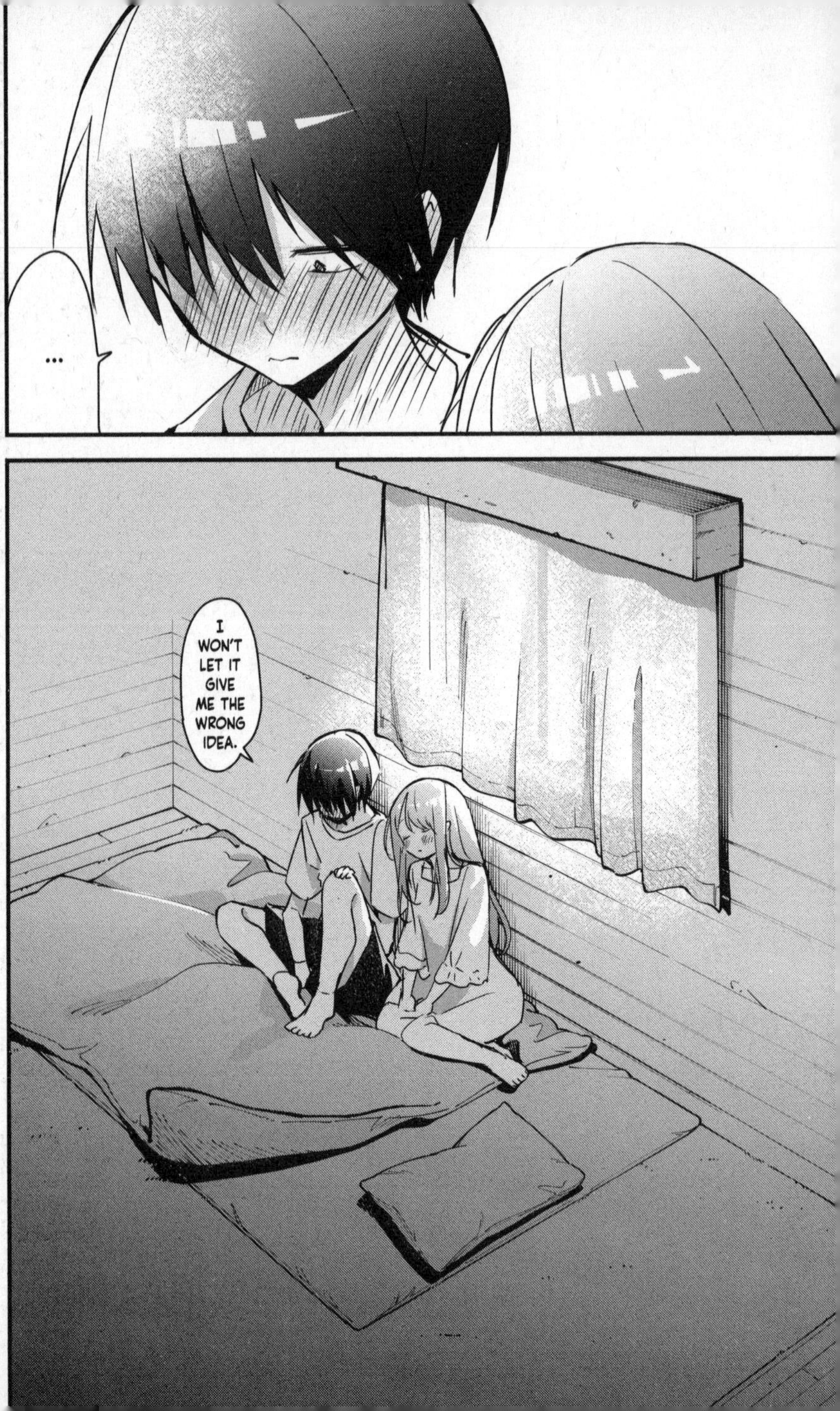
...
I WON'T LET IT GIVE ME THE WRONG IDEA.

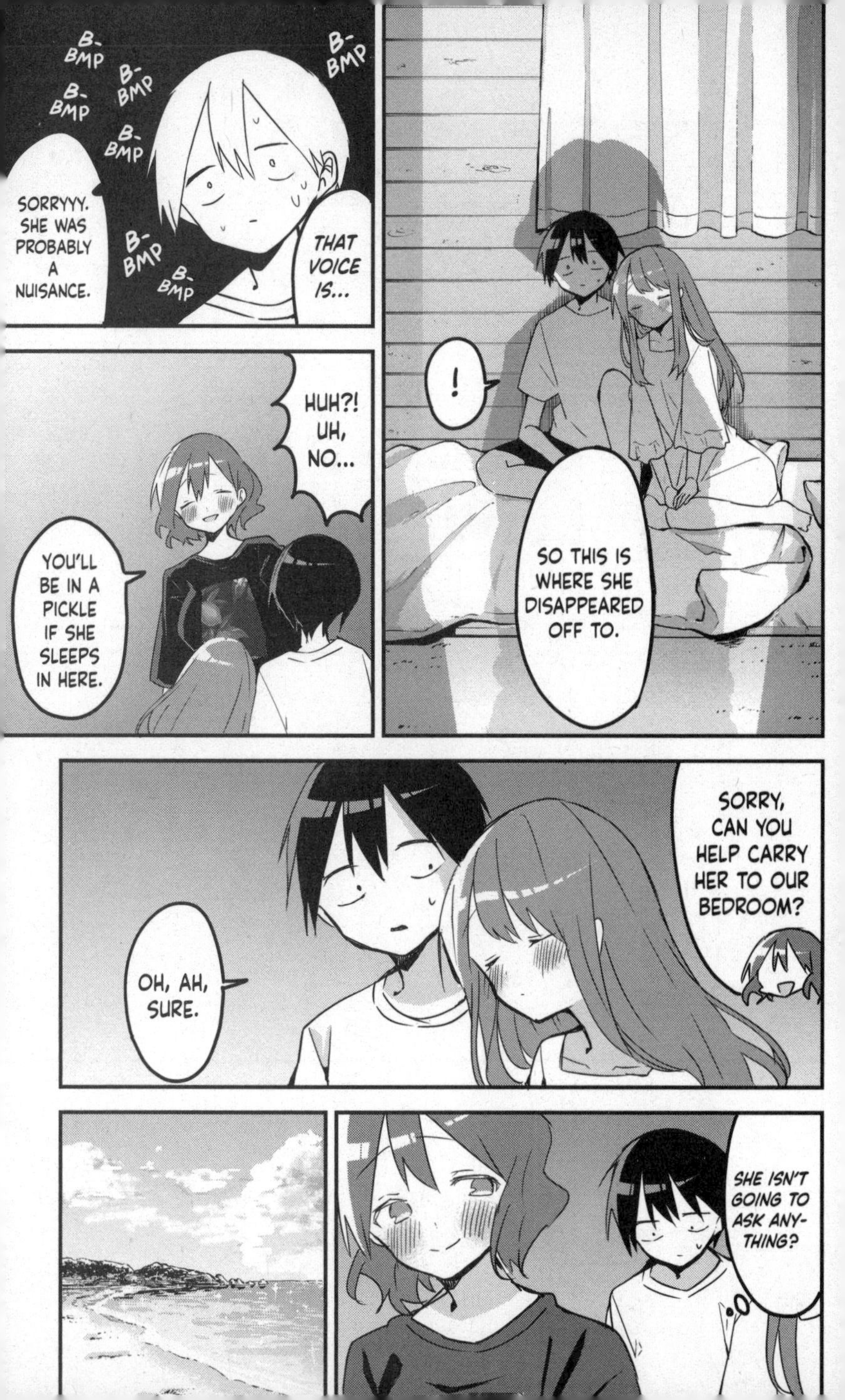
!
SO THIS IS WHERE SHE DISAPPEARED OFF TO.
B-BMP
B-BMP
B-BMP
B-BMP
B-BMP
B-BMP
B-BMP
THAT VOICE IS...
SORRYYY. SHE WAS PROBABLY A NUISANCE.
HUH?! UH, NO...
YOU'LL BE IN A PICKLE IF SHE SLEEPS IN HERE.
SORRY, CAN YOU HELP CARRY HER TO OUR BEDROOM?
OH, AH, SURE.
SHE ISN'T GOING TO ASK ANYTHING?

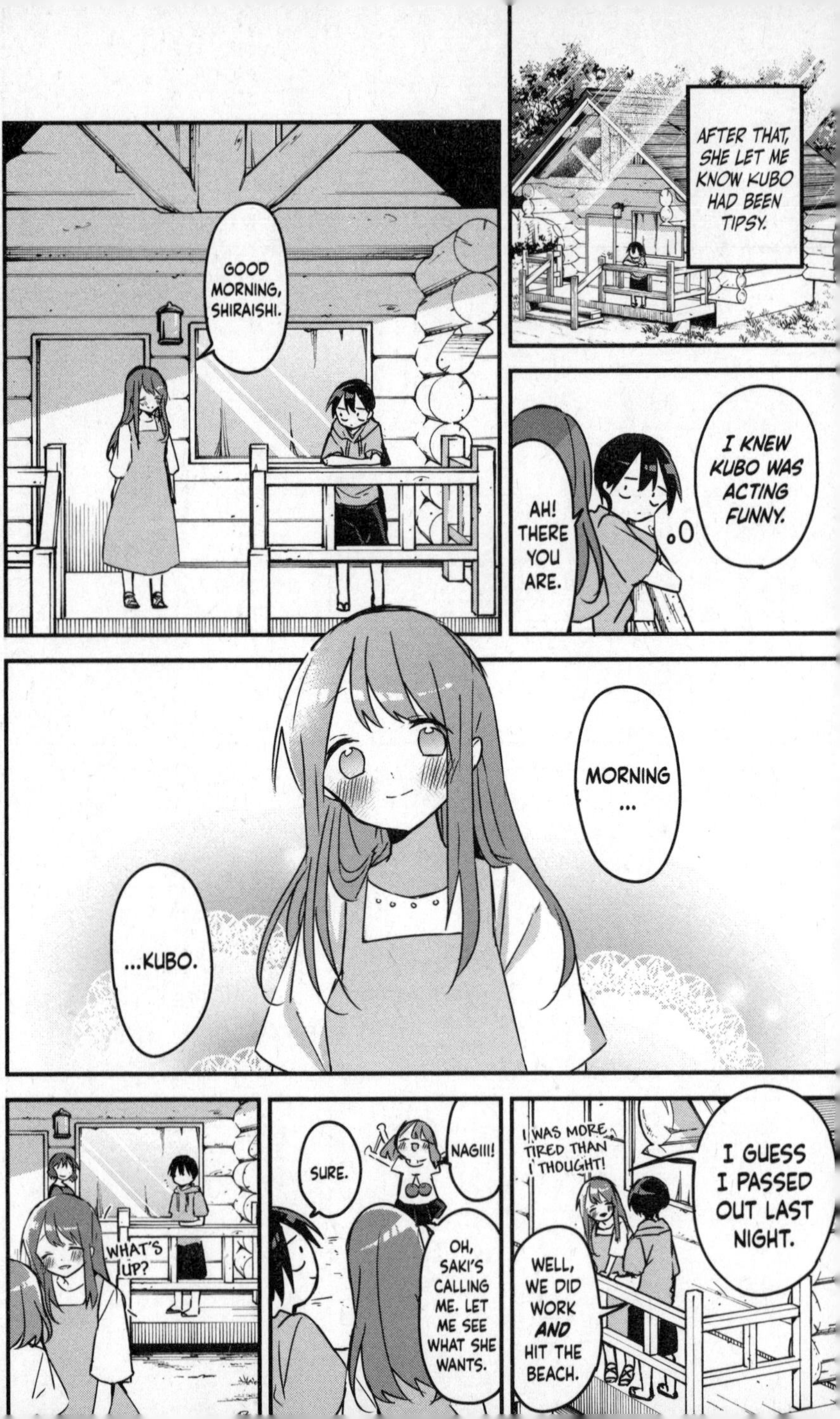
AFTER THAT, SHE LET ME KNOW KUBO HAD BEEN TIPSY.
I KNEW KUBO WAS ACTING FUNNY.
AH! THERE YOU ARE.
GOOD MORNING, SHIRAISHI.
MORNING...
...KUBO.
I GUESS I PASSED OUT LAST NIGHT.
I WAS MORE TIRED THAN I THOUGHT!
WELL, WE DID WORK *AND* HIT THE BEACH.
NAGIII!
OH, SAKI'S CALLING ME. LET ME SEE WHAT SHE WANTS.
SURE.
WHAT'S UP?

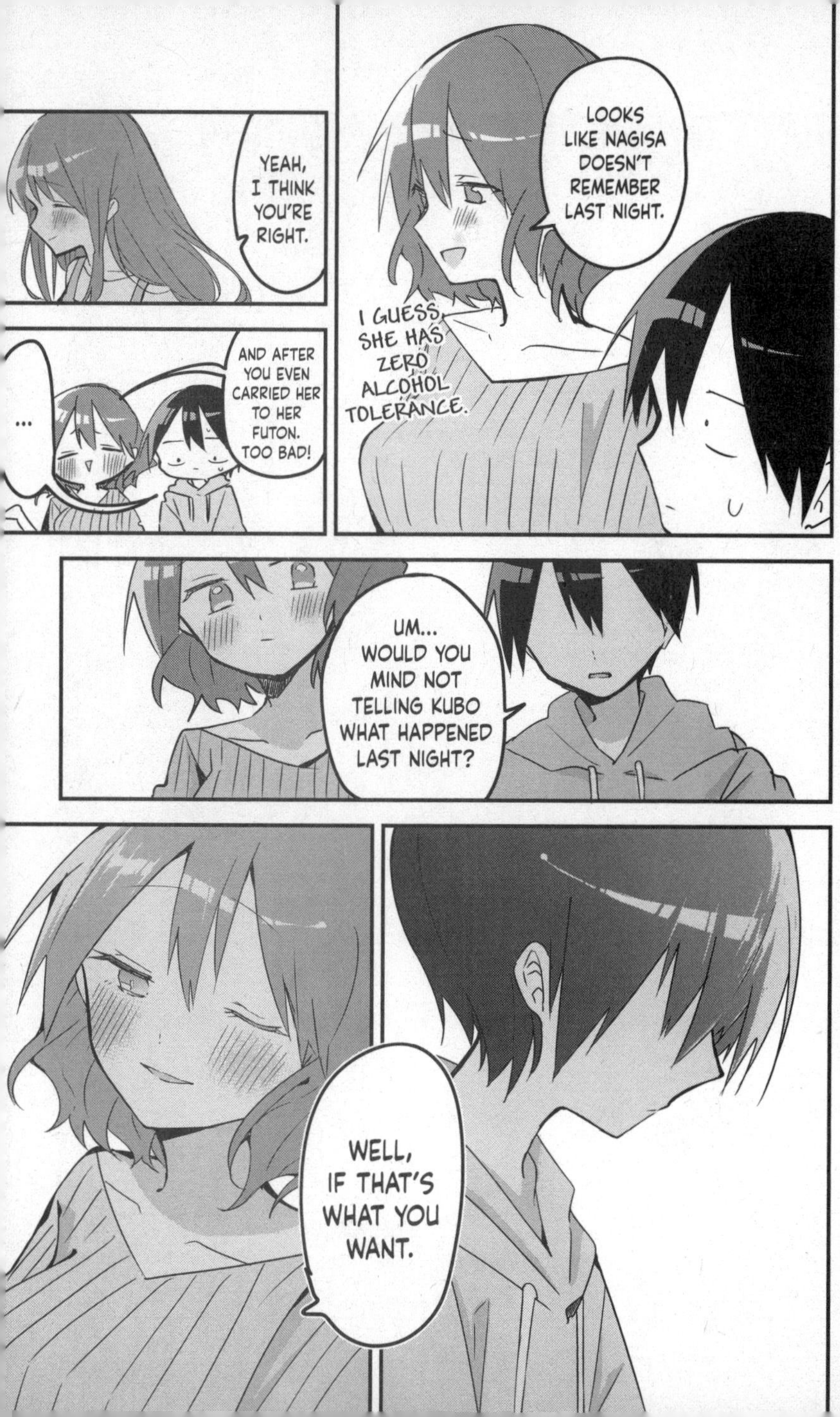
LOOKS LIKE NAGISA DOESN'T REMEMBER LAST NIGHT.
I GUESS SHE HAS ZERO ALCOHOL TOLERANCE.
YEAH, I THINK YOU'RE RIGHT.
AND AFTER YOU EVEN CARRIED HER TO HER FUTON. TOO BAD!
...
UM... WOULD YOU MIND NOT TELLING KUBO WHAT HAPPENED LAST NIGHT?
WELL, IF THAT'S WHAT YOU WANT.

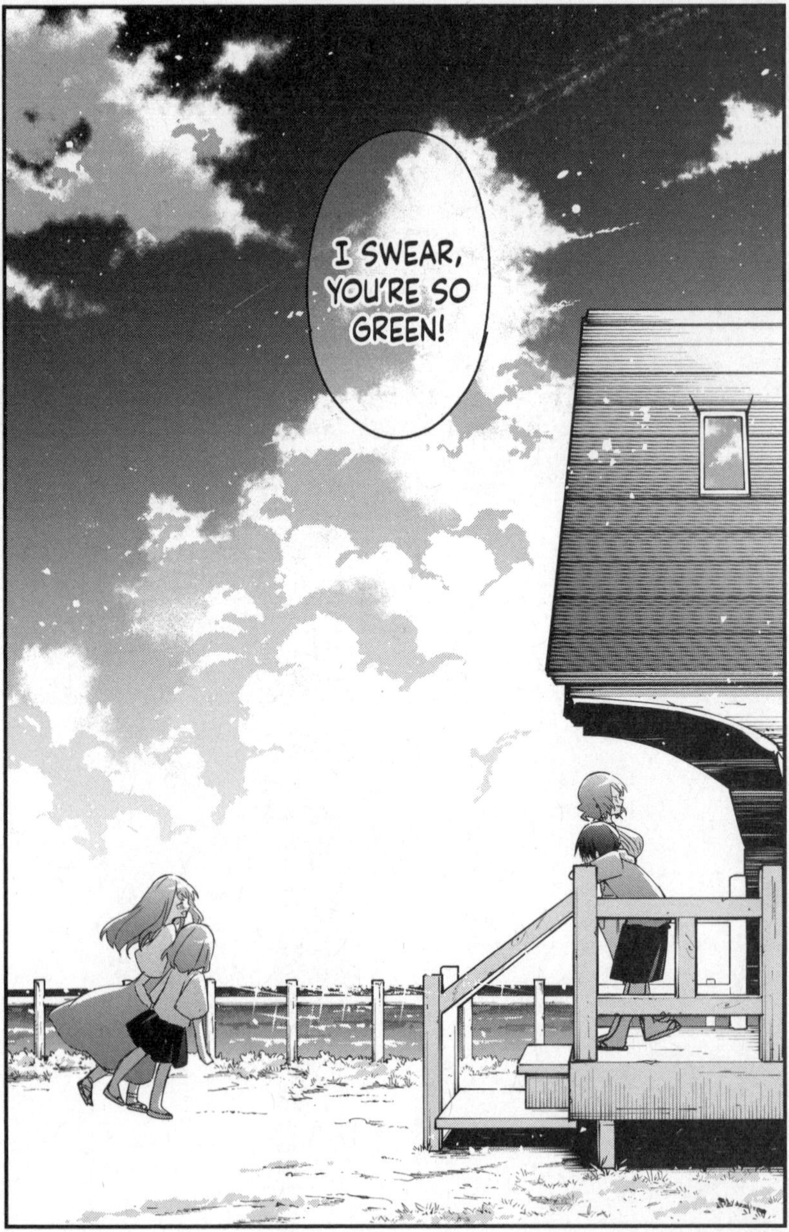
I SWEAR, YOU'RE SO GREEN!

I'VE WANTED TO DRAW THE BEACH SHACK ARC FOR THE LONGEST TIME. I HAD A LOT OF FUN FINALLY GETTING TO DRAW IT! I'VE WANTED TO DRAW IT FOR A LONG TIME!

DRUNK KUBO FROM THE ROUGH DRAFT.

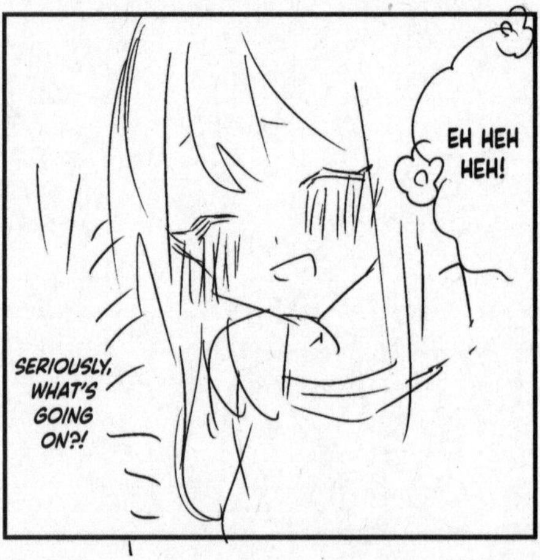
EH HEH HEH!
SERIOUSLY, WHAT'S GOING ON?!

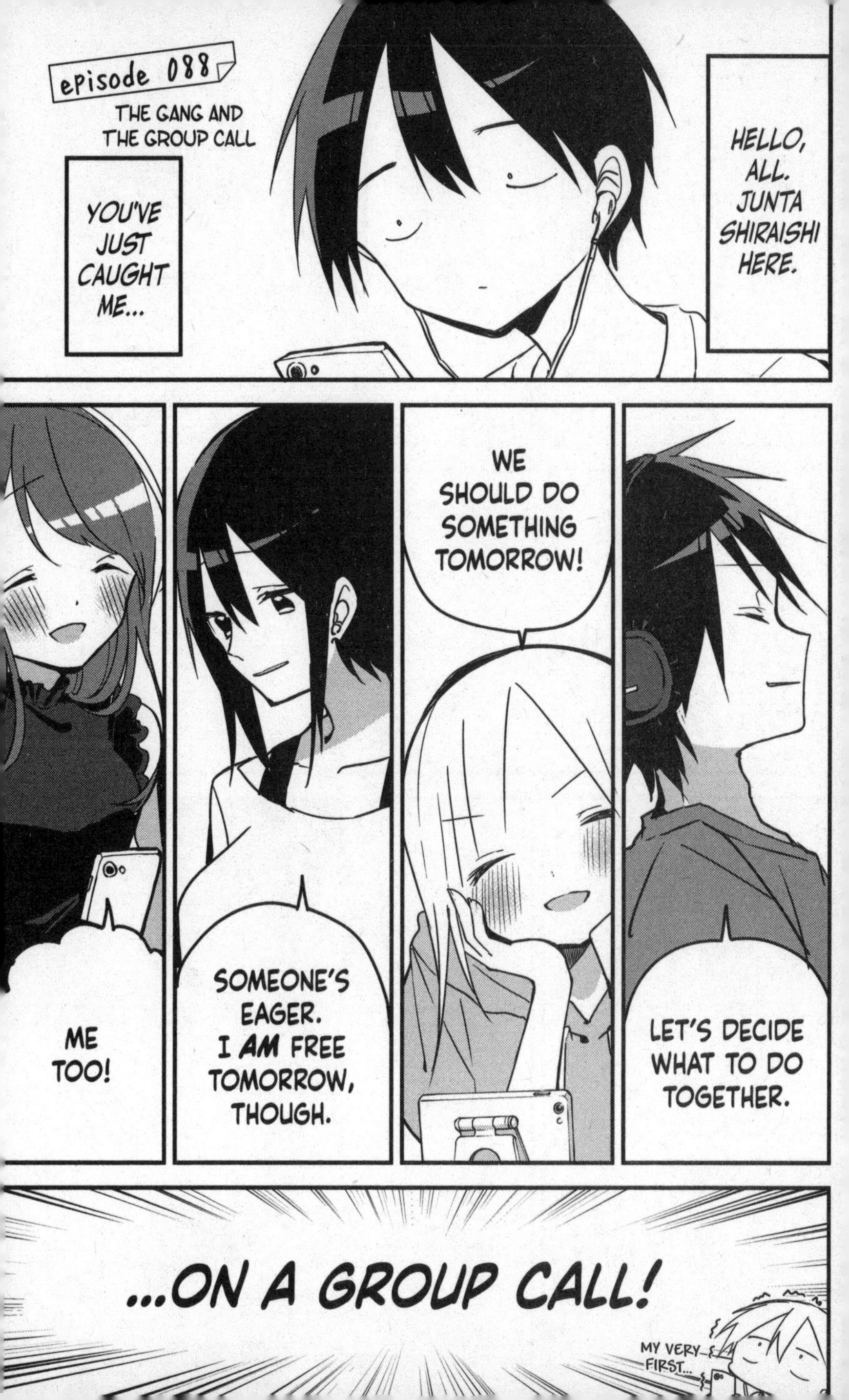
episode 088
THE GANG AND THE GROUP CALL
HELLO, ALL. JUNTA SHIRAISHI HERE.
YOU'VE JUST CAUGHT ME...
LET'S DECIDE WHAT TO DO TOGETHER.
WE SHOULD DO SOMETHING TOMORROW!
SOMEONE'S EAGER. I AM FREE TOMORROW, THOUGH.
ME TOO!
...ON A GROUP CALL!
MY VERY FIRST...

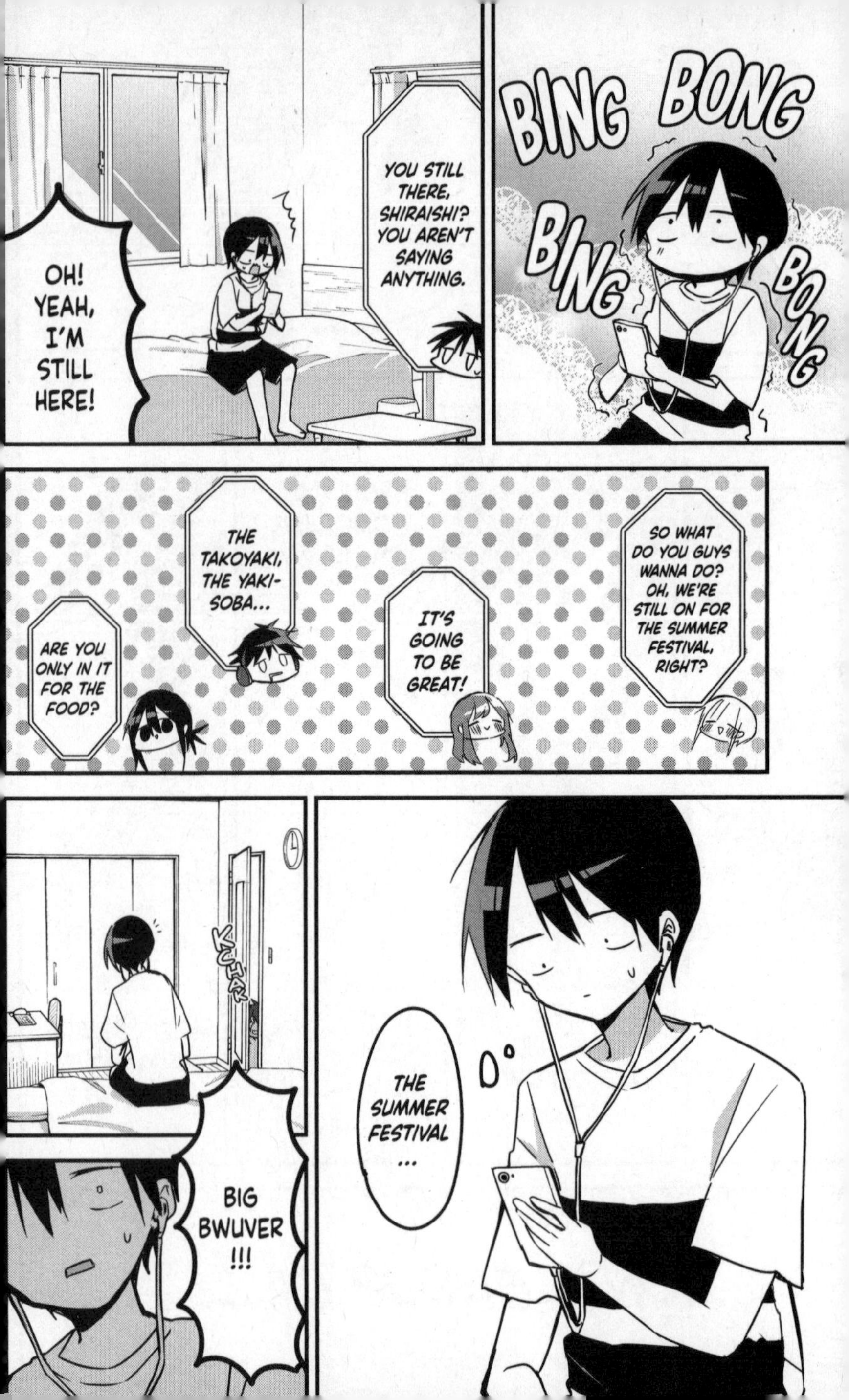
BING BONG
BING BONG
YOU STILL THERE, SHIRAISHI? YOU AREN'T SAYING ANYTHING.
OH! YEAH, I'M STILL HERE!
SO WHAT DO YOU GUYS WANNA DO? OH, WE'RE STILL ON FOR THE SUMMER FESTIVAL, RIGHT?
IT'S GOING TO BE GREAT!
THE TAKOYAKI, THE YAKI-SOBA...
ARE YOU ONLY IN IT FOR THE FOOD?
THE SUMMER FESTIVAL...
KCHAK
BIG BWUVER!!!

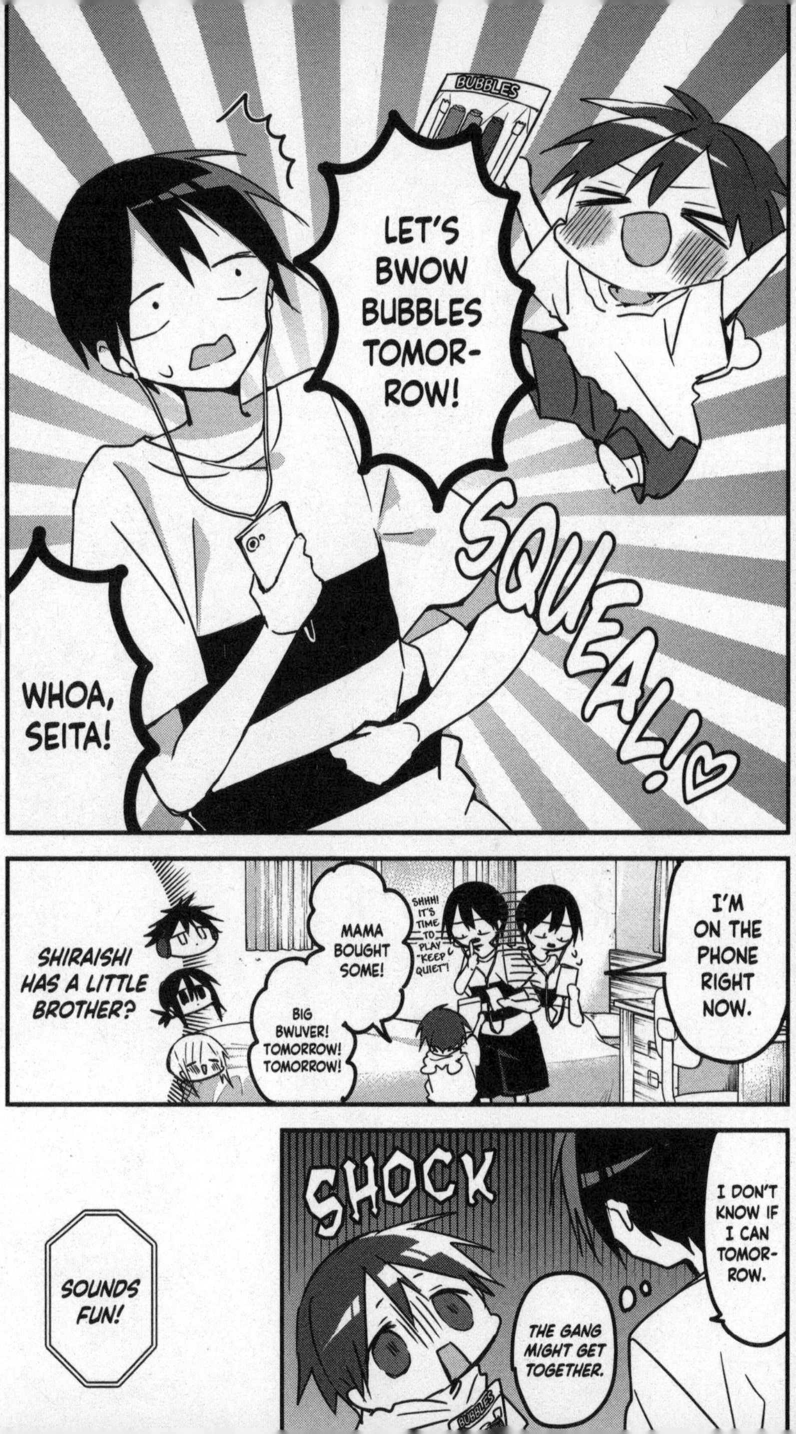
BUBBLES
LET'S BWOW BUBBLES TOMOR-ROW!
SQUEAL!♡
WHOA, SEITA!
I'M ON THE PHONE RIGHT NOW.
SHHH! IT'S TIME TO PLAY "KEEP QUIET"!
MAMA BOUGHT SOME!
BIG BWUVER! TOMORROW! TOMORROW!
SHIRAISHI HAS A LITTLE BROTHER?
I DON'T KNOW IF I CAN TOMOR-ROW.
THE GANG MIGHT GET TOGETHER.
SHOCK
BUBBLES
SOUNDS FUN!

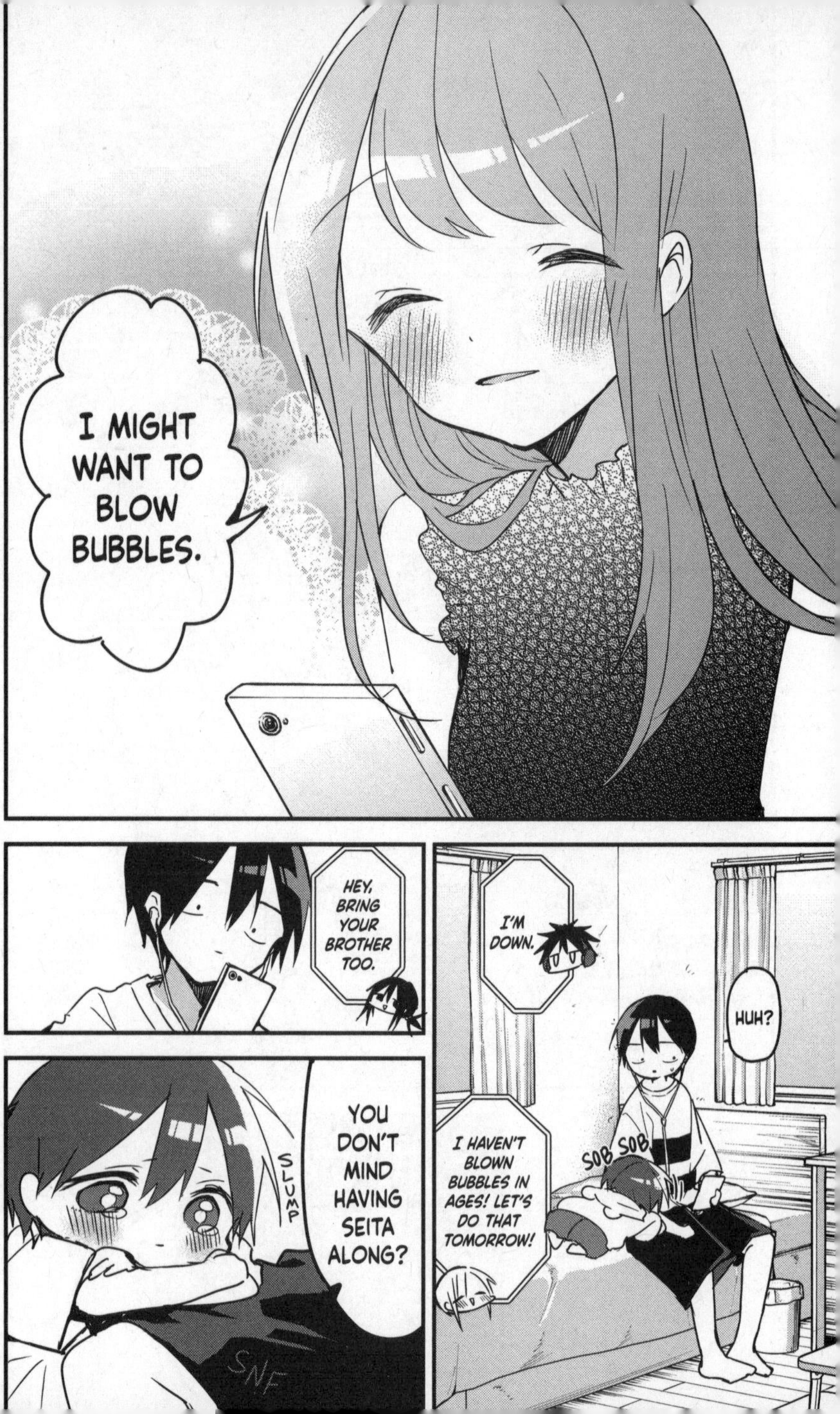
I MIGHT WANT TO BLOW BUBBLES.
I'M DOWN.
HUH?
SOB SOB
I HAVEN'T BLOWN BUBBLES IN AGES! LET'S DO THAT TOMORROW!
HEY, BRING YOUR BROTHER TOO.
YOU DON'T MIND HAVING SEITA ALONG?
SLUMP
SNF

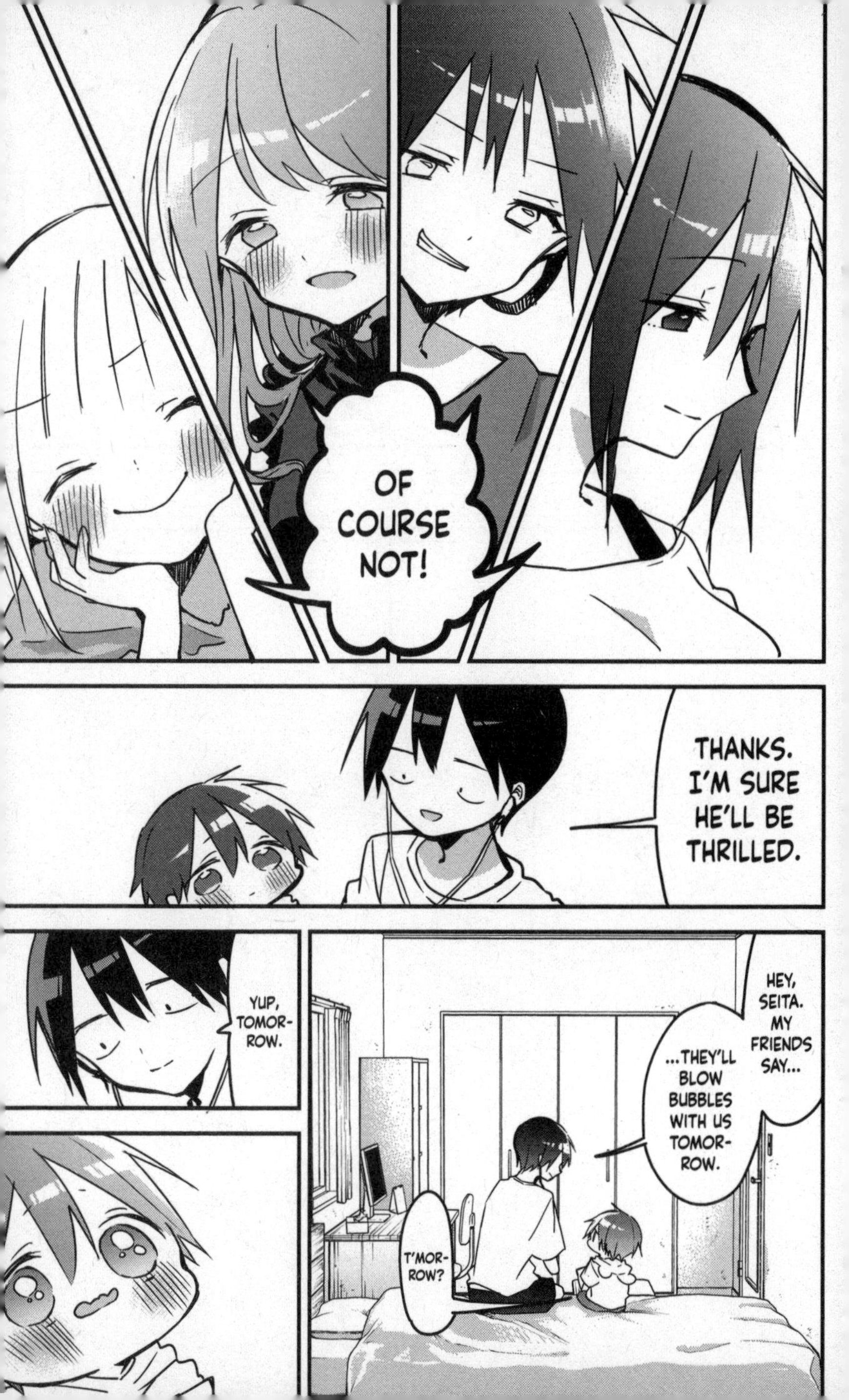
OF COURSE NOT!
THANKS. I'M SURE HE'LL BE THRILLED.
HEY, SEITA. MY FRIENDS SAY...
...THEY'LL BLOW BUBBLES WITH US TOMOR-ROW.
T'MOR-ROW?
YUP, TOMOR-ROW.

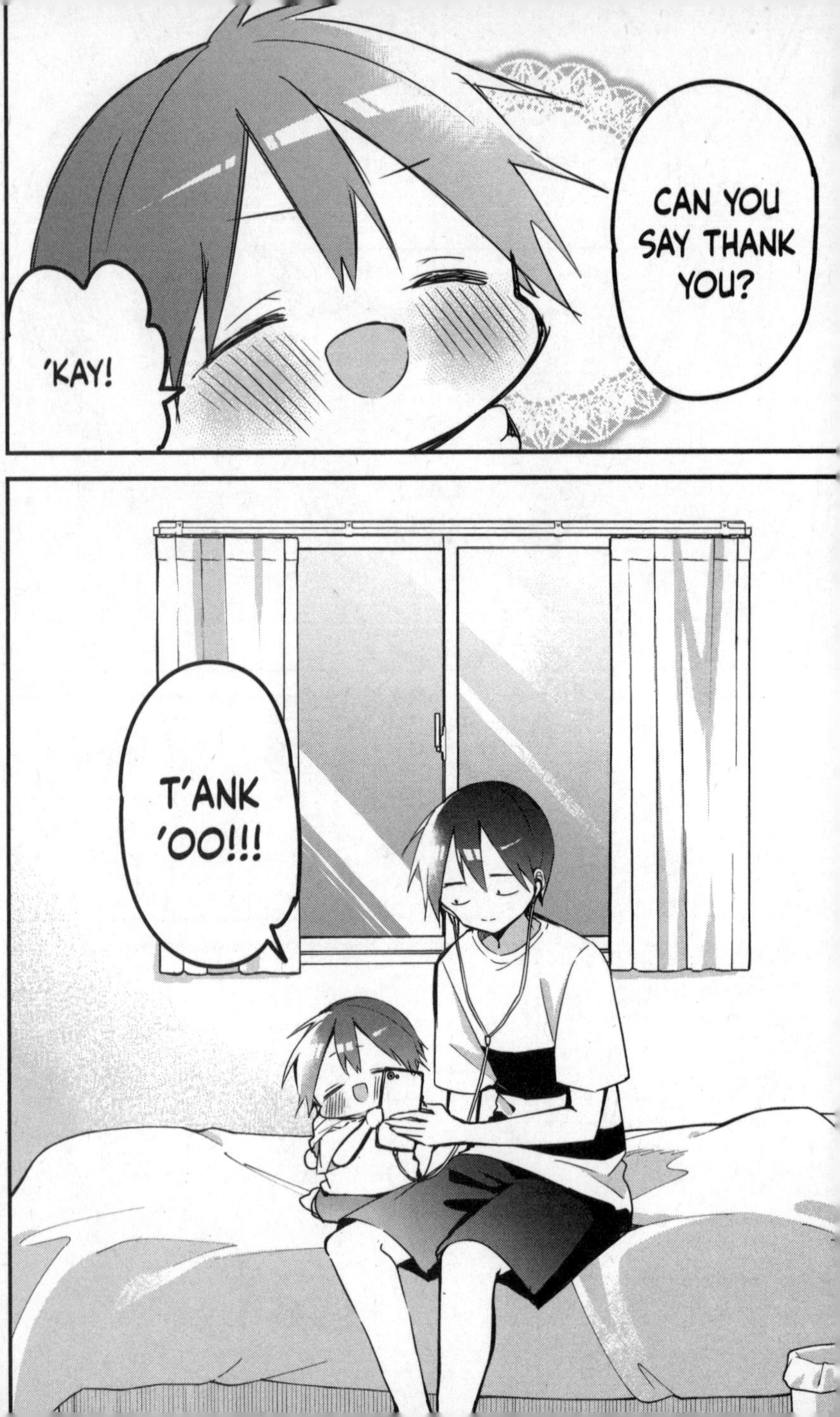
CAN YOU SAY THANK YOU?
'KAY!
T'ANK 'OO!!!

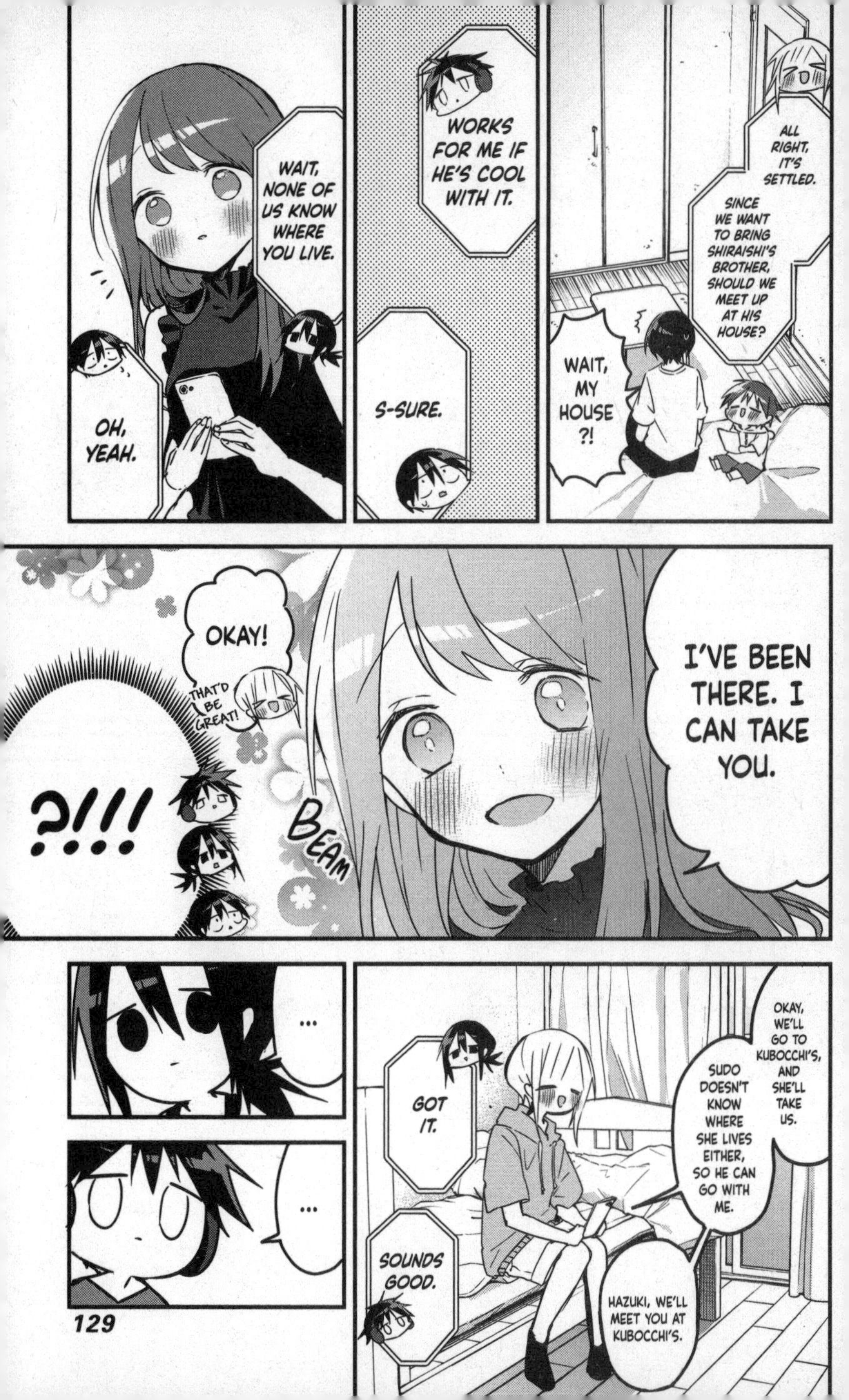
ALL RIGHT, IT'S SETTLED.
SINCE WE WANT TO BRING SHIRAISHI'S BROTHER, SHOULD WE MEET UP AT HIS HOUSE?
WAIT, MY HOUSE ?!
WORKS FOR ME IF HE'S COOL WITH IT.
S-SURE.
WAIT, NONE OF US KNOW WHERE YOU LIVE.
OH, YEAH.
I'VE BEEN THERE. I CAN TAKE YOU.
OKAY!
THAT'D BE GREAT!
BEAM
?!!!
OKAY, WE'LL GO TO KUBOCCHI'S, AND SHE'LL TAKE US.
SUDO DOESN'T KNOW WHERE SHE LIVES EITHER, SO HE CAN GO WITH ME.
GOT IT.
HAZUKI, WE'LL MEET YOU AT KUBOCCHI'S.
SOUNDS GOOD.
...
...

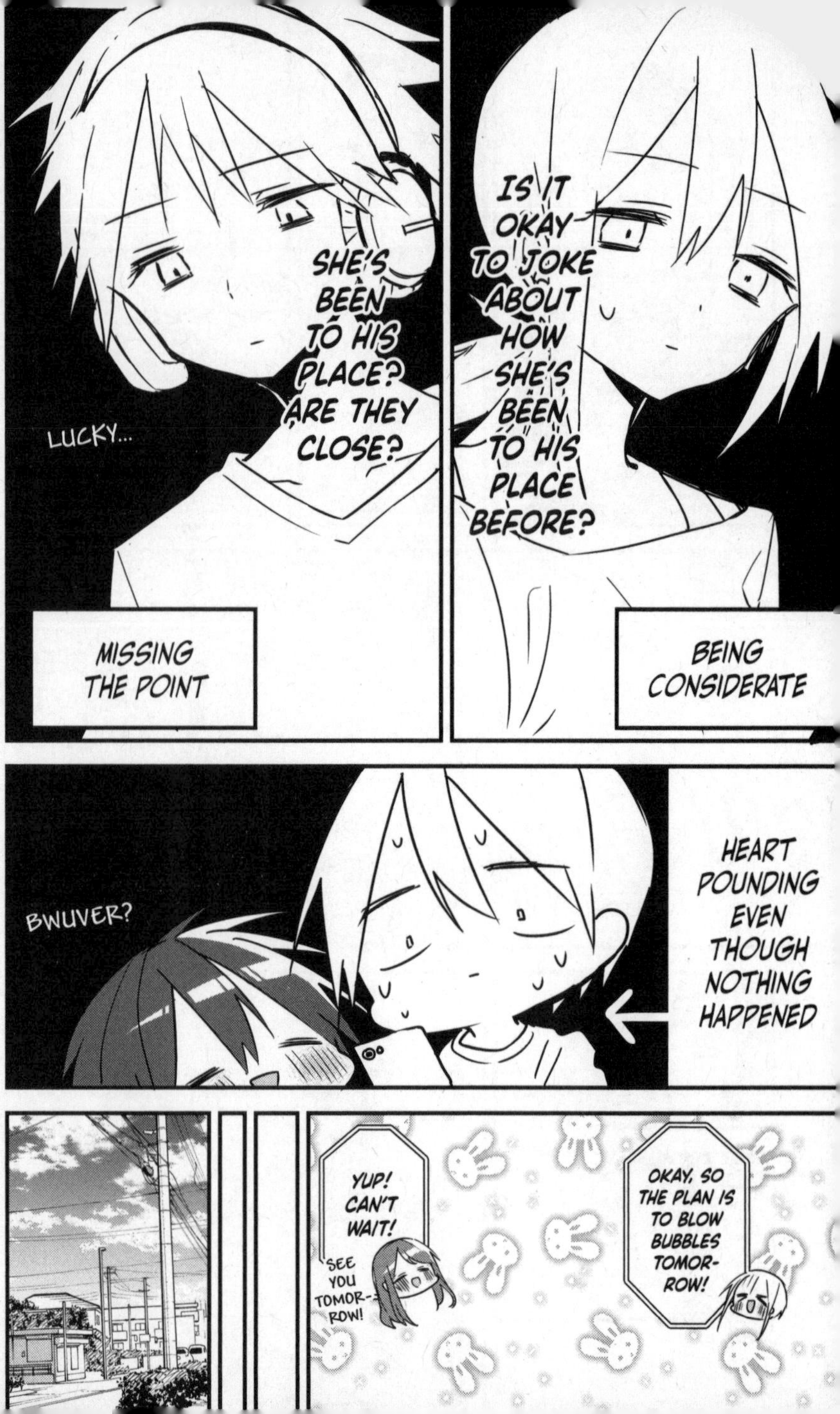
IS IT OKAY TO JOKE ABOUT HOW SHE'S BEEN TO HIS PLACE BEFORE?
BEING CONSIDERATE
SHE'S BEEN TO HIS PLACE? ARE THEY CLOSE?
LUCKY...
MISSING THE POINT
HEART POUNDING EVEN THOUGH NOTHING HAPPENED
BWUVER?
OKAY, SO THE PLAN IS TO BLOW BUBBLES TOMOR-ROW!
YUP! CAN'T WAIT!
SEE YOU TOMOR-ROW!

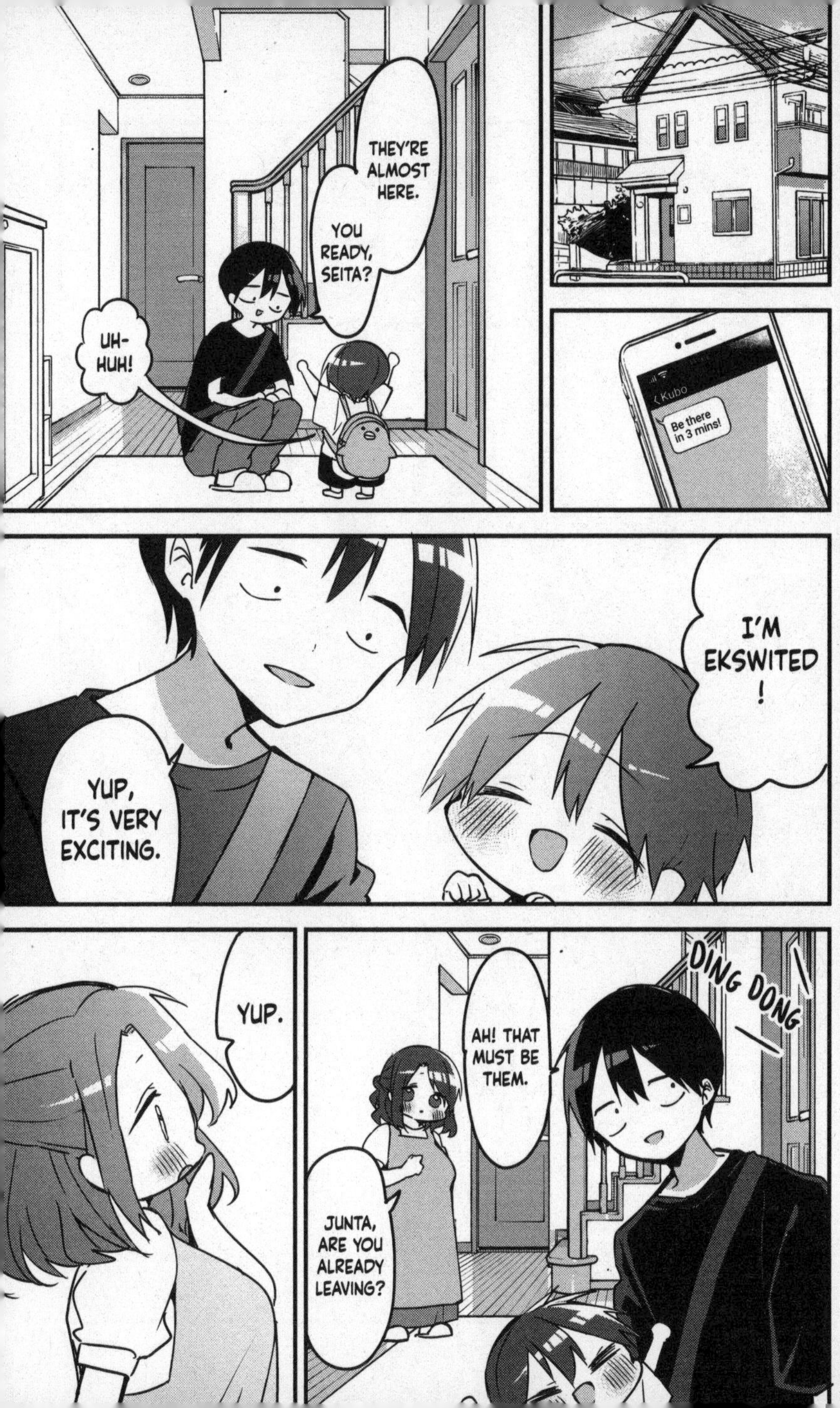
Kubo
Be there in 3 mins!
THEY'RE ALMOST HERE.
YOU READY, SEITA?
UH-HUH!
I'M EKSWITED!
YUP, IT'S VERY EXCITING.
DING DONG
AH! THAT MUST BE THEM.
JUNTA, ARE YOU ALREADY LEAVING?
YUP.

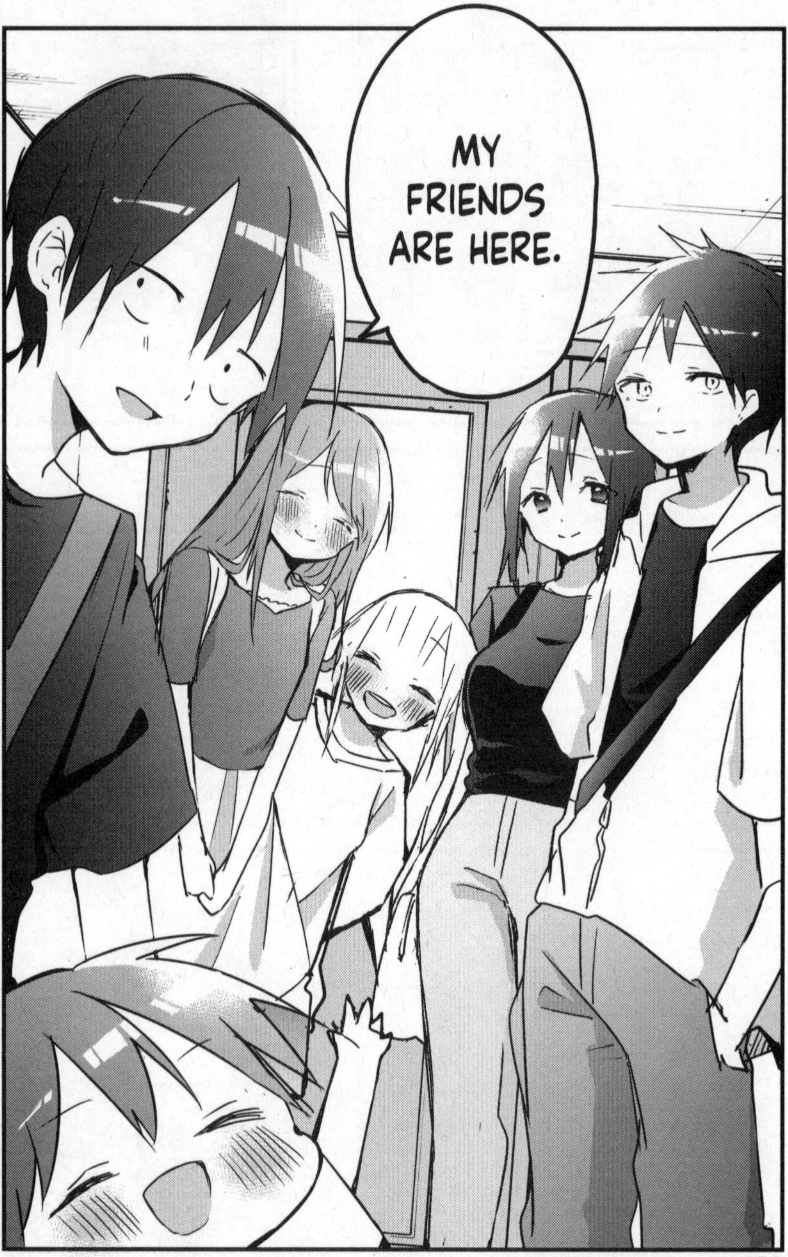
MY FRIENDS ARE HERE.

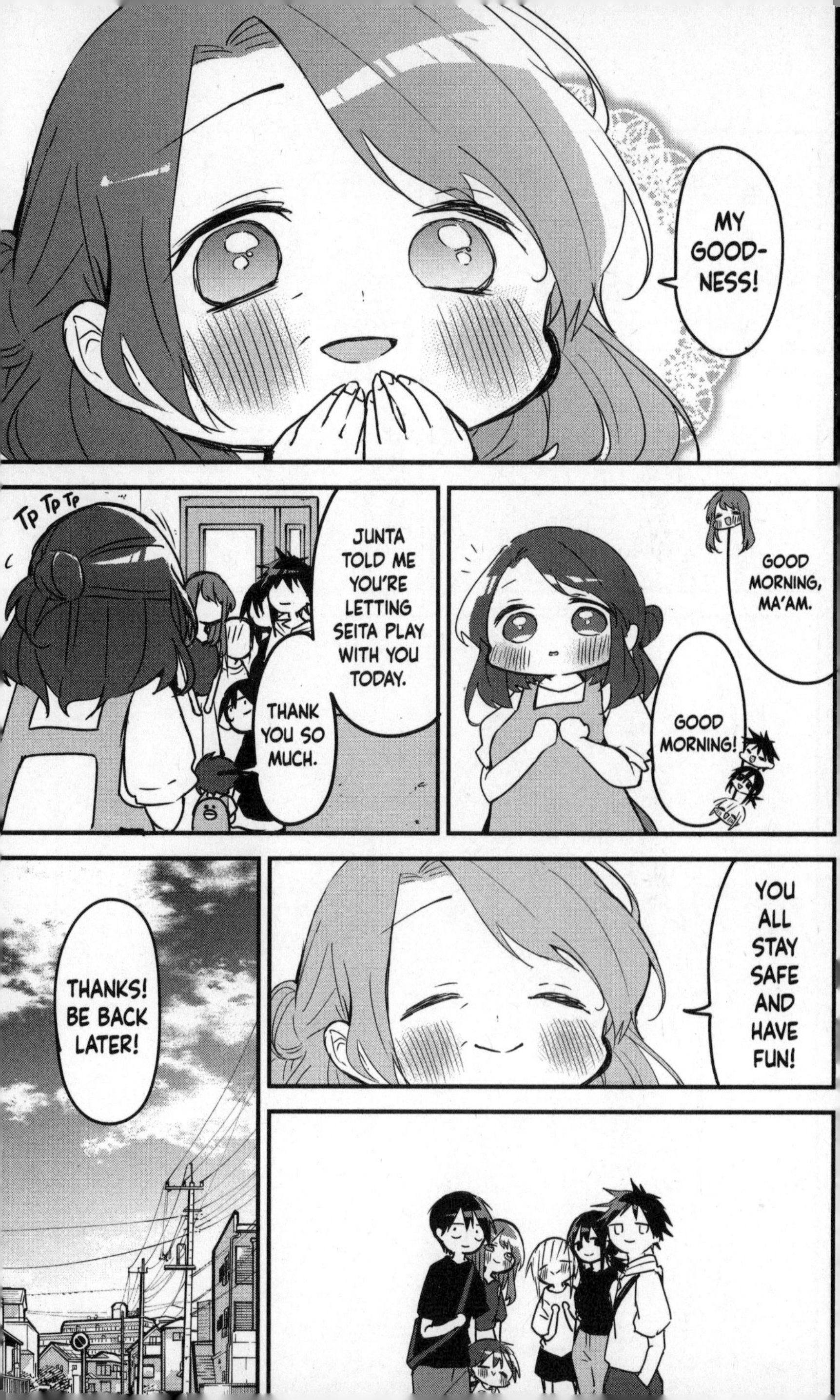
MY GOOD-NESS!
GOOD MORNING, MA'AM.
GOOD MORNING!
Tp Tp Tp
JUNTA TOLD ME YOU'RE LETTING SEITA PLAY WITH YOU TODAY.
THANK YOU SO MUCH.
YOU ALL STAY SAFE AND HAVE FUN!
THANKS! BE BACK LATER!

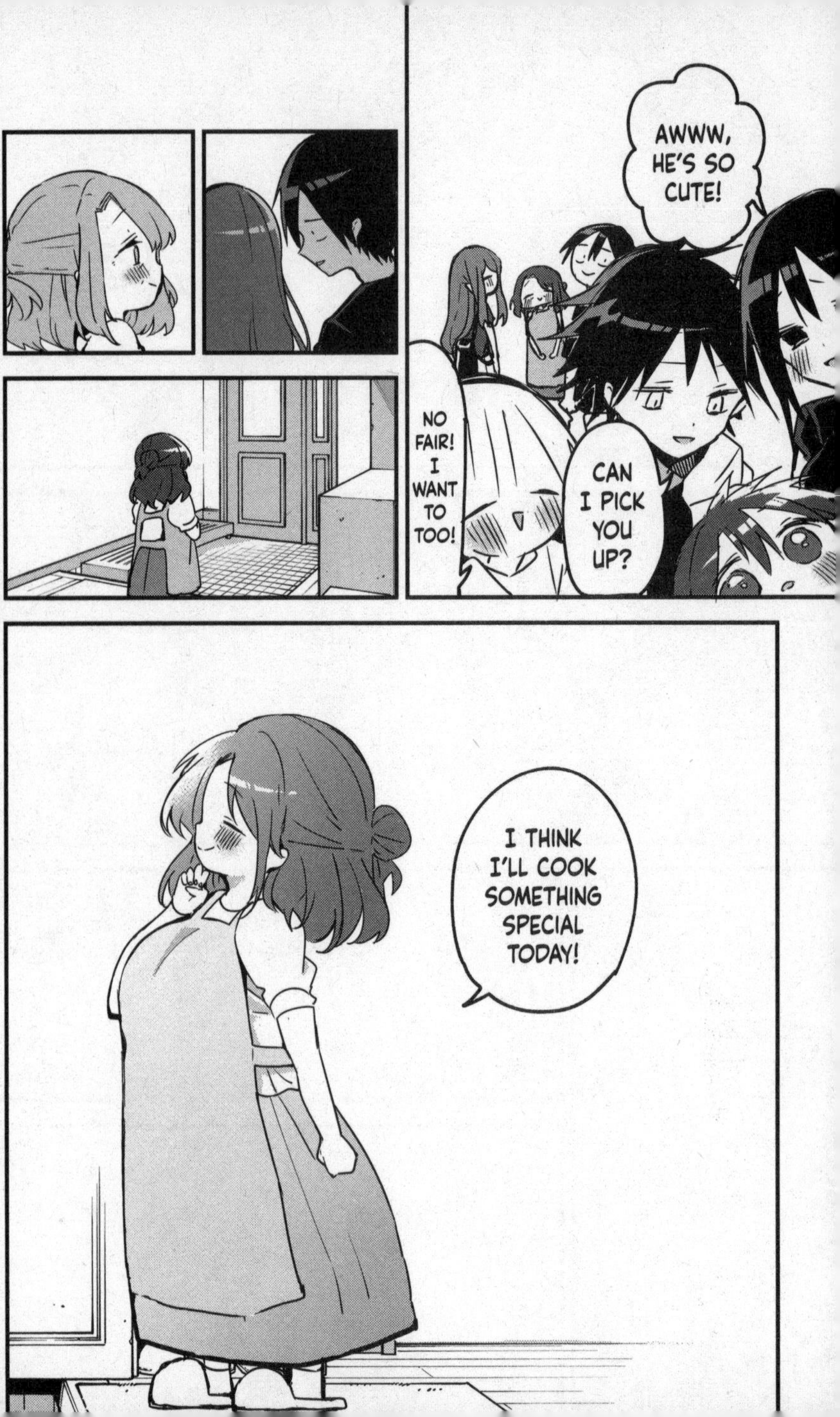
AWWW, HE'S SO CUTE!
CAN I PICK YOU UP?
NO FAIR! I WANT TO TOO!
I THINK I'LL COOK SOMETHING SPECIAL TODAY!

episode 089 BUBBLES AND IRIDESCENCE

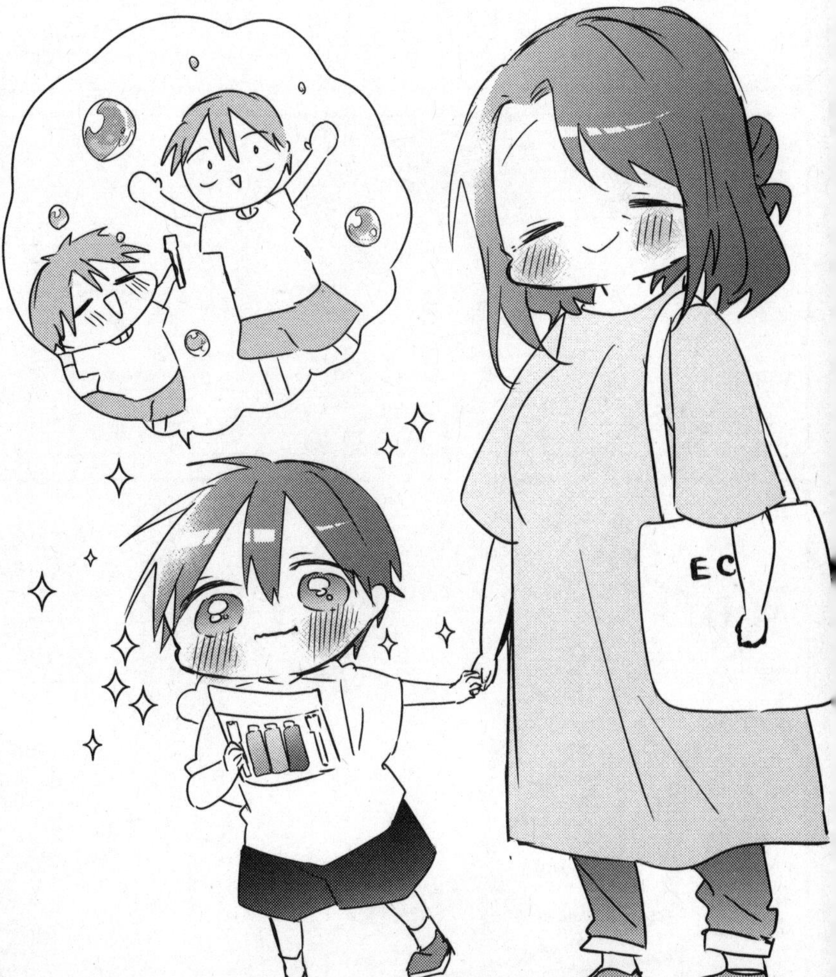
EC

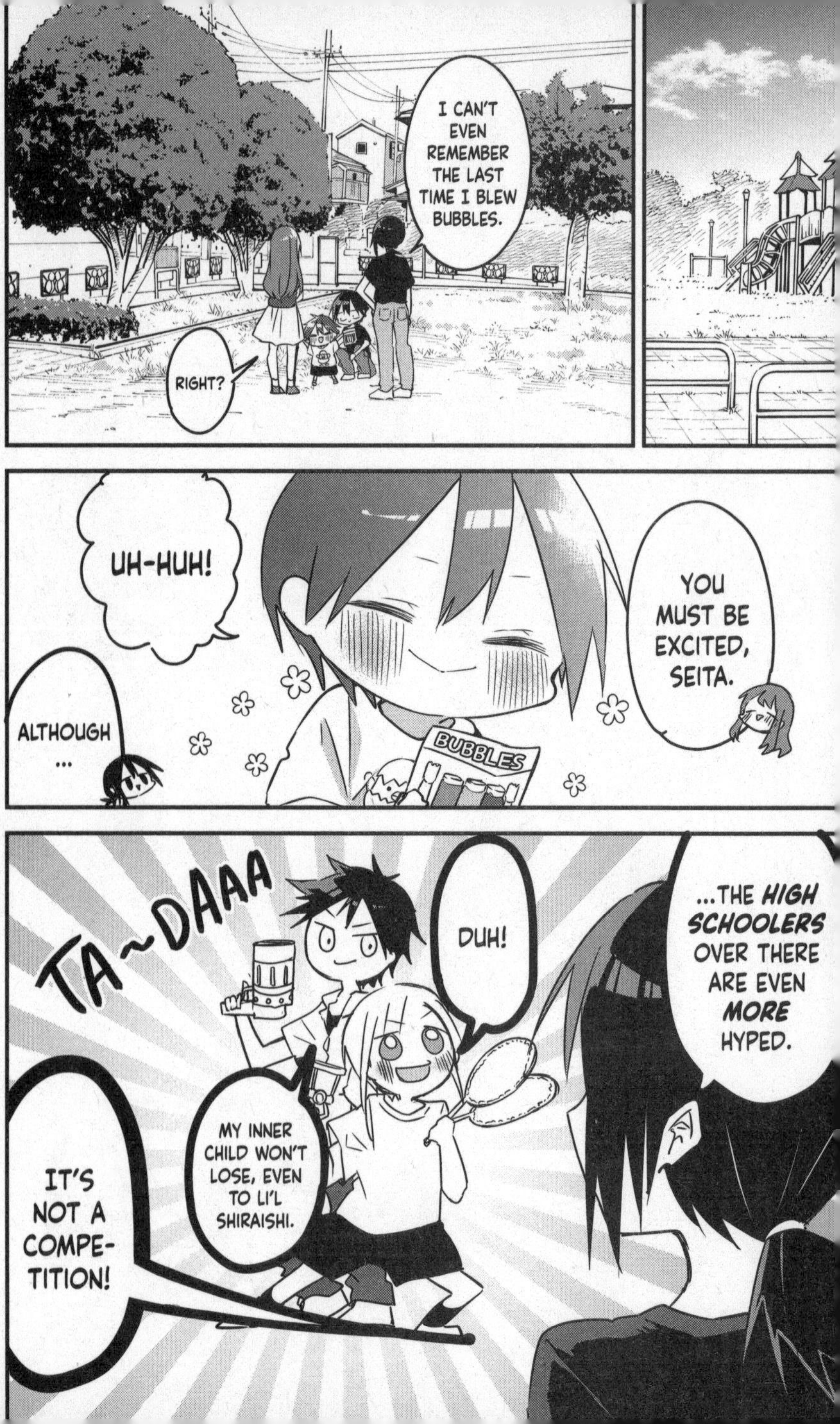
I CAN'T EVEN REMEMBER THE LAST TIME I BLEW BUBBLES.
RIGHT?
YOU MUST BE EXCITED, SEITA.
UH-HUH!
BUBBLES
ALTHOUGH ...
...THE *HIGH SCHOOLERS* OVER THERE ARE EVEN *MORE* HYPED.
DUH!
TA~DAAA
MY INNER CHILD WON'T LOSE, EVEN TO LI'L SHIRAISHI.
IT'S NOT A COMPE-TITION!

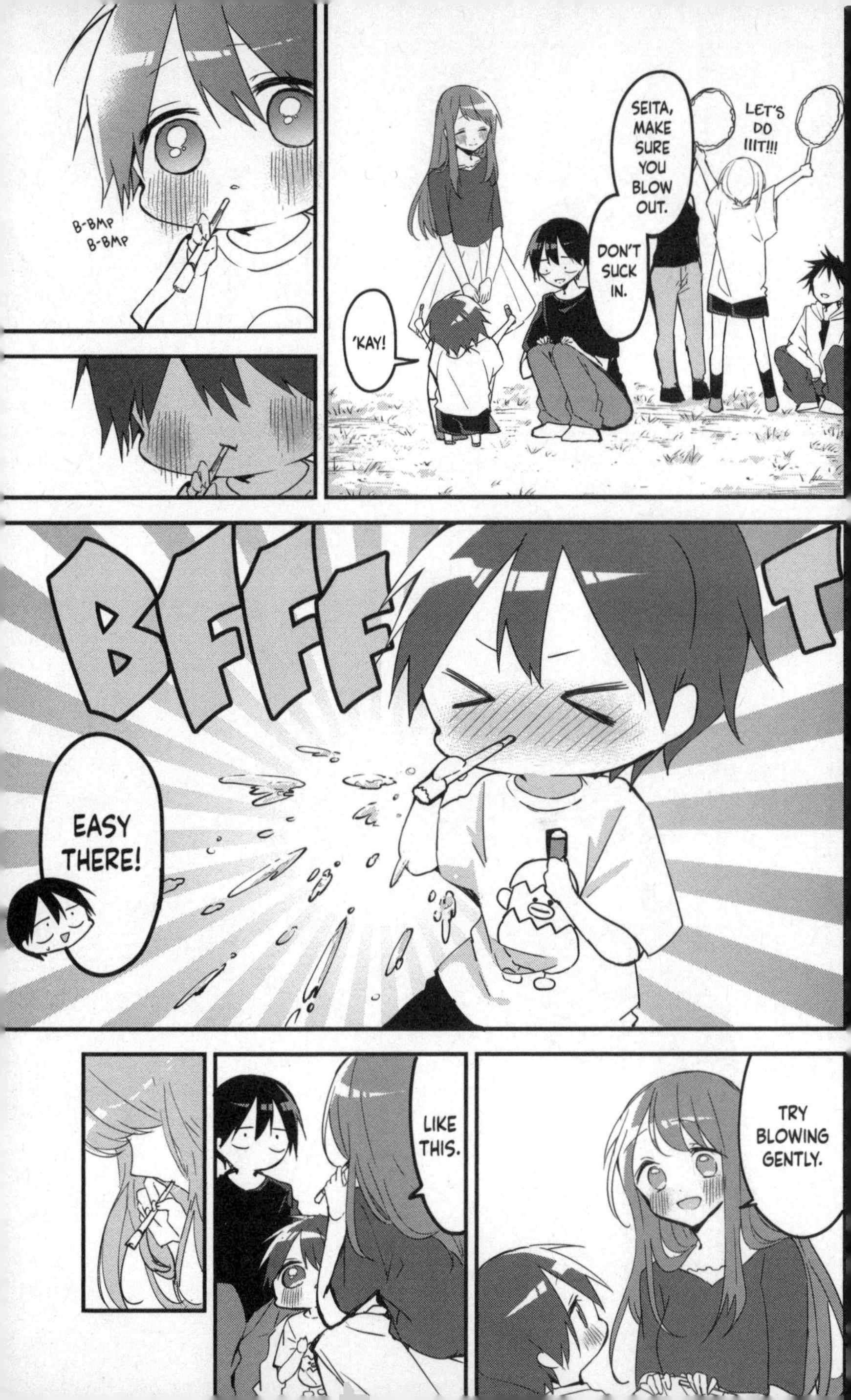
LET'S DO IIIT!!!
SEITA, MAKE SURE YOU BLOW OUT.
DON'T SUCK IN.
'KAY!
B-BMP B-BMP
BFFFT
EASY THERE!
TRY BLOWING GENTLY.
LIKE THIS.

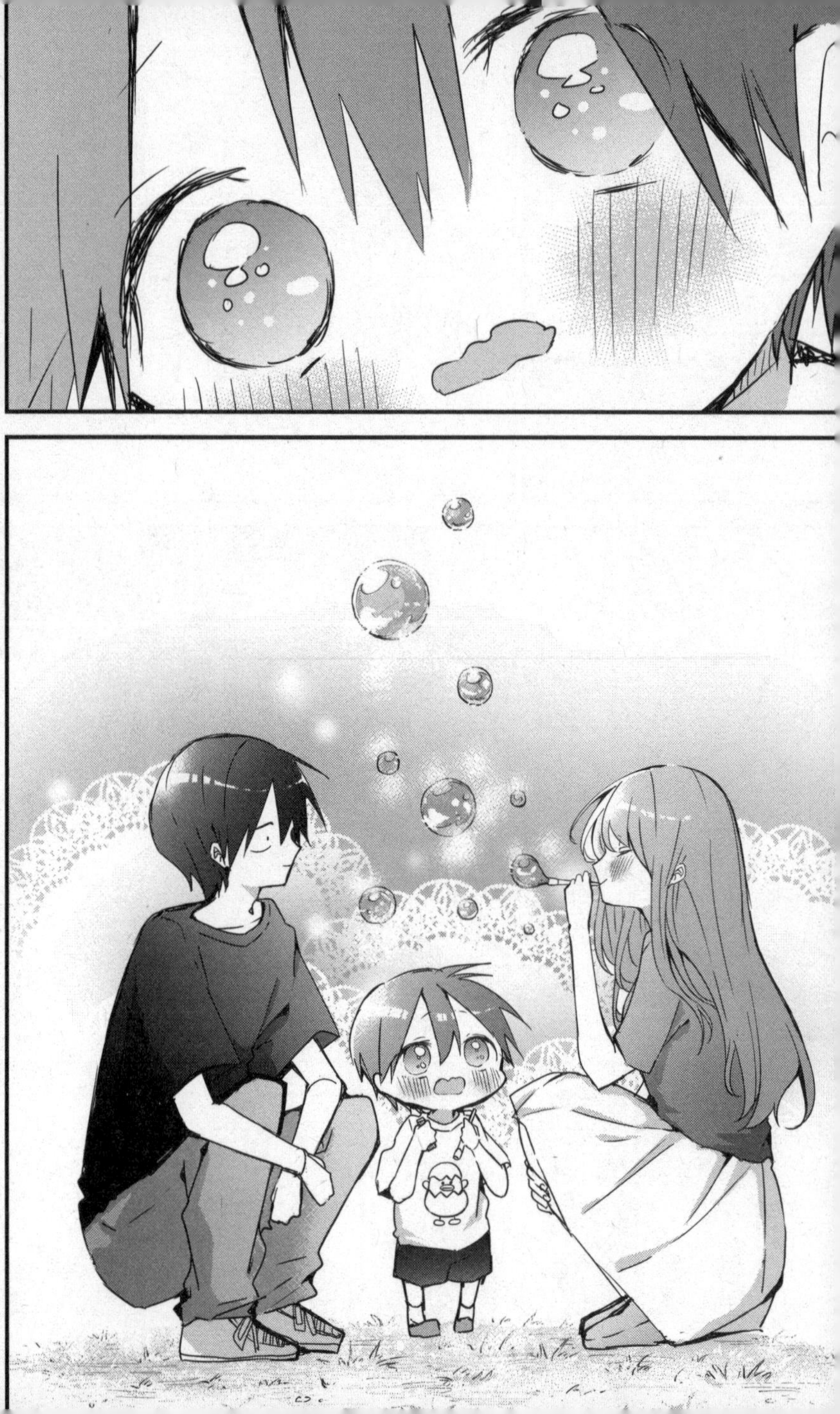

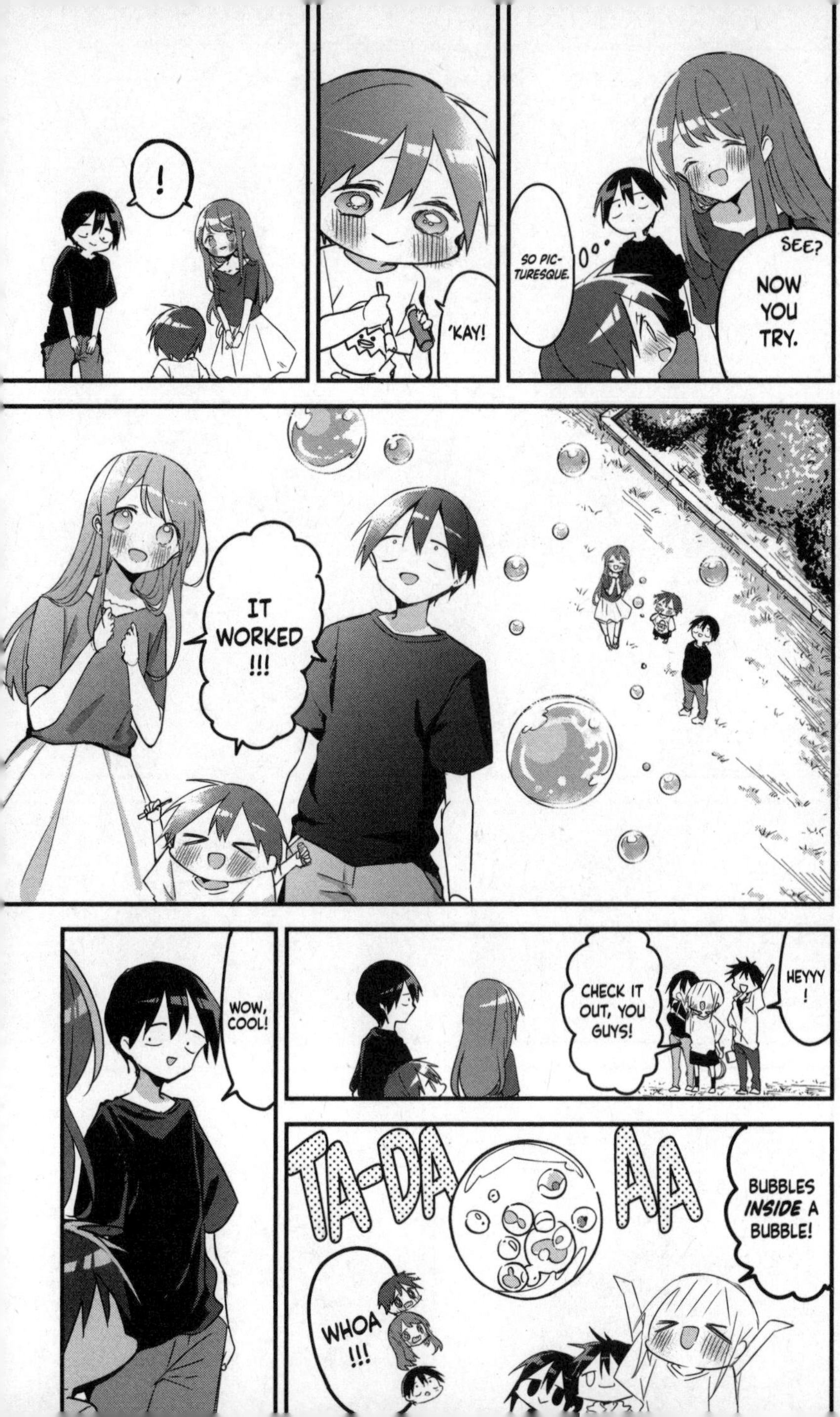
SEE? NOW YOU TRY.
SO PIC-TURESQUE.
'KAY!
!
IT WORKED!!!
HEYYY!
CHECK IT OUT, YOU GUYS!
BUBBLES *INSIDE* A BUBBLE!
TA-DAAA
WHOA!!!
WOW, COOL!

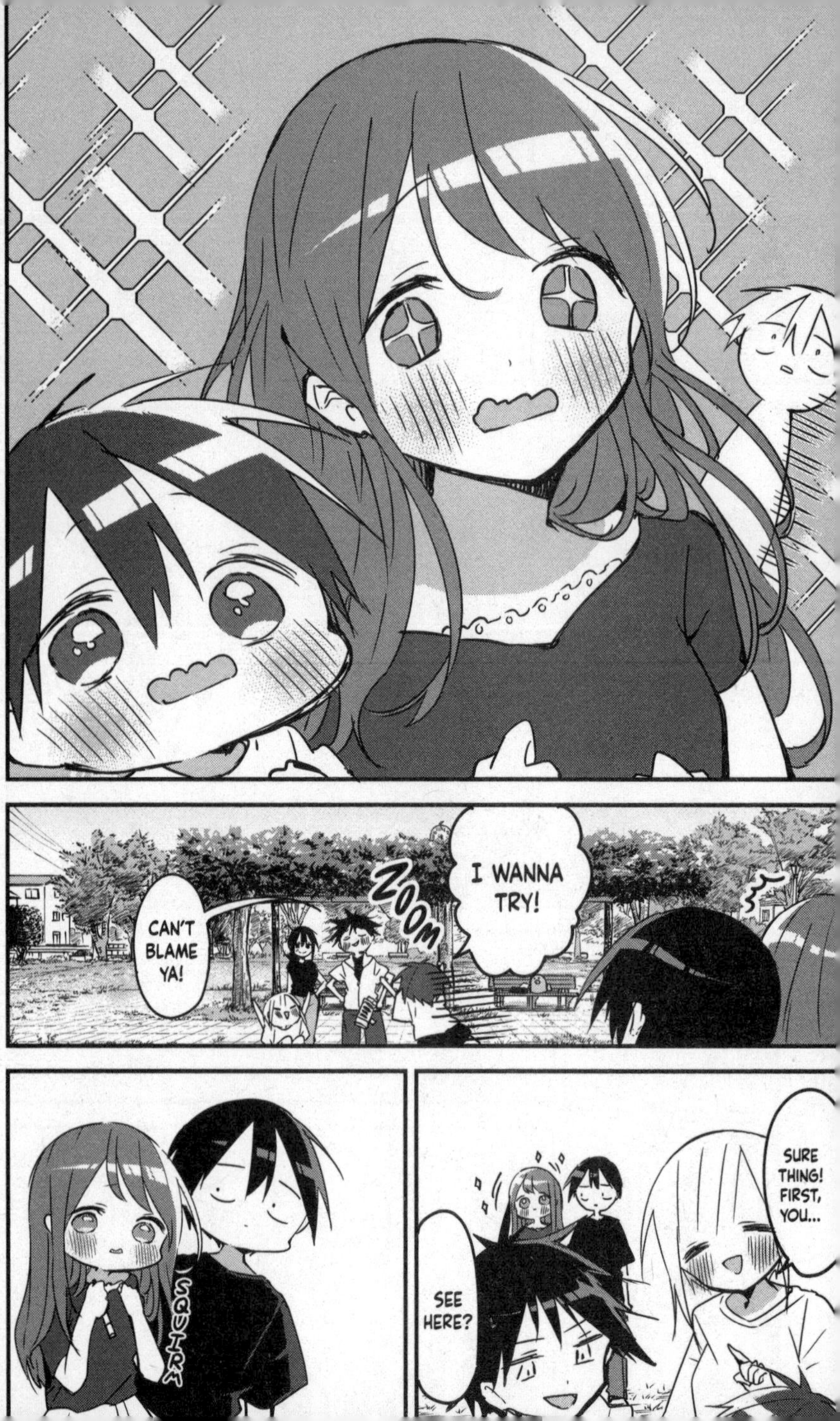
I WANNA TRY!
ZOOM
CAN'T BLAME YA!
SURE THING! FIRST, YOU...
SEE HERE?
SQUIRM

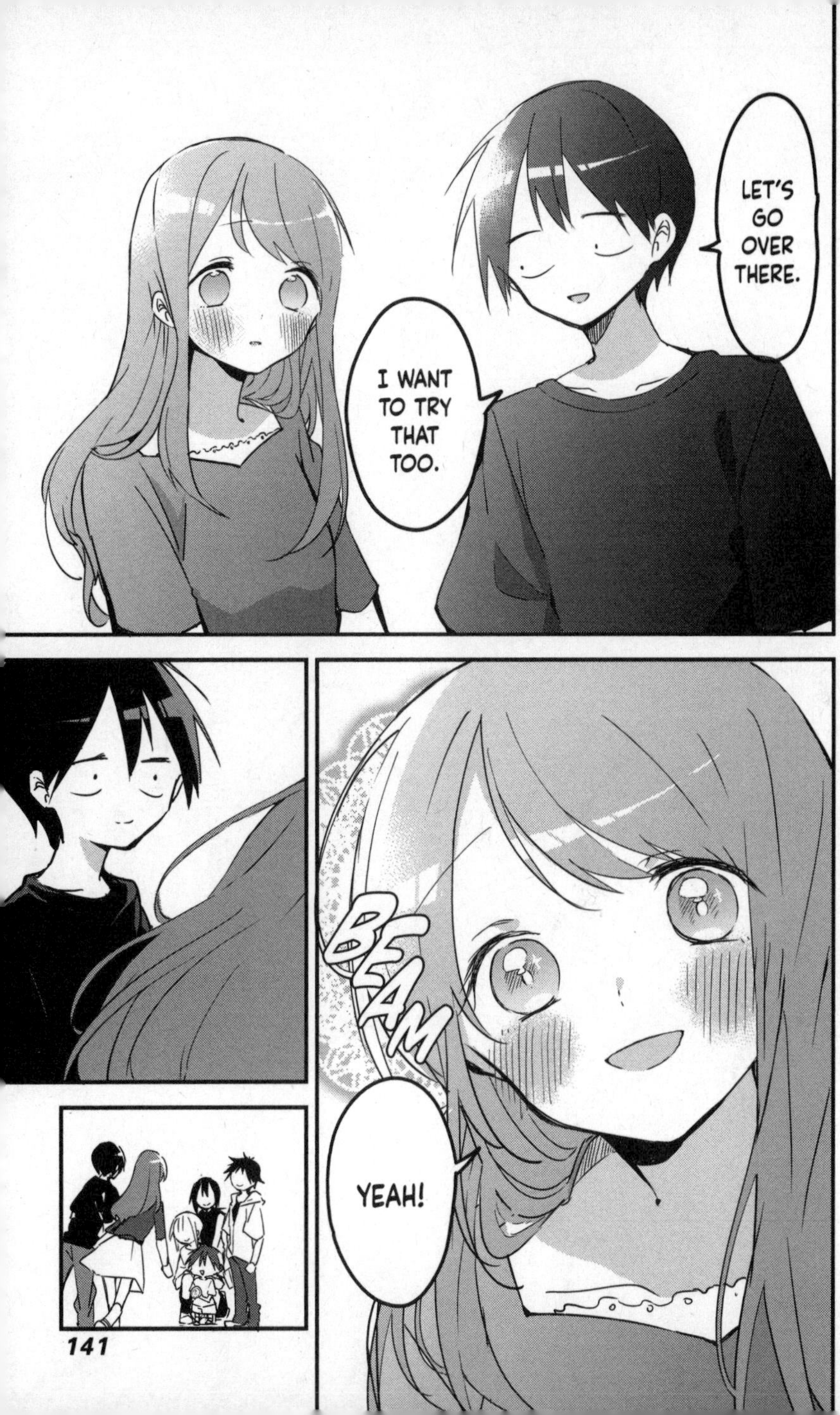
LET'S GO OVER THERE.
I WANT TO TRY THAT TOO.
BEAM
YEAH!

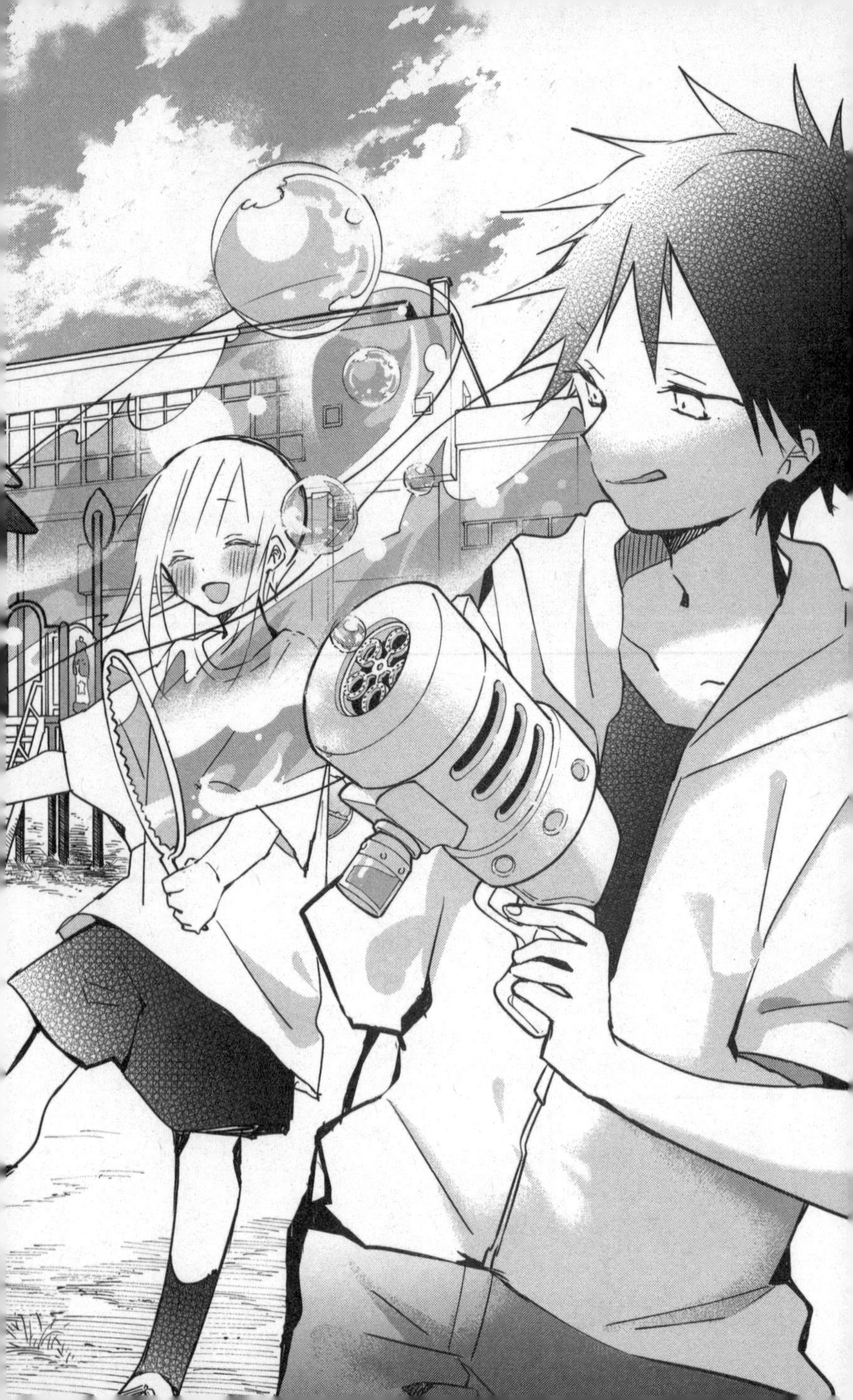

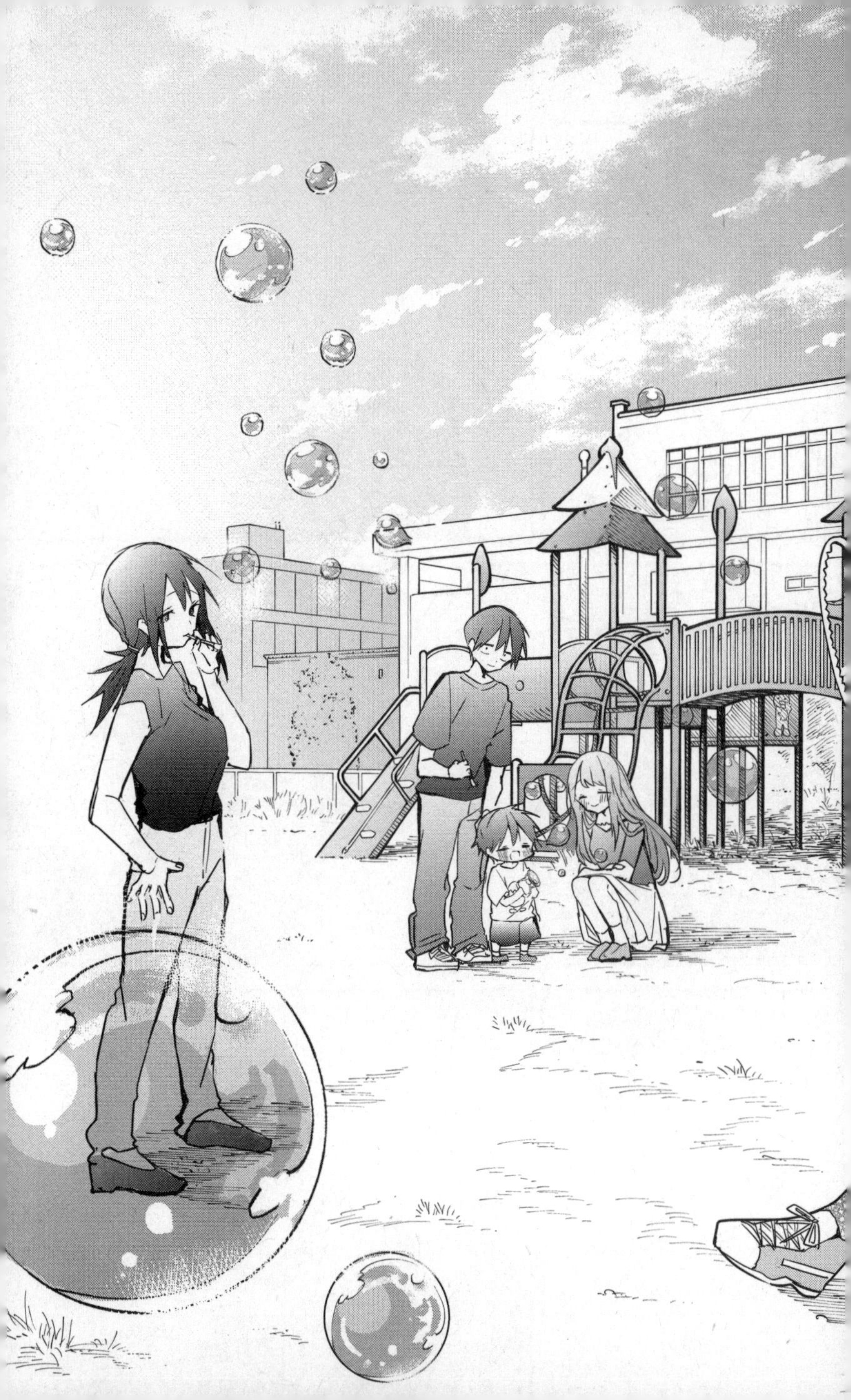

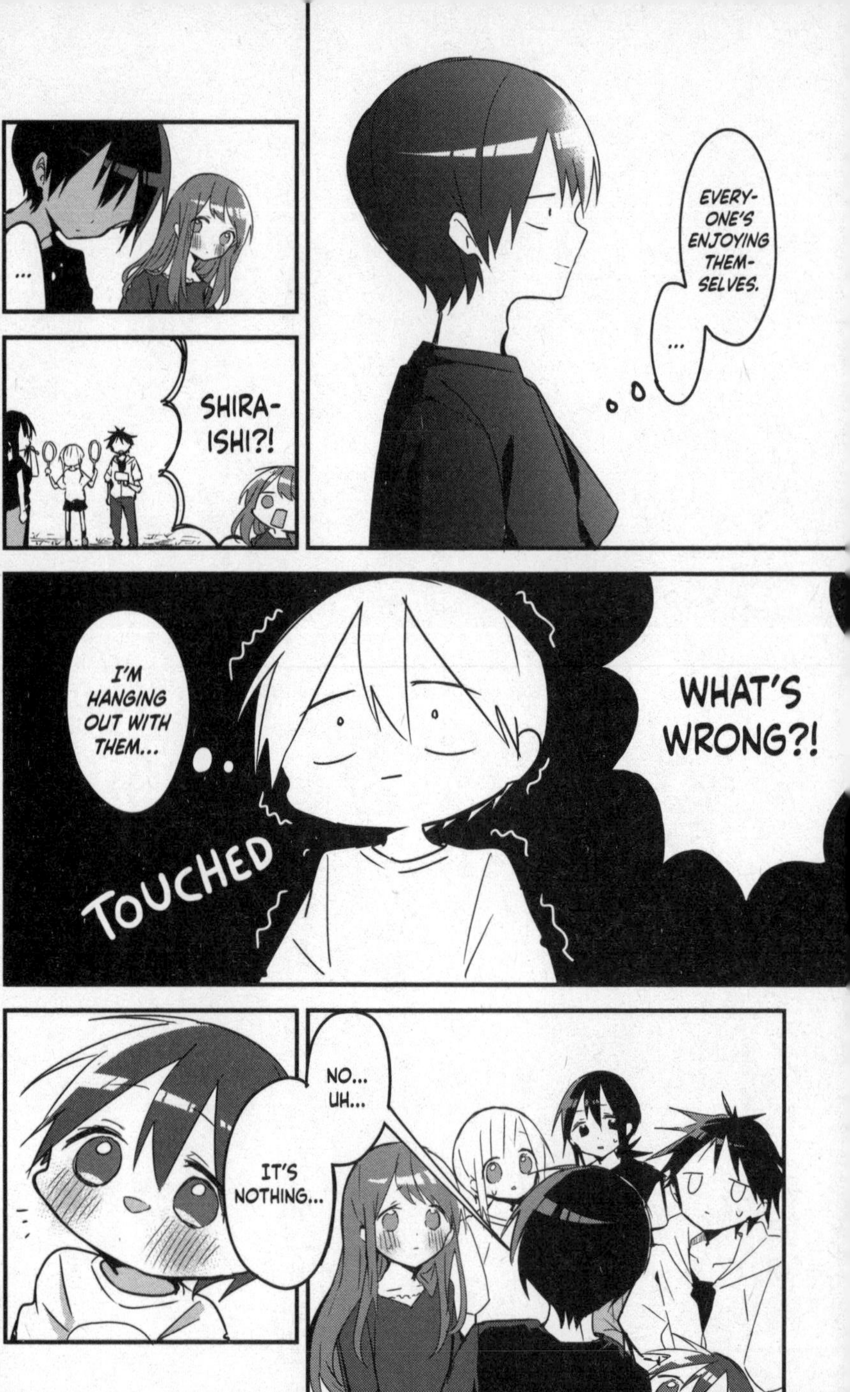
EVERY-ONE'S ENJOYING THEM-SELVES.
...
...
SHIRA-ISHI?!
WHAT'S WRONG?!
I'M HANGING OUT WITH THEM...
TOUCHED
NO... UH...
IT'S NOTHING...

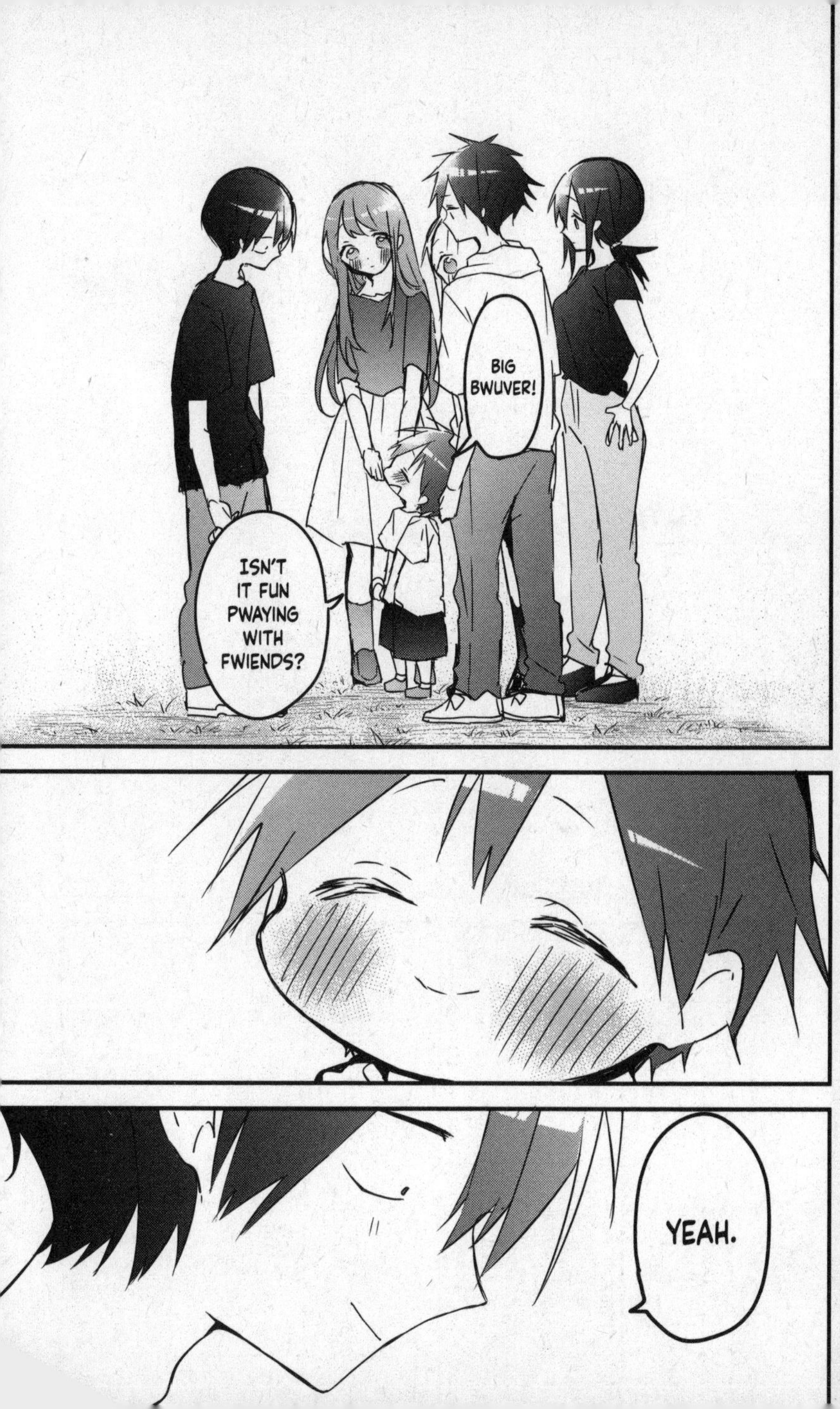
BIG BWUVER!
ISN'T IT FUN PWAYING WITH FWIENDS?
YEAH.

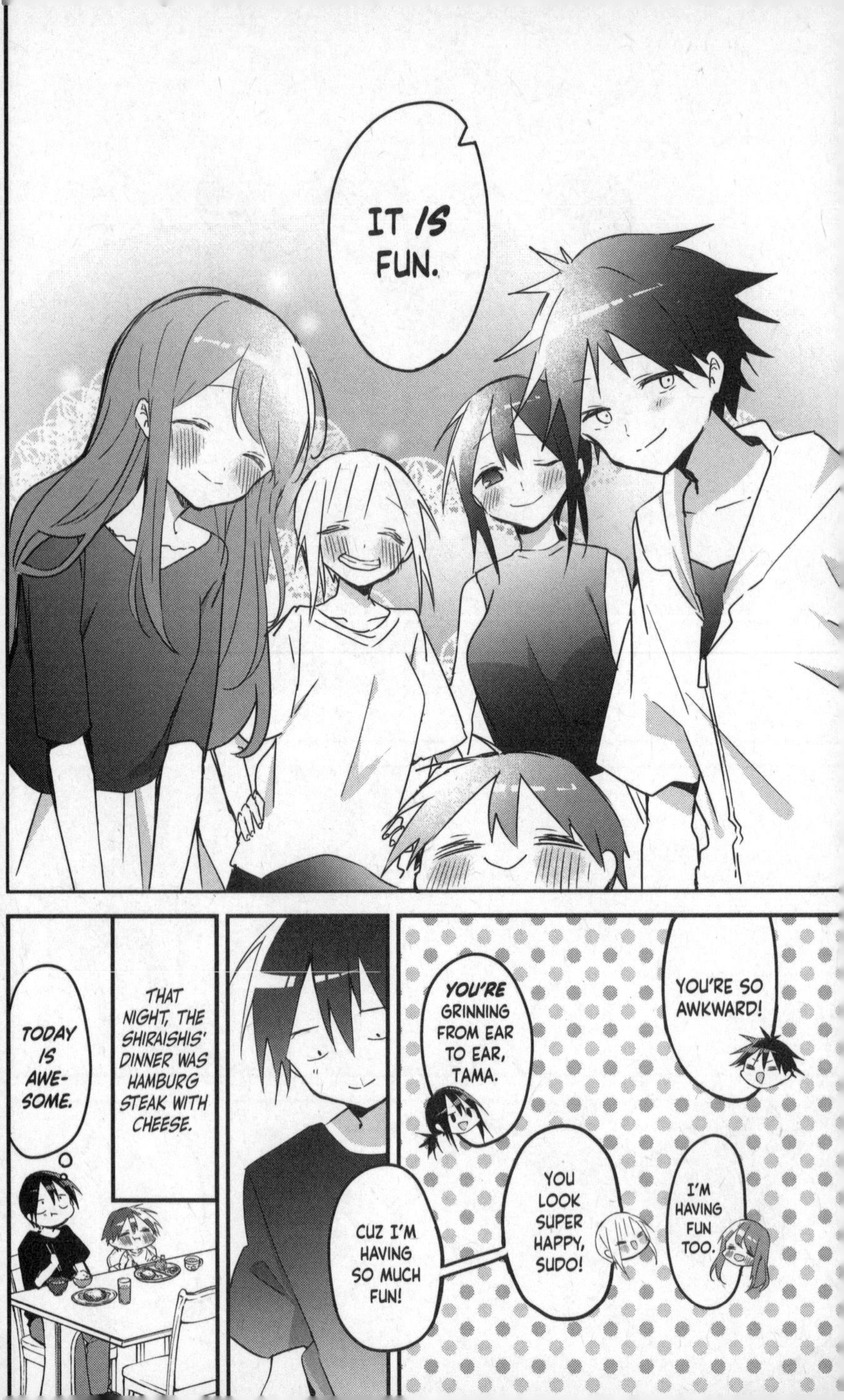
IT *IS* FUN.
YOU'RE SO AWKWARD!
YOU'RE GRINNING FROM EAR TO EAR, TAMA.
I'M HAVING FUN TOO.
YOU LOOK SUPER HAPPY, SUDO!
CUZ I'M HAVING SO MUCH FUN!
THAT NIGHT, THE SHIRAISHIS' DINNER WAS HAMBURG STEAK WITH CHEESE.
TODAY IS AWE-SOME.

episode 090

PRESENT AND TWO BOYS

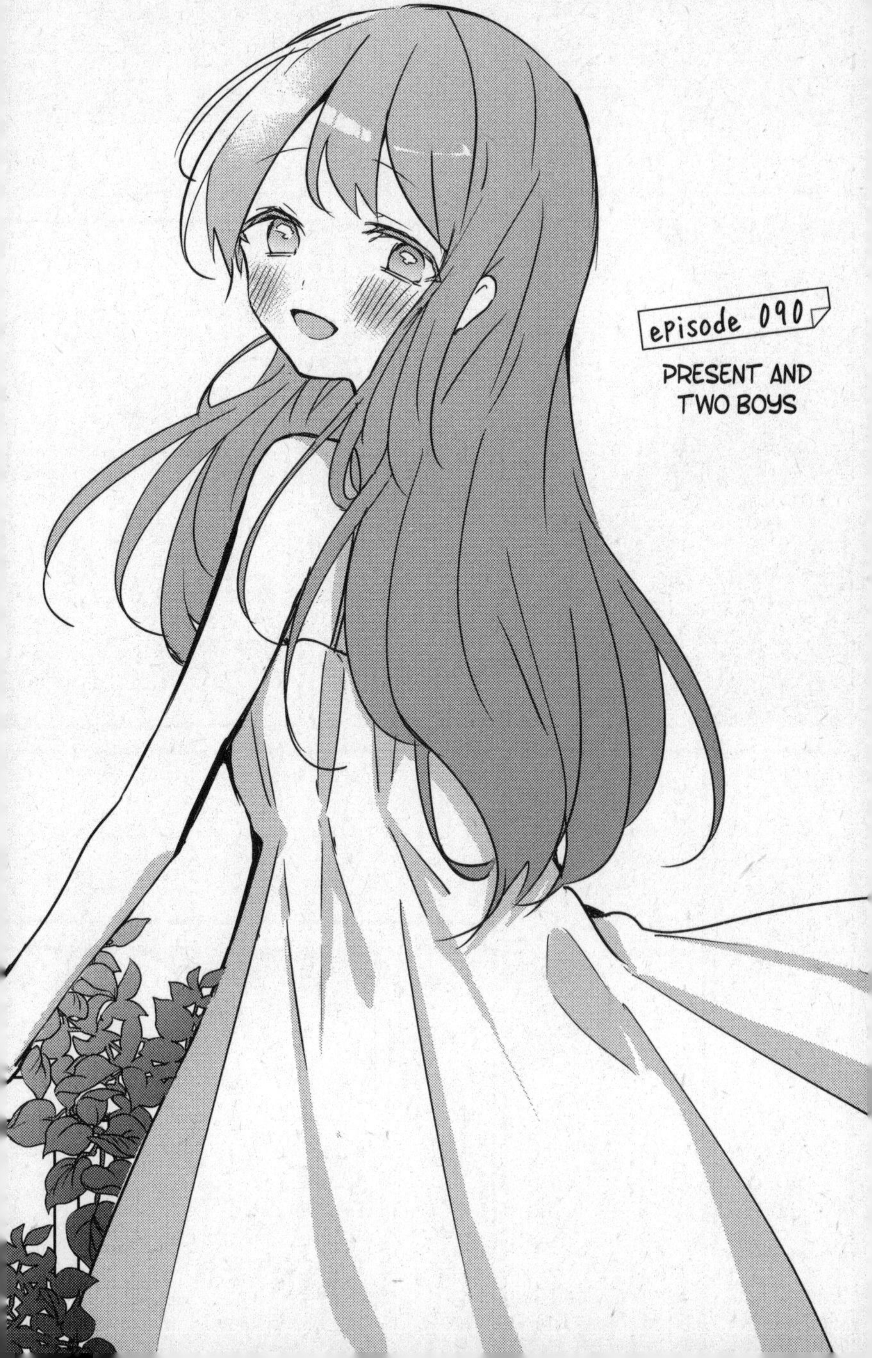

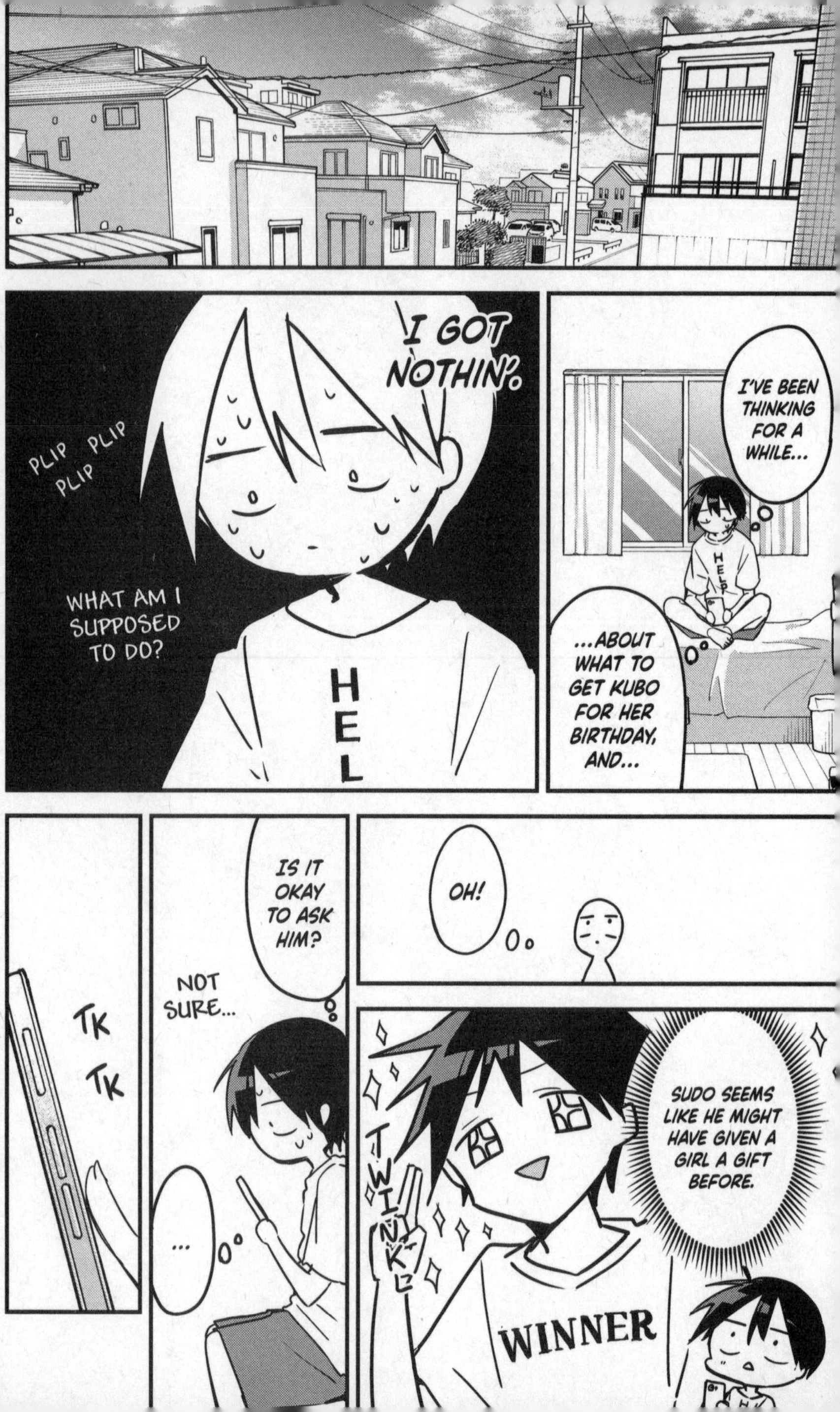
I'VE BEEN THINKING FOR A WHILE...
HELP
...ABOUT WHAT TO GET KUBO FOR HER BIRTHDAY, AND...
I GOT NOTHIN'.
PLIP PLIP PLIP
WHAT AM I SUPPOSED TO DO?
HEL
OH!
SUDO SEEMS LIKE HE MIGHT HAVE GIVEN A GIRL A GIFT BEFORE.
TWINKLE
WINNER
IS IT OKAY TO ASK HIM?
NOT SURE...
...
TK
TK

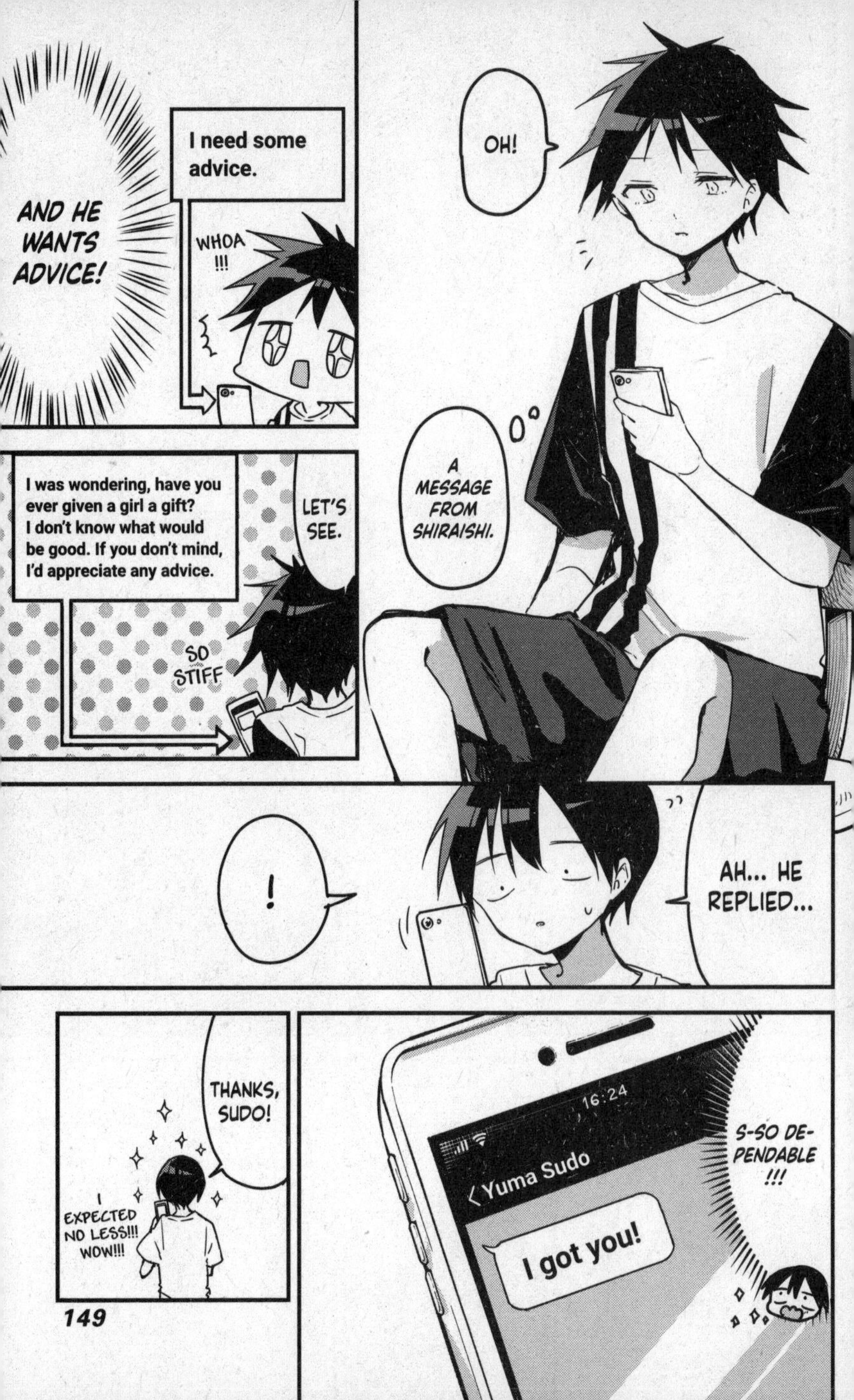
OH!
A MESSAGE FROM SHIRAISHI.
I need some advice.
AND HE WANTS ADVICE!
WHOA!!!
I was wondering, have you ever given a girl a gift? I don't know what would be good. If you don't mind, I'd appreciate any advice.
LET'S SEE.
SO STIFF
AH... HE REPLIED...
!
16:24
Yuma Sudo
I got you!
S-SO DEPENDABLE!!!
THANKS, SUDO!
I EXPECTED NO LESS!!! WOW!!!

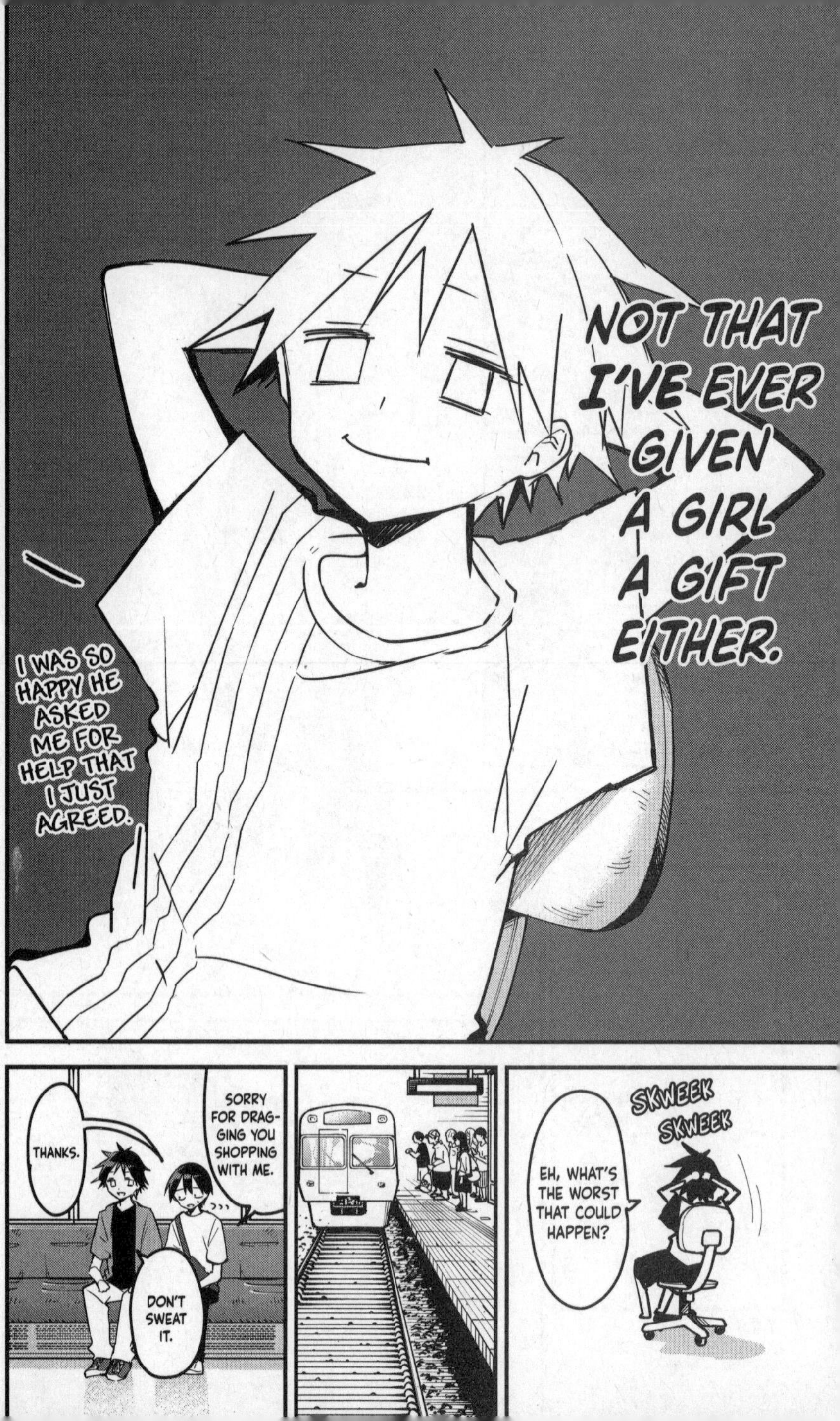
NOT THAT I'VE EVER GIVEN A GIRL A GIFT EITHER.
I WAS SO HAPPY HE ASKED ME FOR HELP THAT I JUST AGREED.
SKWEEK SKWEEK
EH, WHAT'S THE WORST THAT COULD HAPPEN?
SORRY FOR DRAG-GING YOU SHOPPING WITH ME.
THANKS.
DON'T SWEAT IT.

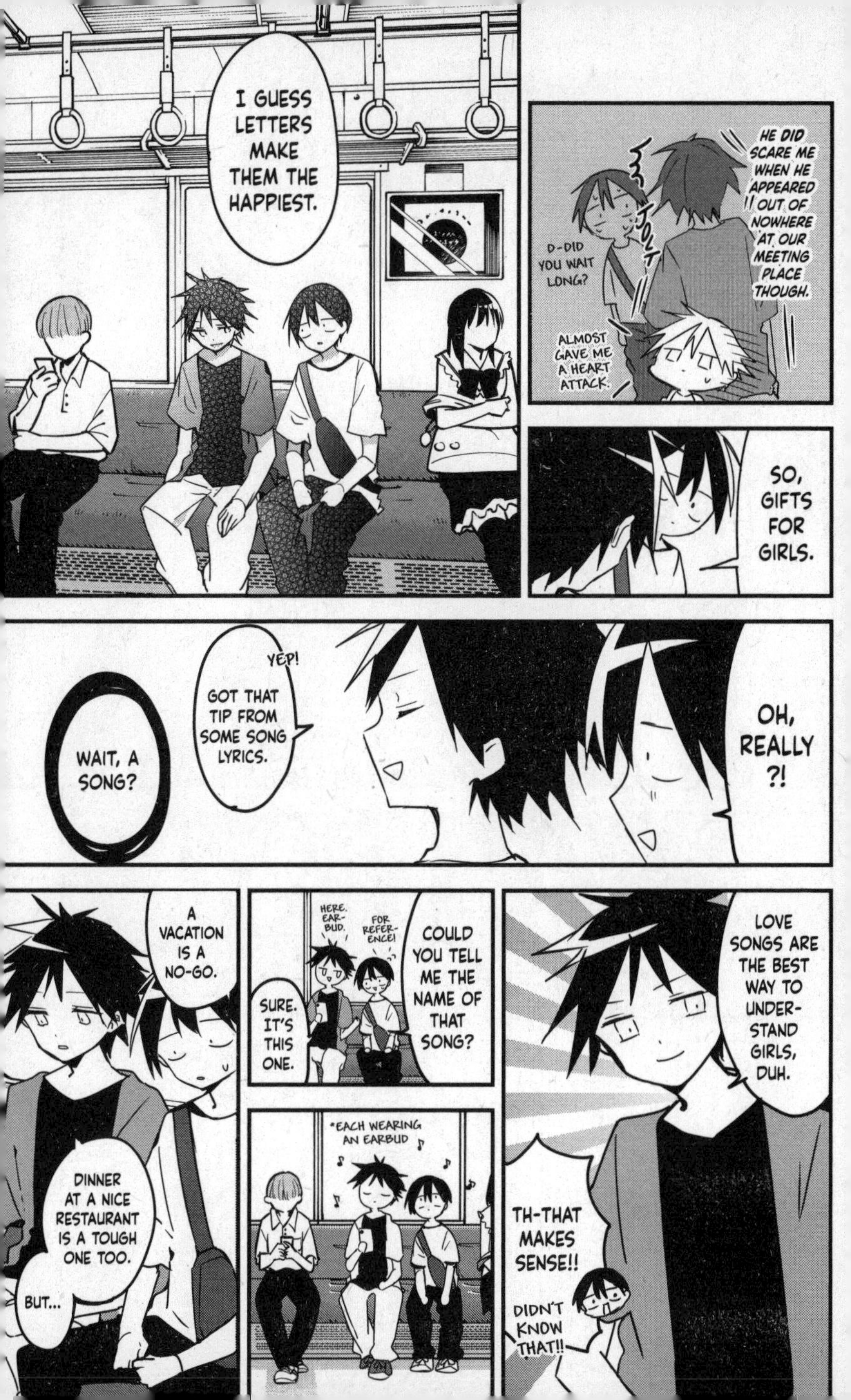
HE DID SCARE ME WHEN HE APPEARED OUT OF NOWHERE AT OUR MEETING PLACE THOUGH.
JOLT
D-DID YOU WAIT LONG?
ALMOST GAVE ME A HEART ATTACK.
SO, GIFTS FOR GIRLS.
I GUESS LETTERS MAKE THEM THE HAPPIEST.
OH, REALLY?!
YEP!
GOT THAT TIP FROM SOME SONG LYRICS.
WAIT, A SONG?
LOVE SONGS ARE THE BEST WAY TO UNDER-STAND GIRLS, DUH.
TH-THAT MAKES SENSE!!
DIDN'T KNOW THAT!!
COULD YOU TELL ME THE NAME OF THAT SONG?
FOR REFER-ENCE!
HERE. EAR-BUD.
SURE. IT'S THIS ONE.
*EACH WEARING AN EARBUD
A VACATION IS A NO-GO.
DINNER AT A NICE RESTAURANT IS A TOUGH ONE TOO.
BUT...

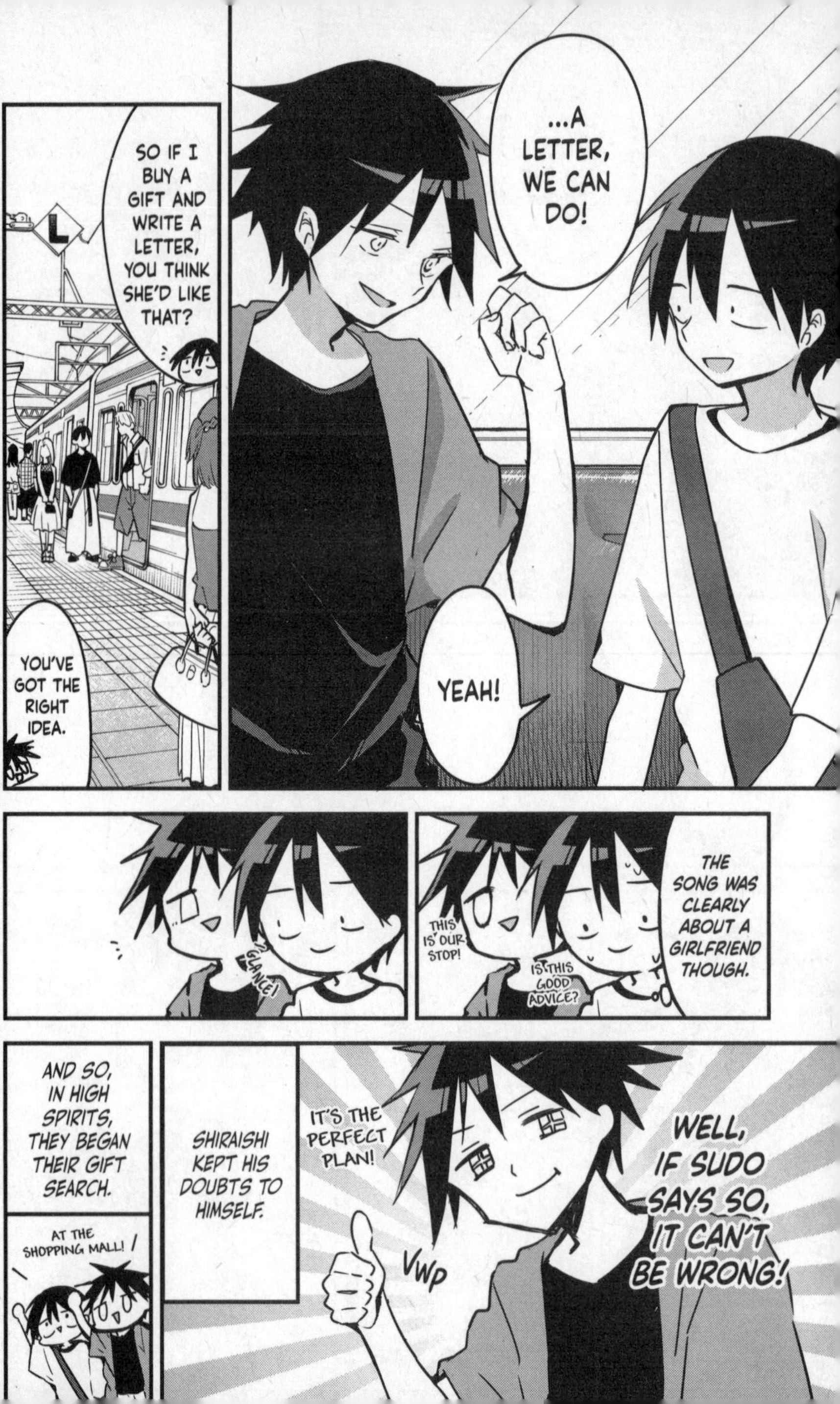
...A LETTER, WE CAN DO!
YEAH!
SO IF I BUY A GIFT AND WRITE A LETTER, YOU THINK SHE'D LIKE THAT?
YOU'VE GOT THE RIGHT IDEA.
THE SONG WAS CLEARLY ABOUT A GIRLFRIEND THOUGH.
IS THIS GOOD ADVICE?
THIS IS OUR STOP!
GLANCE!
WELL, IF SUDO SAYS SO, IT CAN'T BE WRONG!
IT'S THE PERFECT PLAN!
VWP
SHIRAISHI KEPT HIS DOUBTS TO HIMSELF.
AND SO, IN HIGH SPIRITS, THEY BEGAN THEIR GIFT SEARCH.
AT THE SHOPPING MALL!

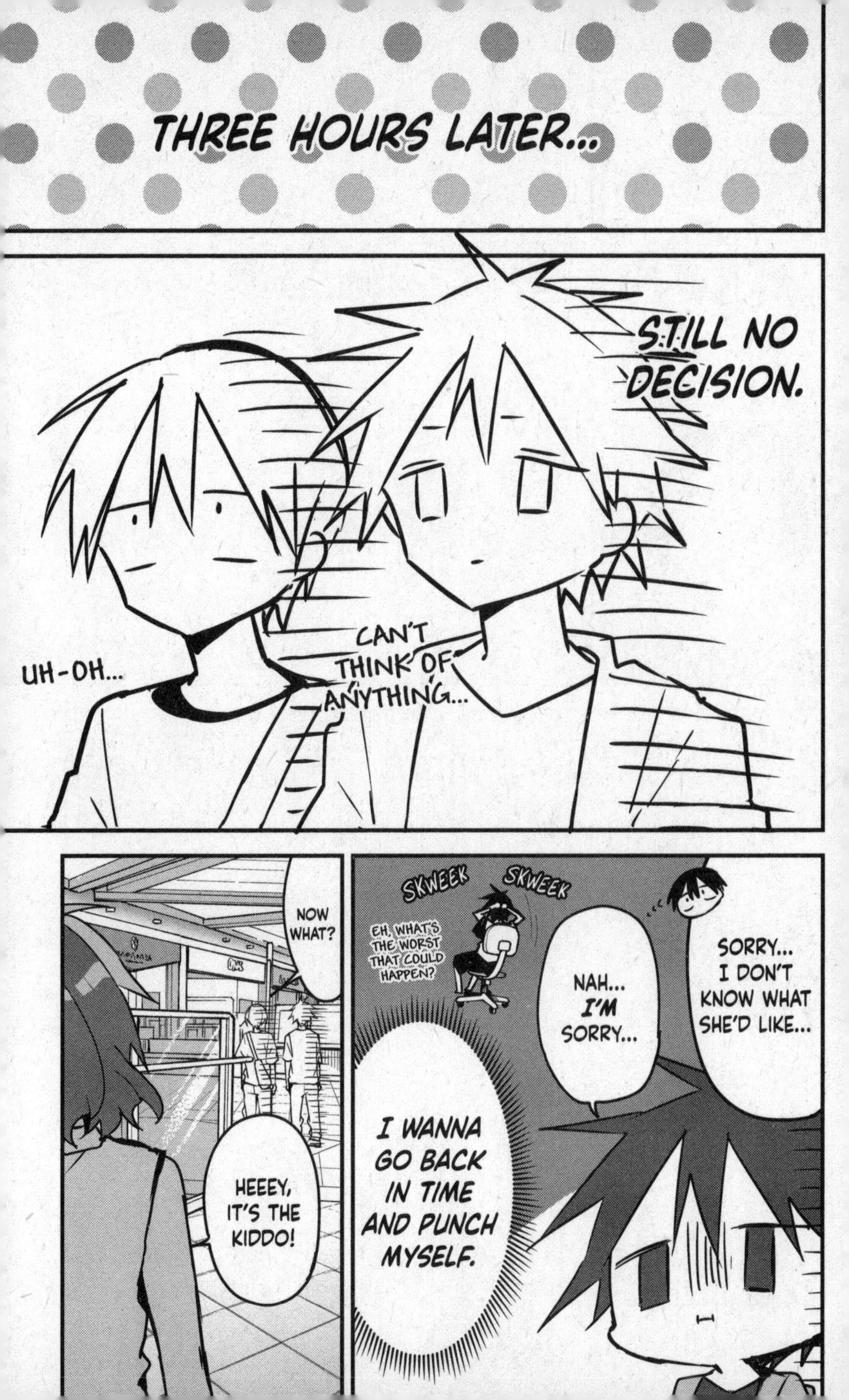
THREE HOURS LATER...
STILL NO DECISION.
CAN'T THINK OF ANYTHING...
UH-OH...
SORRY... I DON'T KNOW WHAT SHE'D LIKE...
NAH... I'M SORRY...
SKWEEK SKWEEK
EH, WHAT'S THE WORST THAT COULD HAPPEN?
I WANNA GO BACK IN TIME AND PUNCH MYSELF.
NOW WHAT?
HEEEY, IT'S THE KIDDO!

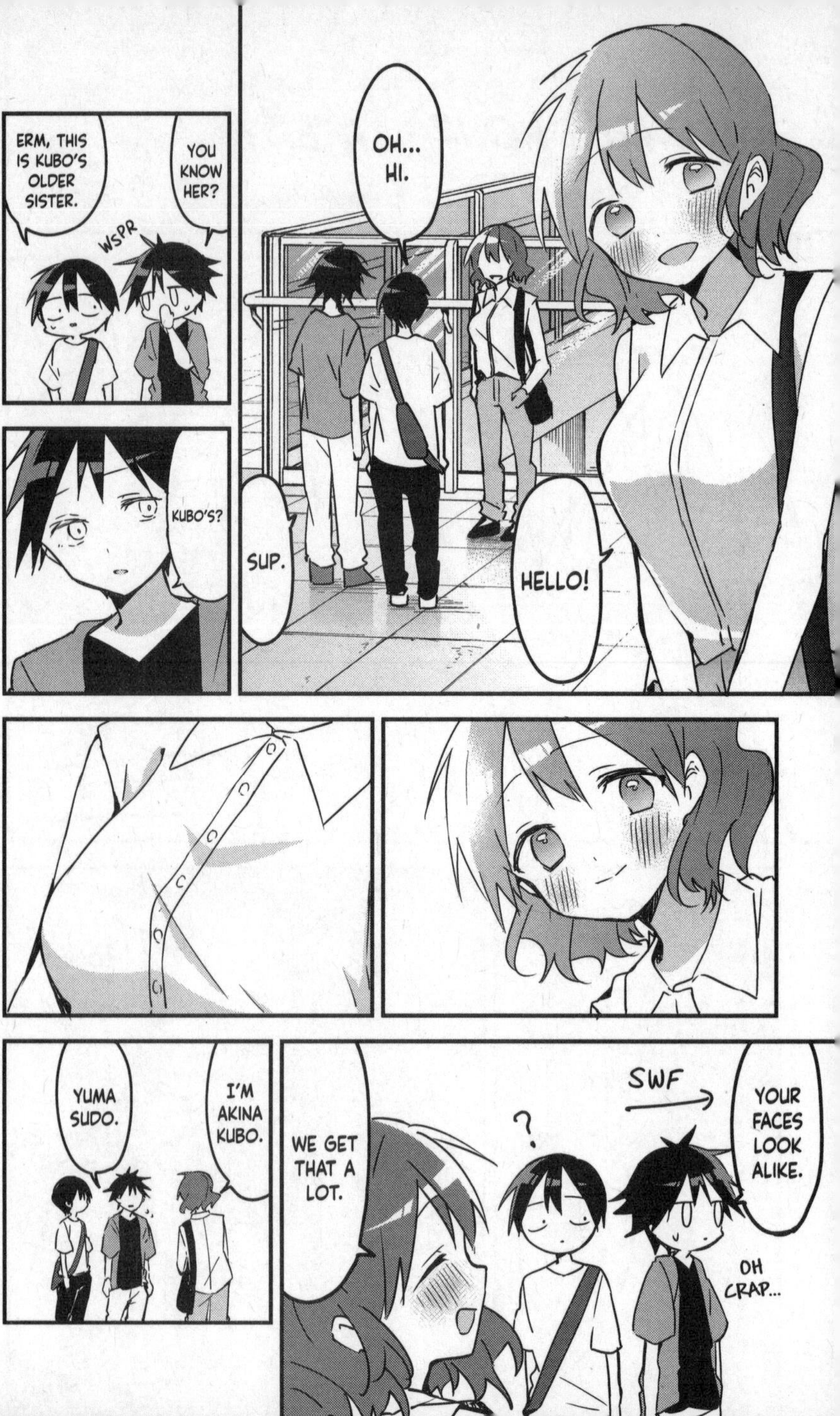
OH... HI.
HELLO!
SUP.
YOU KNOW HER?
ERM, THIS IS KUBO'S OLDER SISTER.
WSPR
KUBO'S?
SWF
YOUR FACES LOOK ALIKE.
?
WE GET THAT A LOT.
OH CRAP...
I'M AKINA KUBO.
YUMA SUDO.

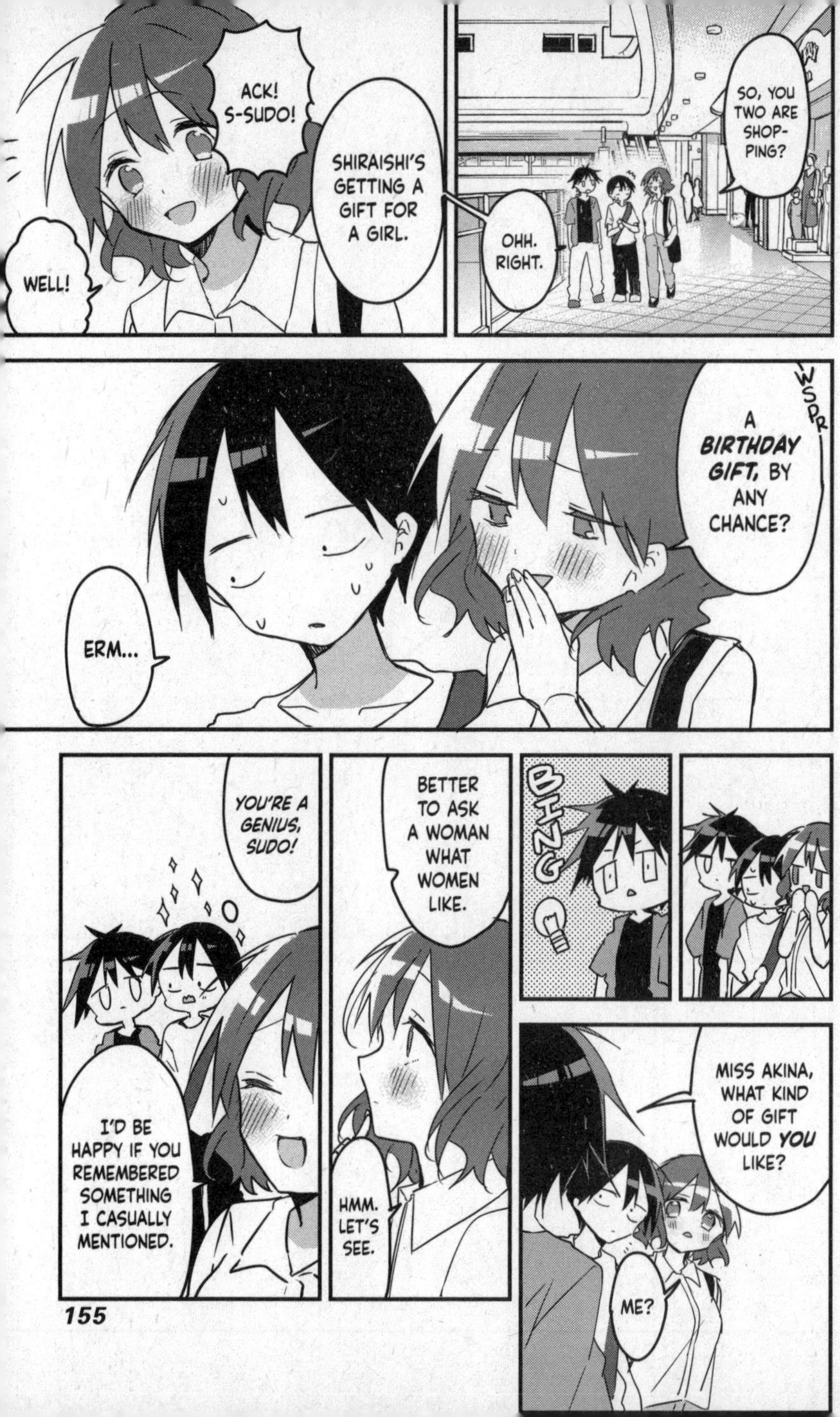
SO, YOU TWO ARE SHOP-PING?
OHH. RIGHT.
SHIRAISHI'S GETTING A GIFT FOR A GIRL.
ACK! S-SUDO!
WELL!
WSPR
A *BIRTHDAY GIFT*, BY ANY CHANCE?
ERM...
BING
MISS AKINA, WHAT KIND OF GIFT WOULD *YOU* LIKE?
ME?
BETTER TO ASK A WOMAN WHAT WOMEN LIKE.
HMM. LET'S SEE.
YOU'RE A GENIUS, SUDO!
I'D BE HAPPY IF YOU REMEMBERED SOMETHING I CASUALLY MENTIONED.

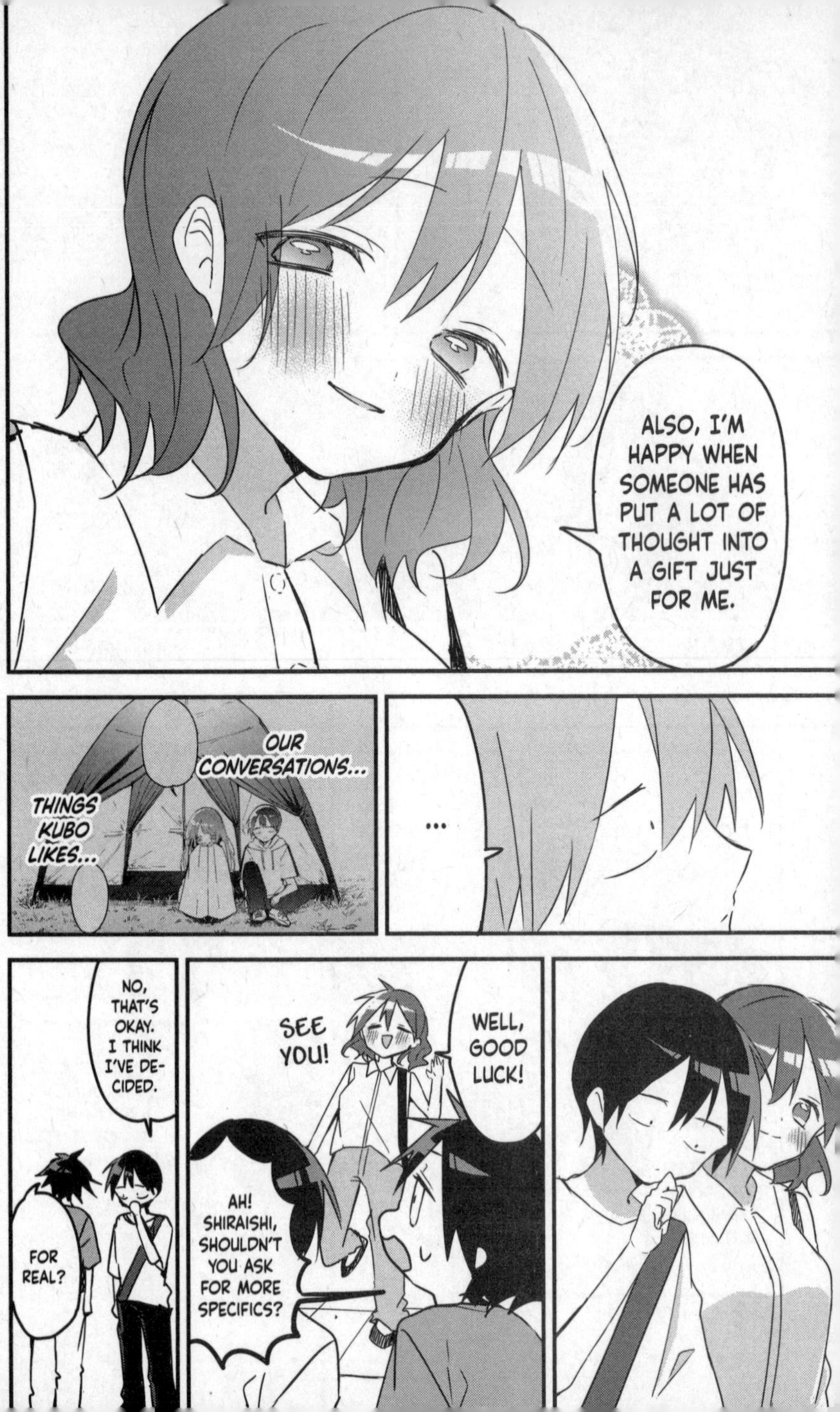
ALSO, I'M HAPPY WHEN SOMEONE HAS PUT A LOT OF THOUGHT INTO A GIFT JUST FOR ME.
...
OUR CONVERSATIONS...
THINGS KUBO LIKES...
WELL, GOOD LUCK!
SEE YOU!
AH! SHIRAISHI, SHOULDN'T YOU ASK FOR MORE SPECIFICS?
NO, THAT'S OKAY. I THINK I'VE DE-CIDED.
FOR REAL?

THERE!!!

ALL RIGHT! THANKS TO THE HELP FROM SUDO AND KUBO'S SISTER, I MANAGED TO BUY A GIFT!

HOW SHOULD I GIVE HER THE GIFT?

DOES SHE HAVE PLANS ON HER BIRTH-DAY?

THAT LEAVES ...

UH...

August

	M	T	W	TH
		1	2	3
			Kubo's birthday	
7		8	9	
	15	16	17	

THAT LEAVES ...

About your birthday

あ か
→ 　 は
さ た な
ら ま

BING!

HOW DO I WORD THIS THOUGH?

IF SHE DOES HAVE PLANS, I'LL CROSS THAT BRIDGE WHEN I GET THERE.

YOUR BIRTHDAY'S THEN, RIGHT?

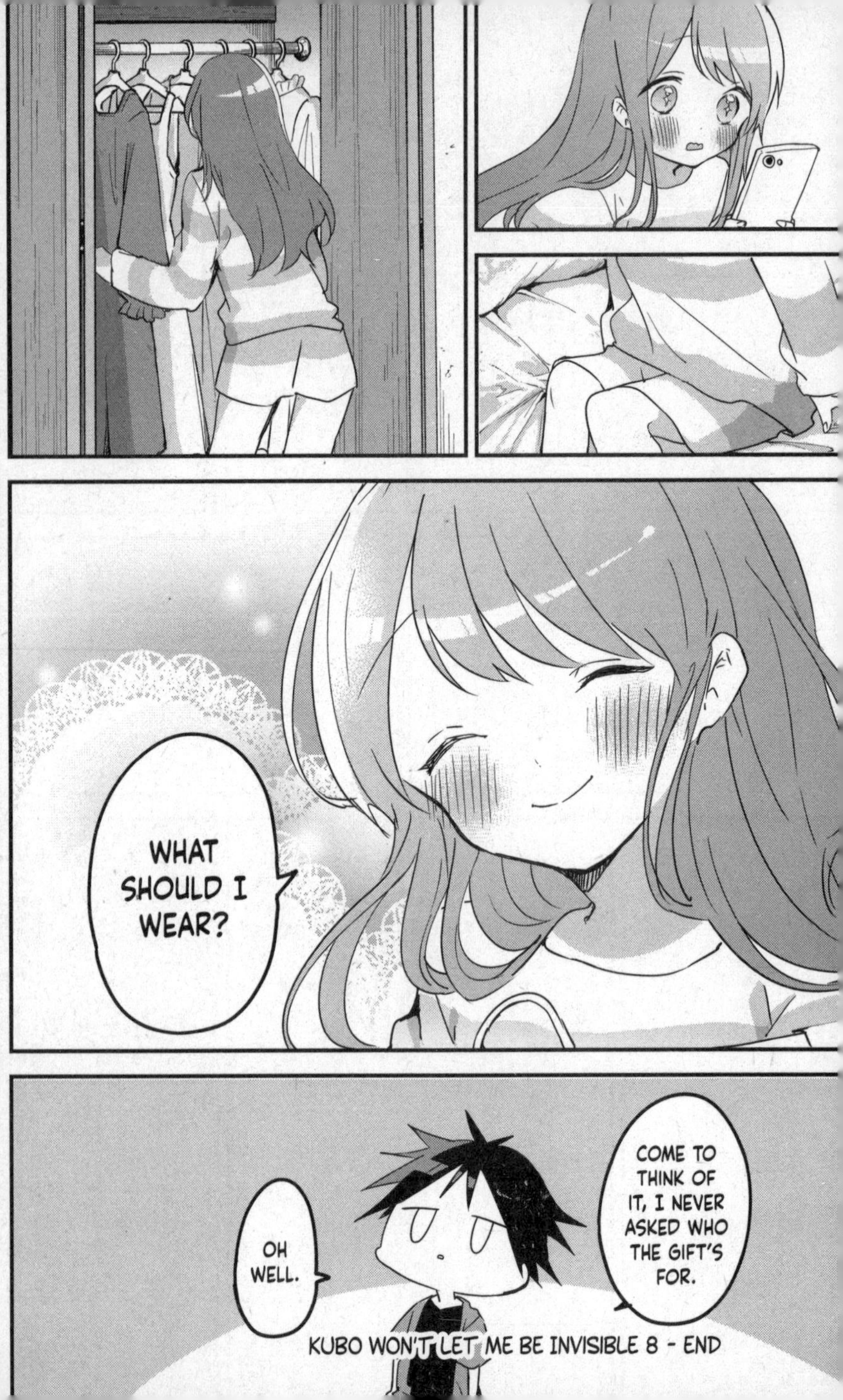
WHAT SHOULD I WEAR?
COME TO THINK OF IT, I NEVER ASKED WHO THE GIFT'S FOR.
OH WELL.
KUBO WON'T LET ME BE INVISIBLE 8 - END

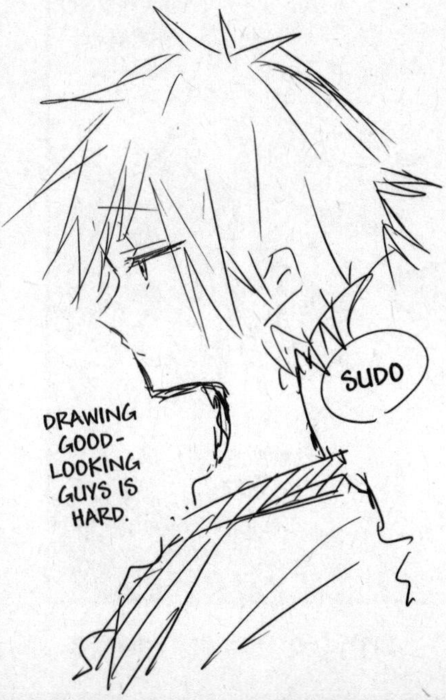
SUDO
DRAWING GOOD-LOOKING GUYS IS HARD.

KUBO WANTS TO SAY MY NAME

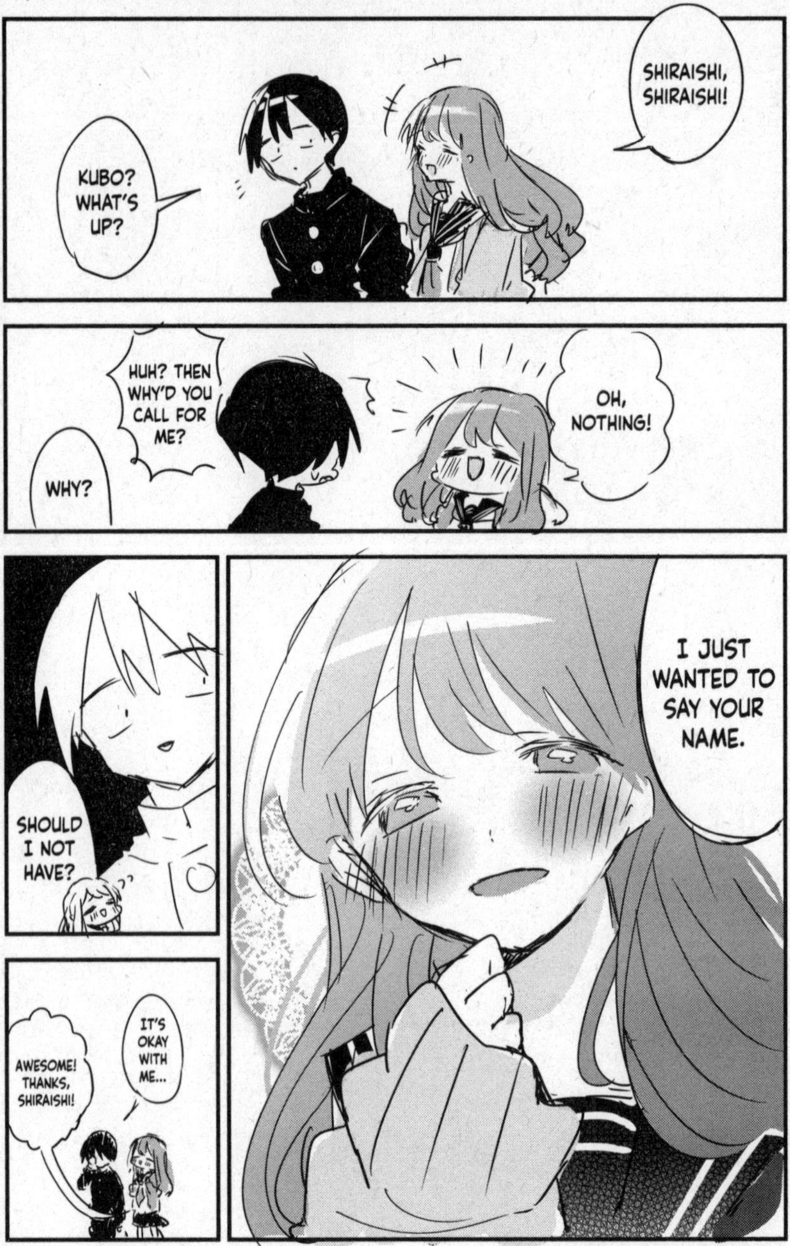
SHIRAISHI, SHIRAISHI!
KUBO? WHAT'S UP?
OH, NOTHING!
HUH? THEN WHY'D YOU CALL FOR ME?
WHY?
I JUST WANTED TO SAY YOUR NAME.
SHOULD I NOT HAVE?
IT'S OKAY WITH ME...
AWESOME! THANKS, SHIRAISHI!

I POSTED THIS ON TWITTER.

Kubo
Won't Let Me Be
Invisible

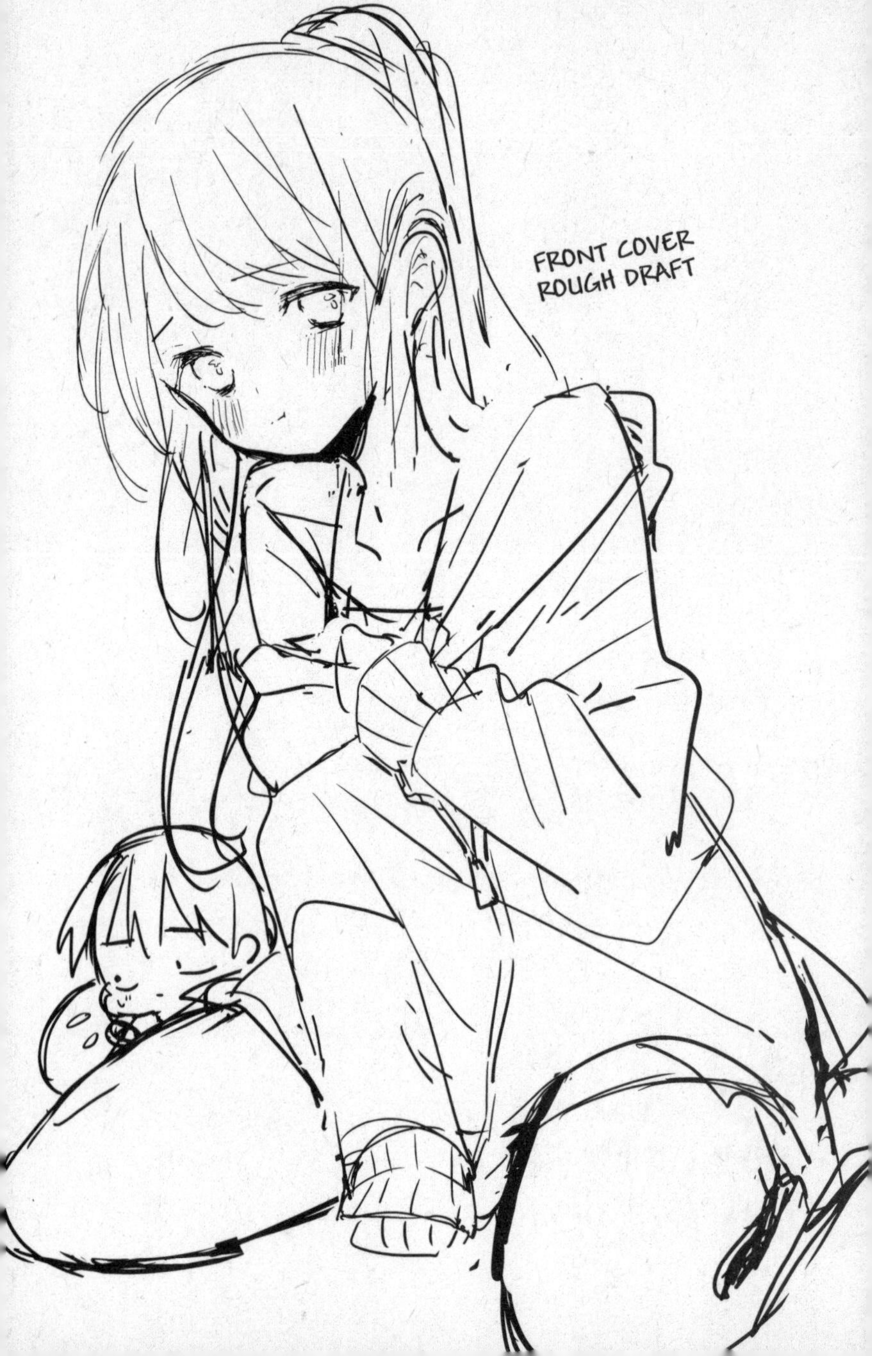
FRONT COVER
ROUGH DRAFT

AFTERWORD

IT'S VOLUME 8! THANKS SO MUCH FOR PICKING THIS UP! I HOPE YOU ENJOYED IT. IN THE MANGA'S STORY, IT'S SUMMER, BUT I'M WRITING THIS AFTERWORD AS I RETURN TO WORK FROM THE WINTER HOLIDAYS. IT SNOWED TODAY. I WISH WINTER VACATION WAS FIVE DAYS LONGER. WELL, I'M LUCKY TO BE PRETTY BUSY WITH WORK RIGHT FROM THE START OF THE YEAR, SO I'M GOING TO BUCKLE DOWN AND GET TO IT. I PRAY THAT THIS WILL BE ANOTHER WONDERFUL YEAR.

I PLAYED A LOT OF VIDEO GAMES IN 2021. THERE ARE ALREADY GAMES I WANT TO BUY IN 2022 TOO. STAR OCEAN, SPLATOON, SUNBREAK... I'M LOOKING FORWARD TO THEM. CURRENTLY, I'M PLAYING TALES OF ARISE. I WANT TO BEAT IT.

I HOPE YOU'LL CONTINUE TO ENJOY *KUBO WON'T LET ME BE INVISIBLE* IN 2022!!! VOLUME 8 IS FUN, AND 9 WILL BE GREAT TOO!!!

MAY WE MEET AGAIN IN VOLUME 9!

NENE YUKIMORI

THANKS

FUKATANI, MASUDA, EDITOR R, HACHIOJI HIGH SCHOOL, ALL MY SUPPORTERS AND YOU!

Morning – aching for a boy.
Afternoon – envying the self that's neither.
Night – dreaming of a girl.

My brain is locked in heated debate,
and you're the topic.
The congress dances. However,
there's but one conclusion.

Very Best
**Editor ℝ's
Title Page Poems**

Vol. 8

Sunscreen blocks summer magic along with the sun,
and I'm newly afraid to take off these clothes.

Welling up, bursting, gliding down, melting,
ringing out, vanishing:
Words reveal me.

My reasons for feeling blue are always wrestling matches with myself
and measuring myself against others.
This self-created melancholy is a stare-down with the me from yesterday.

If we can share without being greedy,
tomorrow is sure to be more fun than today.

Too unreliable for a wish, too insubstantial for a desire,
merely a sweetness like a prayer.

Let's begin class.
We timidly add to the list of each other's words on the blank page of a textbook.

I like the nights when there's no giving, no taking, only sharing.

This is Editor R's Very Best Poems Collection, Vol. 8.

It's just incredible. I suspect that when some people think of *Kubo Won't Let Me Be Invisible*, these poems are the first thing to come to their mind.

I hope the number of things people associate with *Kubo* will continue to grow.

Side note, on the rare occasion that I draw Shiraishi for a title page illustration, R apparently has to rack his brain to come up with a poem for it.

Nene
Yukimori

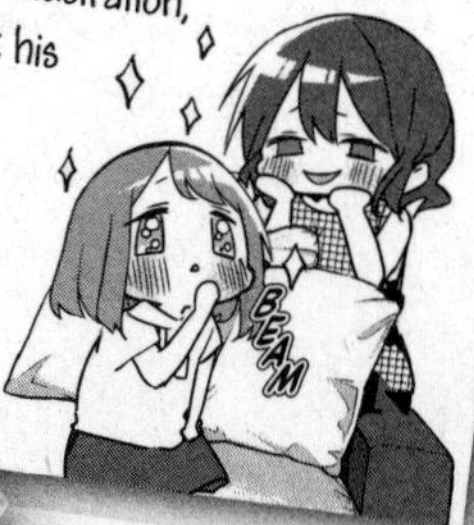
BEAM

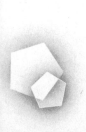

Nene Yukimori

I'm a long way from the future I'd imagined. I mean that in a very good way.

Nene Yukimori earned the right to serialize *Kubo Won't Let Me Be Invisible* in *Young Jump* after the manga's one-shot version won the magazine's Shinman GP 2019 Season 5 contest. The manga then began serialization in October 2019. The work is Yukimori's first to receive an English release.

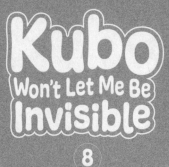

Kubo Won't Let Me Be Invisible

8

SHONEN JUMP EDITION

STORY AND ART BY
NENE YUKIMORI

TRANSLATION
AMANDA HALEY

TOUCH-UP ART & LETTERING
SNIR AHARON

DESIGN
PAUL PADURARIU

EDITOR
JULIA WALCHUK

Printed in the U.S.A.

Published by VIZ Media, LLC
P.O. Box 77010
San Francisco, CA 94107

10 9 8 7 6 5 4 3 2 1
First printing, July 2023

ratings.viz.com
RATED T+ OLDER TEEN

PARENTAL ADVISORY
KUBO WON'T LET ME BE INVISIBLE is rated T+ for Older Teen and is recommended for ages 16 and up. This volume contains suggestive themes.

VIZ MEDIA
viz.com

SHONEN JUMP

STOP!

YOU MAY BE READING THE WRONG WAY!

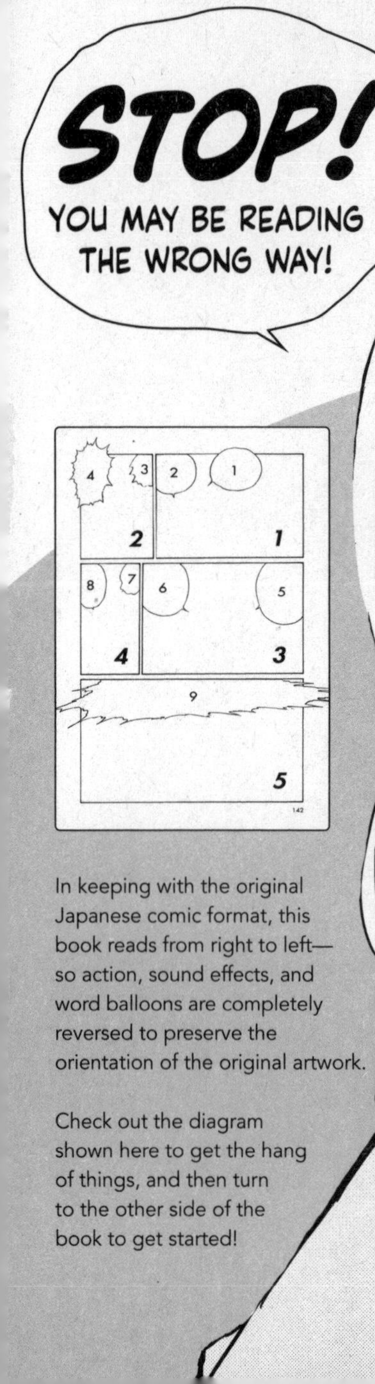

1
2
1
3
4
2
5
6
3
7
8
4
9
5
142

In keeping with the original Japanese comic format, this book reads from right to left—so action, sound effects, and word balloons are completely reversed to preserve the orientation of the original artwork.

Check out the diagram shown here to get the hang of things, and then turn to the other side of the book to get started!

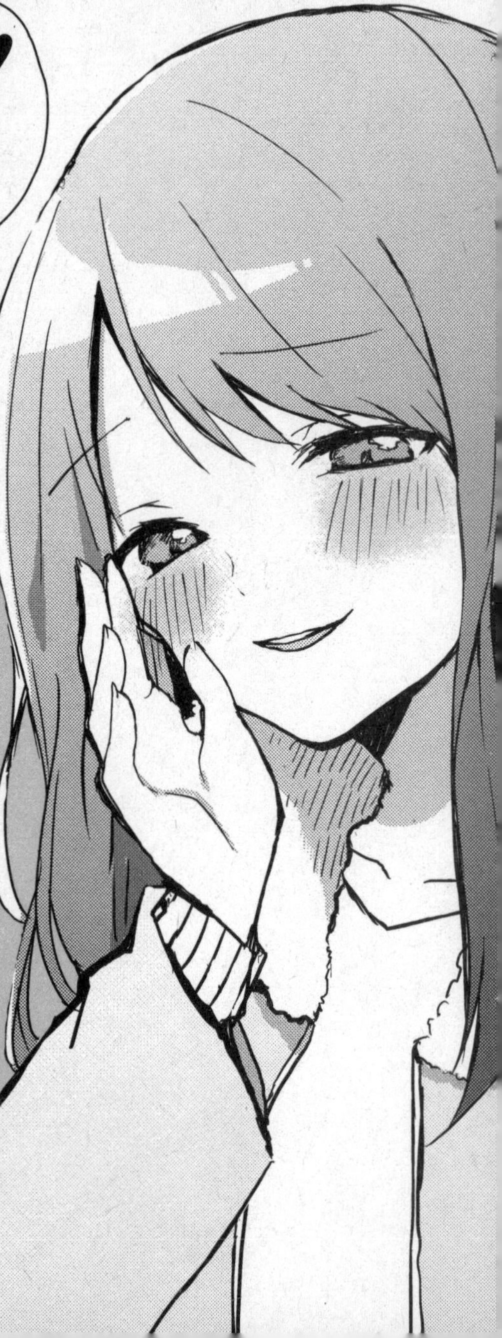